Beyond Imagination

Beyond Imagination

A Simple Plan to Save the World

Dick Eastman

 Chosen Books

A Division of Baker Book House Co
Grand Rapids, Michigan 49516

Published by Chosen Books
a division of Baker Book House Company
P.O. Box 6287, Grand Rapids, MI 49516-6287

Third printing, October 2002

Printed in the United States of America

Library of Congress Cataloging-in-Publication Data

Eastman, Dick
    Beyond imagination : a simple plan to save the world / Dick Eastman.
      p. cm.
    Includes bibliographical references and index.
    ISBN 0-8007-9250-5 (pbk.)
    1. Great Commission (Bible) 2. Evangelistic work. I. Title.
BV2074.E27 1997
266—dc20   96-43777

For security reasons, certain names, locations and details have been altered to protect people involved in remarkable works around the globe.

For current information about all releases from Baker Book
House, visit our web site:
                http://www.bakerbooks.com/

To Jack and Hazel McAlister,
cofounders of Every Home for Christ/
World Literature Crusade,
without whom this collection of inspiring testimonies
could not have been written.

Now to him who is able to do immeasurably more than all we ask or imagine, according to his power that is at work within us, to him be glory in the church and in Christ Jesus throughout all generations, for ever and ever! Amen.

Ephesians 3:20–21

Contents

Part 4: Harvest Finishers
The Closure Factor in Reaching Our World for Jesus

Acknowledgments

It is customary with the publication of a work such as this to thank those by name who made it possible. But that leaves me with a challenging dilemma.

The pages that follow are literally the result of an army of thousands of "foot soldiers" (some of whom have now gone to be with the Lord) who have taken the good news of Jesus to nearly one billion homes in more than 170 nations. That number easily represents as many as five thousand new volunteer participants each year (along with hundreds of full-time staff). Further, because Every Home for Christ (the basis of many of the stories in this book) celebrated its fiftieth anniversary in October 1996, the number of participants involves several hundreds of thousands. Their names alone would easily fill several volumes of a book this size.

But I do wish to specifically acknowledge a considerably smaller group who sacrificially shared their assistance in research-gathering, editing, rewriting and the like to help make possible these pages.

To my wife, Dee, who let me travel around the world eight times in the year of information-gathering just prior to the compiling of these pages, thanks for your patience and partnership—and for all 32 happy years of our life together.

My secretary, Debbie Lord, also deserves special recognition. She retyped the manuscript so many times she had to develop a special system to remember what chapter belonged to which draft.

Faustino Ruivivar Jr., a gifted editor and professional linguist on our staff, helped much in editing the manuscript carefully, as did Gary Martyn, one of Every Home for Christ's talented writers.

I also gratefully acknowledge Garrett Lee for his editorial advice and Marie Reyes for typing the first draft of the book. And to Matt Doerle, thanks for your idea to title the book *Beyond Imagination.* Jane Campbell, editor of Chosen Books, also deserves recognition for her excellent editorial insight.

I also wish to thank a gracious Norwegian brother, Frank Kaleb Jansen of Adopt-a-People Clearing House. It was his exposition of Matthew 24:14 during an EHC chapel that ultimately gave birth to the concepts in this book referred to as the *Oikos* Agenda.

Very special acknowledgment goes to our EHC global executive staff, including Denys Blackmore (Canada); Pierre Clement (France/Europe); Fred Creighton (Middle East/South Asia); Jörg Enners (Germany); Brad Fallentine (U.S.A.); Paul Goodwin (international office); Hennie Hanekom (South Africa/Anglo-Africa); Paul Ilyin (Russia/CIS); Suliasi Kurulo (Fiji/Pacific); Eric Leach (Australia); M. M. Maxon (India); Diafwila-dia-Mbwangi (Zaire/French Africa); Faustino Ruivivar, Sr. (international office); David Tamez (Mexico/Latin America); Enoch Tan (Malaysia/East and Southeast Asia); T. V. Thomas (Canada); Jerry Wiles (U.S.A.); Martin Wilson (U.S.A.); Wes Wilson (international office); and Mell Winger (U.S.A.).

I also gratefully acknowledge Every Home for Christ's board of directors in the United States, particularly Andy Duda, chairman, and Tom McGehee, vice chairman, as well as those boards of respected leaders serving as a covering for the EHC ministry in more than one hundred nations around the world.

Introduction

Try to imagine every family, household by household, in every village of Nepal, including remote Sherpa villages high in the shadows of Mount Everest, being visited by bold believers who present the Gospel of Jesus Christ personally to each household.

Further imagine the same visiting not only in our needy nation, but throughout every remote region on earth, touching every least-evangelized or unreached people group yet to have any contact with the Gospel.

As hard as it is to imagine, this is all happening even now. In fact, with the publication of this book, Nepal is only a few villages from being totally finished—all 75 districts. The same miracle has also happened in eighty additional nations.

It is all part of a sweeping global revival and accelerating harvest of souls, marked by amazing signs and wonders, that I trust will inspire you to believe that the Great Commission may well be accomplished in our generation—quite literally. I am convinced God does have a plan to save the world, and that it is very simple—and well on its way to completion.

Many of the unusual testimonies shared on the pages that follow, some almost beyond imagination, are the result of dedicated foot soldiers (full-time and volunteer) participating with the global ministry of Every Home for Christ (now in its fiftieth year) to take the good news of Jesus to every family in every village, town and city on earth. These pages also include encouraging testimony from many other ministries to show that God is knitting them together to see His "kingdom come, [his] will be done on earth" (Matthew 6:10; see Revelation 11:15).

In writing these accounts, I have sought to verify every testimony possible. In the twelve months prior to the publication of this book, for example, I traveled at least eight times around the world to speak with eyewitnesses to these reports or with people who were in direct contact with eyewitnesses. Some were flown to Every Home for Christ's international headquarters in Colorado Springs, Colorado, for extensive interviews.

In several instances pseudonyms have been given to individuals to protect their continuing work in certain dangerous areas, or for a more readable flow of the narrative. (The latter technique has been used in a few places when eyewitnesses did not know the names of those involved.)

The vignettes preceding each chapter describing the conversions of two chiefs in distant rain forests, and the resulting mass conversion to Christ in their respective tribes, include some written dramatizations of their pasts based on cultural characteristics of those peoples and how they would have lived and matured during their early years. This is especially true in the writing of the story of the earliest years of Chief Haribo, who was born in the late 1800s. The actual events surrounding Haribo's dramatic angelic visitation and conversion in 1990, well after his one hundredth year, are based on an account of one who was in Haribo's village the day of his conversion with whom I spoke.

Further, over a recent two-month period, I traveled to both rain forests mentioned in the vignettes to see firsthand the fruit of the brave evangelists with "beautiful feet" (see Isaiah 52:7; Romans 10:15) who helped take the good news of Jesus to these previously unreached peoples.

For these peoples and multitudes like them, the promise of God to "pour out my Spirit on all people" (Acts 2:17) seems to be drawing ever closer to its fulfillment. As impossible as it may be to imagine, every unreached people group on earth may soon have had an opportunity to experience God's supernatural love and encounter the transforming power of Jesus Christ, His Son.

Dick Eastman, International President
Every Home for Christ

Harvest Strategy

*The Simplicity Factor
in Reaching Our World for Jesus*

Early in my ministry, a wise colleague and mentor told me, "Dick, God's plans are always incredibly simple and unusually inexpensive. So if things start getting terribly complex and amazingly expensive, you might rethink whether it's God's plan after all."

The early Church must have understood this principle when it came to reaching the world for Jesus. All the believers had was a commission from Christ to go everywhere to everybody (see Mark 16:15) and a caution from Him to do it without monetary encumbrances or materialistic concerns (see Matthew 10:9–10).

As I explain in Part 1 of this book, those New Testament believers ultimately reached entire cities and regions with the Gospel of Jesus so that "everybody" heard (see Acts 4:16; 5:28; 19:10) without benefit of modern technology. Their method was unusually simple and amazingly economical. And I believe, as we will shortly see, that it is coming back into fashion.

Imagining the Impossible

The old high priest lay dead. Chief Haribo had lived through more than one hundred seasons of the annual rains, and had seen more than one hundred yam harvests, before anyone told him about Jesus. Now he had died soon after repeating a simple prayer of confession prayed over him by two followers of Jesus.

The young evangelists had traveled a great distance over rough seas and rocky mountains to reach the chief's rugged, hilly island in a distant part of the South Pacific. They could tell the old man was easily one hundred years old and near death, but they were trusting God to provide a miracle that would prove His power to heal.

The elderly village leader had never heard about Jesus. Neither had anyone else in this remote part of their island. But that was soon to change.

The numerous village elders—spiritual heads of at least five villages in this region—looked on, nearly naked, as they heard their own chief pray a prayer unlike any they had ever heard. In fact, it was the only prayer to the "one true God" anyone in the interior of this island had ever heard. Haribo had asked someone called Jesus, the only Son of the Living God, to come into his heart, just as the two evangelists had suggested.

But instead of being restored to life, which the young men said could happen through the power of their God, the old chief died soon after he prayed the sinner's prayer.

The elders saw him die and began preparing his body for ceremonial burial. But what happened next, a full eight hours later, was beyond imagination, changing this village forever. It could well change your thinking about the miraculous.

Back in Fashion

It was our very first missionary journey, and my wife, Dee, and I were excited. We were in our early twenties, serving as youth pastors of a growing church in southern Wisconsin while I finished my studies at Moody Bible Institute in Chicago. It was 1966. Our denomination had decided to begin a new program for young people, letting them experience missions firsthand on a short-term basis. We would have the joy of leading one of these very first teams of youth, just four in number, to a distant mission field. (Years later that number would grow to more than ten thousand.)

Our assignment was the Central American nation of British Honduras (now known as Belize). During our briefing sessions with veteran missionaries, including one long-term missionary from the region of our destination, we were informed that few mission fields in the world were more rugged than British Honduras. It was called the Africa of Central America. Indeed, when the veteran missionary from the region heard that a team of young people was going into British Honduras, he seriously questioned the wisdom of choosing such a location for so new a program, especially one that involved youth. We were told to expect the worst of conditions and not too many results.

Before we left on our journey, another veteran missionary suggested that distributing evangelistic literature might be the best thing we could do on our visit, since more and more Central Americans were learning to read. In fact, they had a passion for reading everything they could get their hands on. So we decided to spend most of our brief mission going home to home distributing literature.

As we walked from house to house in the shimmering heat of Belize City, the capital of British Honduras, we noticed people's hunger for the printed page. Not one person rejected the literature. Often those who were home wanted to hear more. We were amazed when more than 450 people in just five weeks invited us inside and prayed to receive Christ as Savior.

Late one night in the sweltering heat, I lay awake thinking about the simplicity of communicating the Gospel house to house and the unusual receptivity of the people. Why wasn't there a worldwide initiative to do just what we were doing? It seemed so logical, especially after 450 people had prayed to receive Christ in just over a month. At that time as many as three million people globally were becoming literate every week. How relatively easy it would be to evangelize the vast majority of the world, I thought, if the global Church went systematically to where people lived, providing them a clearly printed message of salvation.

And if this strategy were to be covered with much prayer, I further reasoned, I was sure the Holy Spirit would open the eyes of at least one reader in every home. And how simple it would be to include decision cards with the literature so people could send a response to a follow-up office and request Bible lessons to help them grow in their understanding of what it means to be a disciple of Jesus Christ.

As I lay awake in the night, the smoke of burning mosquito repellent filling the air, I wondered if world evangelism could really be this simple. Could Jesus have envisioned such a strategy when He gave His Great Commission to the early Church?

> "Go and make disciples of all nations, baptizing them in the name of the Father and of the Son and of the Holy Spirit, and teaching them to obey everything I have commanded you."
>
> Matthew 28:19–20 (see Mark 16:15)

Little did I realize that night, as I pondered a home-to-home strategy for the fulfillment of the Great Commission, that God had already birthed just such a strategy. In fact, by this time it had been in place for more than thirteen years. Nor could I have known that in thirty years I would be involved in its international leadership, observing signs and wonders beyond imagination (as you will soon discover) that clearly indicate fulfilling the Great Commission could well be within reach of this generation.

A Biblical Pattern for Evangelizing the World

When Jesus discussed His ultimate return to earth and the establishment of His eternal Kingdom among humankind, He made it clear that one primary sign was central to the culmination of these events. The record of Christ's words to His disciples concerning this sign can be found in at least two key passages in the Gospels.

And both New Testament writers describe Him reaching the same conclusion about the primary sign that must precede His return.

Mark records Jesus as describing a variety of events that would occur as indicators that the time of His return was approaching. Jesus prophesied, "Many will come in my name . . . and will deceive many" (Mark 13:6). "Wars and rumors of wars" and "earthquakes . . . and famines" (verses 7–8) would occur. Yet Jesus was careful to explain, when highlighting these specific coming calamities, that "such things must happen, but the end is still to come" (verse 7).

Then our Lord made a succinct, foundational statement declaring one primary sign that had to occur first. He said, "The gospel must first be preached to all nations" (verse 10).

Matthew's description of the same occasion adds further insight. Here we read these words of Jesus:

> "This gospel of the kingdom will be preached in the whole world as a testimony to all nations, and then the end will come."
>
> Matthew 24:14

Note especially the six additional words in Matthew's account: *And then the end will come.*

A careful, word-by-word review of Matthew's record of this vital declaration, looking in particular at the Greek words employed in the text, reveals some amazing insights into precisely how the world might eventually be evangelized, quite literally, prior to Christ's return.

This Gospel

First we note the expression *this gospel*. The word *gospel* comes from the Greek word *euangelion,* which simply means "a good message." *Euangelion* is related to the Greek verb *euangelizo,* meaning "to announce, bring, declare, show a good message or good news." Here Christ is speaking of "a good message" that in its simplicity declares, shows and announces the existence and reality of His Kingdom.

The message or proclamation need not be complex, nor does it have to be spoken. Its purpose is simply to present the salvation message clearly. That is the Good News!

Of the Kingdom

Then we discover that this "good message" is "of the kingdom"— meaning it concerns the kingdom of heaven. *Kingdom* is from the Greek word *basileia*, meaning "rule, realm, royalty." It is related to *basileus*, which describes "a foundation of power" or "a sovereign."

Thus, Jesus is speaking of a good message that declares, shows or announces the reality of the Kingdom—which is the realm, royalty and rulership of heaven, the basis of all our power.

Shall Be Preached

Next we discover that this "good message," in simplicity, is to be preached or announced. We first note, of course, the words *shall be*, which declare finality. It will happen—the "it" being the global preaching (or communicating) of this good message of the Kingdom.

The Greek word translated "preached" is *kerusso*, meaning to "proclaim, publish or herald." It does not necessarily mean declaring the Gospel through spoken words, such as from a pulpit, as we traditionally interpret the word *preach*. It actually refers to any form of communicating this "good message," so long as it announces the reality of God's realm and rulership as the basis of our power to be saved.

All the World

Now we discover the scope of the publishing or heralding of this Good News. It will be accomplished throughout "all the world." The Greek form of this word for *all* is *holos,* meaning "whole or complete." As a noun or adverb the word means "altogether, every whit, or throughout."

19

All appears 5,456 times in the Bible, or an average of almost five times per chapter. Clearly it is one of the most vital words in Scripture. As someone wisely said, "All means all, and that's all all means!" Here it simply means, "In and throughout the whole, entire or complete world."

But we note that this adjective precedes the noun *world*. And it is at this point in our text that we discover something most interesting.

The World

At first glance Christ's use of the expression *the world* seems clear. *All the world* means all the world, right? The Greek word translated "world"—*oikoumene*—means in its most basic sense "inhabited globe" or "populated land." But its makeup from other Greek roots suggests it is not merely our globe as a created and inhabited geological entity that is to be evangelized, but the *individual dwellings* where people live.

In fact, a more careful look at the related roots of *oikoumene* adds even more depth to our definition. The verb *oikeo*, for example, means "to occupy a house; to reside or inhabit." It comes from the Greek word *oikos*, meaning "a dwelling, a family." In some cases it may suggest "a sphere of influence." By using the word *oikoumene*, the Lord might actually have been suggesting that "this gospel" (or good message) that announces the reality and existence of His Kingdom would be "published and heralded in and throughout the whole globe—dwelling by dwelling, family by family, occupant by occupant."

Frank Kaleb Jansen, global mission strategist and leader of Adopt-a-People Clearing House, says of Christ's use of the word *oikoumene* in Matthew 24:14: "I believe Jesus is actually saying that this gospel of the Kingdom shall be proclaimed to *every home!*"[1]

Jansen appears to have support from W. E. Vine in his *Expository Dictionary of New Testament Words*. Vine suggests the word *oikos* ("dwelling"), which is a root of *oikoumene* when used in such texts as Acts 5:42 (where the disciples are said to have proclaimed the Gospel "house to house"), can actually mean "every home."[2]

Reaching every family or inhabited dwelling makes sense in the completion of Christ's Great Commission because the Lord clearly wants everyone to have access to the Gospel. Recall Peter's declaration that God is "not willing that any should perish, but that all should come to repentance" (2 Peter 3:9, KJV). Paul described the sweep of God's intention when He told Timothy that He desires "all men to be saved, and to come unto the knowledge of the truth" (1 Timothy 2:4, KJV).

As a Witness

The purpose of communicating or heralding the Gospel throughout the whole world, "dwelling by dwelling," is that it might become a witness to all who receive it. The word *witness* used here is from the Greek noun *marturion*, meaning "evidence given" or "testimony." *Marturion* is derived from the Greek word *martus*, meaning "a witness, record, martyr."

This "good news," the Lord is saying, will be communicated literally to all the inhabited world as "evidence given" to the reality of His Kingdom.

To All Nations

Once again a Greek expression translated "all" is used—but this is a different word from the one employed earlier in the text. Here the expression used is *pas,* meaning "all, any, every, the whole, whosoever, thoroughly." It is an adjective preceding *nations*, making it clear Christ's Good News will reach *every* nation or people group thoroughly before the end comes. Jesus is saying *the whole* of each people group or nation will hear. None will be missed.

Nations

Nations in our text means considerably more than mere geographical entities with boundaries that we think of today when looking at a map of the world. The Greek word used here for nation is *ethnos,* meaning "race, tribe, people, family of people, clan or subclan." Again note the unusual scope of the use of the word *ethnos.* Jesus was speaking of the reality of taking the Gospel not only to all people, right where they live (their *oikos*), but to all "peoples, races, tribes, groupings, clans and even subclans."

Ethnos is the Greek equivalent of the Hebrew *mispahot* used in Genesis 12:3, in which God promised Abraham that through him all the families (*mispahot*) of the earth would be blessed. *Mispahot* refers to "races or subdivisions of ethnic and national groups." Jesus was suggesting here that all peoples everywhere, even in small subclans, will receive the Good News.

Isn't it apparent that for this to happen, the Gospel must be taken literally to where these people live—their *oikos?*

The End Will Come

Only after all the preceding phases occur, according to Jesus, can we anticipate the full culmination of God's plan. Only then will "the end" come.

When our Lord spoke of "the end" ultimately coming, the Greek word used is *telos,* meaning "goal, ultimate objective, conclusion, result or purpose." *Telos* here speaks of Christ's ultimate objective or purpose of His coming Kingdom. *Heko,* translated "come" in our text, means "to arrive" or "come into fruition." Jesus was saying that when all the requirements of the text have been met, His ultimate goal or objective will arrive or come into fruition.

A Summary Paraphrase

There we have it. A detailed and significantly amplified look at all Jesus was saying in Matthew 24:14 might read as follows:

> "And this good message [that declares, shows and announces the existence and reality] of this Kingdom, which is the realm, royalty and rulership of heaven [the basis of our power], shall be proclaimed, published and heralded in and throughout the whole and completely inhabited globe or land [dwelling by dwelling, family by family, occupant by occupant] as

a witness and testimony [of the reality of this Kingdom] to all, any and every race, nation, tribe, people group, clan and subclan, and then [and only then] the ultimate goal, objective and purpose of the Kingdom will fully arrive [and come into fruition]."

We can abbreviate the paraphrase as follows:

"This good message from the realm of heaven must be presented personally and completely to every family in every part of the inhabited world—right where people live—and only then God's purpose, as well as the ultimate goal of the Church, will be fulfilled."

The Old-Fashioned Way

Smith-Barney, the prestigious American investment company, tells would-be investors, "We make money the old-fashioned way. We earn it!" They are suggesting that no matter how many gimmicks and trendy ideas other agencies might use to increase investments for their clients, ultimate success will come because their organization works hard. That is "the old-fashioned way"!

Such is a principle we might apply to emerging strategies of world evangelization. In the midst of today's explosive technological developments in communication, it is easy to overlook the biblical simplicity with which the early Church employed her strategies of evangelism. Yet if we are ever to measure the completion of the task of taking the Gospel to "every creature" (Mark 16:15, KJV), we must not neglect evangelism the old-fashioned way.

True, technological advances may speed up the process of evangelism significantly, as well as confirm the fruit, but the only truly measurable way to finish the task is the old-fashioned way: *The Church must go where people live.*

In Acts 4 we read about the dramatic results following the healing of a crippled man at the Gate Beautiful (Acts 3:1–10). Because of this miracle, the religious authorities were worried, noting the ever-increasing impact the preaching of the Gospel was having on the city of Jerusalem. After bringing Peter and John before the San-

23

hedrin (the ruling council) for questioning, the authorities realized that even though these two men were "unschooled, ordinary men" (Acts 4:13), their strange doctrine was spreading. So they conferred privately regarding the matter.

> "What are we going to do with these men?" they asked. "Everybody living in Jerusalem knows they have done an outstanding miracle, and we cannot deny it."
>
> Acts 4:16

The expression *everybody living in Jerusalem knows* is significant. It sets the tone for an even more sweeping declaration from the same group of religious leaders in the next chapter.

There we discover the apostles still proclaiming the Good News boldly everywhere they went. Once again they were arrested and taken before the Sanhedrin for questioning. Angrily the high priest declared, "We gave you strict orders not to teach in this name. Yet you have filled Jerusalem with your teaching . . ." (Acts 5:28).

Note especially the accusation "You have filled Jerusalem with your teaching." What prompted the high priest to use the word *filled?* Was he exaggerating or speaking loosely, or did this religious leader have something more literal in mind?

Part of the answer can be found in the same chapter. The very last verse paints a picture of New Testament evangelism as orchestrated by the early Church leaders: "Day after day, in the temple courts and from house to house, they never stopped teaching and proclaiming the good news that Jesus is the Christ" (Acts 5:42). The Authorized Version says, "Daily in the temple, and in every house, they ceased not to teach and preach Jesus Christ."

The suggestion here is one of totality—"house to house" (NIV) or "in every house" (KJV)—which might explain why the high priest spoke of Jerusalem as being "filled" with the apostles' teaching. Not a single *oikos* was missed.

Commenting on this passage in his excellent book *That None Should Perish,* Ed Silvoso suggests, "There is only one way to 'fill a city' and that is by doing it house to house."[3]

Simply stated, this is evangelism the old-fashioned way! It is going where people live—to each individual *oikos.*

The Early Church Method of Evangelism

A more careful look at this early Church method of evangelism reveals several characteristics that help us understand not only why it was so successful, but why it will be essential for the completion of Christ's Great Commission.

It Was Simple

First, the early Church method was *simple.* Its scope was sweeping while its focus was specific: Just go where the people live and don't miss anyone. Progress can be measured, quite simply, because everyone lives someplace. In New Testament days, of course, the disciples lacked the ability to leave a printed or recorded Gospel message, yet we see them carefully visiting "every house." They seemed to realize that going house to house was the logical way of responding to Christ's Commission to provide everyone reasonable access to the Good News.

Indeed, the author of Acts would later describe the results of Paul's extended ministry that began in Ephesus: "This went on for two years, so that all the Jews and Greeks who lived in the province of Asia heard the word of the Lord" (Acts 19:10). The only way this report (indicating that all had heard) could be received in any literal sense is if Paul had trained the early Church disciples to go to every *oikos.* And we do know that when Paul finally left Ephesus, he told the church elders, "You know that I have not hesitated to preach anything that would be helpful to you but have taught you publicly and from house to house" (Acts 20:20).

So Paul himself set an example by going from *oikos* to *oikos.*

25

It Was Systematic

The method of the early Church was also *systematic*. This alone would explain how Jerusalem could be "filled" with the apostles' doctrine or how "every house" could be visited.

Perhaps the disciples remembered the systematic manner by which Jesus had fed the five thousand. His systematic approach is evident in Mark's and Luke's records of this miracle. Mark refers to Christ's organization of the great crowd into companies of hundreds and fifties (6:40). Luke speaks of a similar approach (see Luke 9:14).

Is it possible that the disciples remembered this miracle when they looked at the task of evangelism, remembering how Jesus had tied the feeding of the five thousand to meeting people's eternal spiritual needs? First He had commanded His disciples to do the impossible—"You give them something to eat" (Mark 6:37; Luke 9:13)—while all they could produce was a small lad's lunch. But the boy's willingness to sacrifice all he had released the miracle. Second, after performing the miracle, Jesus had declared, "Do not work for food that spoils, but for food that endures to eternal life, which the Son of Man will give you" (John 6:27).

This is the context, then, in which Christ employed a systematic strategy for feeding the multitude. Had the disciples not seated the crowd in companies of hundreds and fifties, those in the first few rows might have received far more food than they needed, perhaps even grabbing a few extra fish and loaves to take home, while those near the back of the crowd might never have been fed at all.

Sadly, this is often a picture of evangelistic endeavors today. Communism in the Soviet Union crumbled, opening this once-closed region to the Gospel. Denominations and mission agencies wanting to report to their constituencies that they were now in Russia hurried in to establish a presence in Moscow. Soon scores of organizations and denominations had established a presence in that city—certainly not a bad thing. But through the planting of these churches and ministries primarily in one city, the same people have been "evangelized" by repeated crusades and a multitude of thrusts;

and pedestrians around Red Square were drenched in a seemingly never-ending array of Gospel encounters (probably noticing that most campaigns include the presence of videocameras capturing these activities for "the folks back home").

In the meantime, less than a two- or three-hour drive in almost any direction from Moscow reveals villages and towns with multitudes far in excess of the crowd Jesus fed who have not received even one presentation of the Gospel. The back rows have already been missed!

It Was Strategic

But there is yet a final vital characteristic of the early Church method of evangelism that we must not overlook. Their plan was clearly *strategic*.

Strategic means "that which counts the most." The New Testament Church went to every *oikos* (home) because they knew this strategy counted the most in obeying the Commission Christ gave His Church to tell everyone about His love. It was probably obvious to the disciples that this was the only way to measure their progress.

Even today in our high-tech society, this is still the surest way to chart our progress in completing the Great Commission. True, television, radio and mass evangelistic crusades are vital, even essential. Television can reach remarkable numbers of people, for example (in nations where it is permitted), in a relatively short time. Radio has an even greater reach. But it is impossible to know exactly which homes scattered across a vast region have TV or radio, or if they are tuned in when the Gospel is proclaimed.

Continued blitzes assure us of greater saturation. But, significant as these media are, it is impossible to measure whether all people have had at least some reasonable contact with the Gospel as a result. We can measure our progress in providing everyone reasonable access to the Gospel only by going physically to where they live.

When coupled with other methods of evangelism in cooperative efforts (such as television, radio, mass evangelistic crusades, film evangelism, etc.), going to every *oikos* becomes even more strategic.

A Veteran Speaks

Few individuals in the twentieth century have had a greater impact on global missions than the late Oswald J. Smith of the renowned People's Church of Toronto, Canada. At a memorial service following the death of Dr. Smith, Billy Graham called him one of the greatest missionary statesmen of our generation. For more than a half-century, literally hundreds of missionaries were supported by the People's Church as a result of Dr. Smith's passionate appeals for missionary advance. Often the church gave three times as much for missions as it kept for local needs. (Most churches today do well to give ten percent of their income for missions.)

As the veteran pastor was transferring the leadership to his son Paul, Dr. Smith offered this assessment of the ultimate challenge of reaching the whole world, literally, for Jesus:

> For more than 30 years I have prayerfully considered the problem: How can we evangelize the world in the space of one generation? Long ago I was convinced that we could never send out enough missionaries. For a while I gave up hope. But there must be a way. After travel and study in nearly 100 countries, I have come to this conclusion—the only way we are going to be able to carry out the Great Commission, 'Go into all the world and preach the gospel to every creature,' will be by means of the printed page. By the systematic use of the printed page we shall be able to enter into every home and thus reach every individual with the gospel message.[4]

Oswald J. Smith understood the significance of *oikos* evangelism, especially through the use of the printed page. He was convinced it was the key to reaching everybody, particularly if methods like audio messages could also be used to reach illiterates. But the focus must be on everybody.

So that is why I am writing this book—and why I am telling the remarkable story of Haribo, the old chief introduced in the vignette at the start of this chapter whose dramatic testimony, in similar vignettes, is woven throughout the book. (Later we will add an equally inspiring account of a Pygmy tribal chief in the equatorial rain forest of Africa whose conversion opened the door for the planting of sixteen Pygmy churches with more than four thousand converts in just thirteen months.)

The purpose of Haribo's story and the many other testimonies in this book is to show that everybody, everywhere, can be reached at their *oikos*—if the Body of Christ has the will to do it. And it can happen soon!

Frankly, the Church must become increasingly uncomfortable with the notion of merely reaching as many people as possible with the Gospel before Jesus comes. We should settle for nothing less than "every creature," since anything less is outside the will of God (see 2 Peter 3:9). We must employ every means and method to reach this goal, especially the simple, old-fashioned New Testament plan to go where people live.

Happily, the Church is catching the vision afresh of *oikos* evangelism. And many groups (as we will see in the pages that follow) are embarking on a bold challenge to finish what the early Church began—in our own generation. I invite you to join me on this journey as we follow in the footsteps of some "beautiful feet" on their way to every dwelling on earth with the Good News!

Seasons of the Rain

Ceremonially he was named Haribo by his parents, who stood naked as they sacrificed the fattest of their pigs to the spirits of the Kwaio Mountains in a remote island in the Solomon Islands. Theirs was a mystic region of the Pacific where headhunters and cannibals still existed. They voiced a prayer to whatever gods might be listening, asking that their tiny son be allowed to see many yam harvests and seasons of the rain.

Marking these annual events was how the Kwaio peoples (for whom yams provided the main staple) measured their years. They had no concept of the modern calendar, even though the Gregorian calendar, instituted by Pope Gregory XIII, had been used throughout much of the world since 1582. Nor did they realize humankind was fewer than two decades from a major turning point—what people of a more developed society called the twentieth century.

As that century was about to dawn half-a-world away, America would be victorious in the Spanish-American War. Her ground forces would defeat the army of Spain at Santiago, Cuba. The most famous of these troops, the Rough Riders led by Teddy Roosevelt, would capture San Juan Hill on July 1, 1898.

Of course, neither Haribo nor his parents knew anything of this. Nor did Haribo know, a mere youth of fifteen yam harvests as the year 1900 arrived, that a new century was dawning. Amazingly, he would see another 95 seasons of the rain, with their accompanying harvests of yams, before tears would fill his eyes and he would understand the reason he had been kept alive for so many years.

Seeds of the Harvest

It was Nepal's monsoon season and the waters of the Daraudi River, usually calm, churned angrily. It would quickly drag into its depths anything caught in its torrents.

As Bishnu Pokhrel stood looking at the raging Daraudi, he told himself it would be better to plunge into the river with his entire family than face the cruel, ongoing vengeance of his offended Hindu god. Only death, he was convinced, would bring deliverance to his entire household by releasing their lives into another cycle of higher, better existence. He had to persuade his wife to join him. And since circumstances had devastated them both in recent days, he was certain she would agree. Besides, Hindu wives always did what they were told.

Bishnu sighed heavily as he thought of his troubles and how the cruelty of his gods had brought him to the river.

A Black Ram Sacrifice

Bishnu Pokhrel was a strict Hindu born in a typical village of Nepal. He was more fortunate than most, for he was able to attend school for several years, long enough to learn to read and write. But at age eleven Bishnu had to help more on his parents' village farm, so his schooling ended. Most of his time now would be spent tending goats.

During his spare moments Bishnu began to read the Hindu scriptures, often chanting them rhythmically for many hours as he watched the goats throughout the day. This way he was able to memorize lengthy passages of the sacred writings of Hinduism. Every morning after a traditional bath for purification, Bishnu repeated special prayers 108 times. He became a devout Hindu, an example to everyone in the small village.

Through his teen years Bishnu sought work by laboring in the fields of neighbors, gaining a reputation as an able worker. Marriage finally came at nineteen, and later the birth of his first child, a son. Bishnu felt truly fulfilled.

But his joy was short-lived as serious emotional problems developed. One day while climbing a tree to cut food for his animals, Bishnu fell. His injuries brought pain, dizziness, loss of appetite and insomnia. Friends and neighbors, even Bishnu himself, attributed his fall to an evil spirit. In the fleeting times when he could sleep, he was haunted by frightful dreams of painful scorpion bites, tiger attacks and stampeding water buffalo. Was insomnia better than sleep with these torturous nightmares?

Bishnu's parents blamed his young wife, Reka, for their trouble, accusing her of bringing into the marriage some terrible god that had to be appeased with sacrifices. So the Pokhrels, in keeping with their tribal tradition, decided that a black ram had to be killed at the pillar of their house. But no relief came. Finally Bishnu was driven from the family home and forced to live in a cow shed. For months no one visited him, for fear of the strange god bringing about all these disasters.

After Reka gave birth to their second child, a girl, Bishnu's troubles only increased. Now there was another mouth to feed, and Bishnu could not find work. In desperation he called the local *jhankri* (witch doctor). The *jhankri* said that a goat must be killed, and in five days all would be well. The *jhankri* would keep the meat as payment.

Bishnu obliged but nothing changed. So other *jhankris* were called, fourteen in all over the next eighteen months. Each demanded payment, depleting Bishnu's resources. His plight continued to worsen until finally he fell into a semiconscious state that lasted nineteen days. When he came back to full consciousness, Bishnu discovered he had lost everything.

So it was that months later, because of the cruelty of his gods, Bishnu found himself returning to the Daraudi River, this time with his equally despondent wife, tiny son and infant daughter. They felt they had no other choice.

Each parent clutching a child, they walked slowly to the hilly overlook above the turbulent Daraudi. For moments Bishnu stood contemplating their fate. Then he said, "It's time!" Both of them, each holding a child, leaped into the raging river below.

A Portrait of Life

Bishnu lost his hold on his son and was tossed violently about for two hundred yards down the treacherous river. Then he was

33

swept onto the shore, where he watched in utter amazement as his entire family, even his infant daughter, washed up safely. Neighbors came running to the water's edge, scolding that it was their fault for "falling" into the river. It was obvious to the villagers that Bishnu and his family had angered the gods.

But some of the villagers took pity on Bishnu and suggested he visit a medical clinic for help. He spent a month at a clinic in Katmandu, Nepal's capital, but returned in the same physical and mental condition.

Later he traveled to a small mission hospital in the Gurkha district, about a day's walk from their home. There a Christian doctor gave him medication, along with some surprising words: "Don't sacrifice to the idols anymore. That won't wash away your sins." She told Bishnu about Jesus Christ and invited him to accept Jesus' wonderful gift of forgiveness and new life.

He took the medicine but rejected the spiritual advice, which he did not understand. But something inside compelled him to stop offering sacrifices to appease his gods.

Bishnu recovered his health but quickly forgot the message about Jesus.

A decade passed. One day two workers from Every Home for Christ passed through his village making "house calls." The workers visited every family and gave them two Gospel messages, one geared to adults, the other to children.

Bishnu was fascinated by the simplicity of one of the messages, *Are You Happy?* He read the booklet carefully several times, then decided to send in the response card to the address in Katmandu for additional information. He had vague memories of the doctor's words about forgiveness and wanted to know more about this "Son of God" called Jesus Christ. Hinduism offered nothing like this.

Soon the first of a four-part Bible lesson came, "The Way to a Happy Life." It provided Bishnu and Reka with an introduction to knowing Jesus Christ personally. Soon another Christian worker traveled to Bishnu's village to give him further nurturing.

So intense was Bishnu's hunger for God's truth that the worker gave him his own personal Bible. Bishnu read it, completed the four Bible lessons and surrendered his life to Christ. Reka followed, as did the children, now almost teenagers.

Weeks later Bishnu and Reka again stood looking into the waters of the Daraudi River. Once again their children were with them. But whereas a decade earlier, a little farther up the river, they had jumped in to die, today they stood at the edge of a more peaceful river, ready for the burial of Christian baptism. The river that a decade earlier had been a picture of death had become a portrait of life.

Is Literature Distribution Effective?

Bishnu's testimony seems to echo that of Jonah's:

> "The engulfing waters threatened me. . . . I sank down. . . . But you brought my life up from the pit, O LORD my God. . . . Those who cling to worthless idols forfeit the grace that could be theirs. But I, with a song of thanksgiving, will sacrifice to you. . . . Salvation comes from the LORD."
>
> Jonah 2:5–7, 9

The decision card Bishnu returned to Nepal's office of Every Home for Christ (EHC is actually called Every Home Concern in Nepal) was only one of 3,282 cards received that month. And in the same month, village evangelists visited more than 42,000 families in Nepal.

The every-home evangelism strategy I described in the last chapter has been instrumental in planting almost two billion printed Gospel "seeds" worldwide, not unlike the small booklet that helped Bishnu and his family come to know Jesus. Since the very first EHC initiative in Japan in 1953 (which we will look at in the next chapter), the planting of these seeds systematically, family by family, has brought a remarkable harvest of more than 22 million returned decision cards, each representing in some cases (like Bishnu's) more

35

than one person's decision to receive Jesus. In a recent twelve-month period, more than four thousand such cards were processed daily—over 1.4 million in a single year!

Still, many missions strategists continue to treat such evangelism as secondary to other methods. Is the printed page, even when used in a carefully developed, systematic strategy, an inferior or less effective means of communicating the Gospel?

Early in the twentieth century, Charles Cowman, missionary to Japan and founder of the Oriental Missionary Society, ran across the testimony of a young man who wrote, "I received a Scripture portion, and it was the first time I ever heard that there was a true and living God. I want Him." Cowman became convinced that the printed page would be essential in the ultimate evangelization of the world.

Here is how he described the simple telling of the Gospel story in his early days in Japan:

> From snow-capped Fuji to coral-reefed Loochu, neglected people are coming by the hundreds to the Savior. The pure gospel message accompanied by faith and prayer makes converts anywhere, even where idolatry has held sway for centuries. The greatest success has not been attained by our most skilled preachers. The simple story, told in the simplest way, has brought the multitudes.[1]

Decades later, toward the end of the twentieth century, we must not discount the amazing global increase of literacy that suggests the presence of at least one reader in the vast majority of families in the world. *USA Today* reported on September 8, 1995, that the present world average of adults who can read is 76 percent. Even in developing countries it is a remarkable 68.3 percent.[2] Except in some very remote areas, every home probably has at least one reader, maybe more.

And fully half the people of the world, according to Patrick Johnstone in his definitive intercessors' guide *Operation World*, attribute their salvation to the printed page.[3]

Gospel Literature Answers the Question

The late respected linguist Dr. Frank Laubach, recognized during his lifetime as the world's leading authority on literacy, once wrote, "The basic problems of teaching the world to read have been solved. But there is one unanswered question: What will these millions read?"[4] A grandson of Mahatma Gandhi told an American audience a generation ago, "Missionaries taught us to read, but Communists gave us the books!"[5]

In our generation we have the opportunity to offer the printed message of salvation.

The late Dr. Paul Smith of the People's Church in Toronto, son of the renowned Oswald J. Smith, wrote this in his book *World Conquest:*

> Aircraft, medicine, radio and records, together with many other devices, have certainly multiplied and accelerated the work of every flesh-and-blood missionary. However, with all of these methods combined, the present staff of missionaries, or even a greatly increased staff, could never reach the entire world with the Gospel in our generation. The hope of getting the task completed lies in literature—the Word of God and the Gospel message printed in the language of the people.[6]

Dr. Robert G. Lee, former pastor of the Bellevue Baptist Church of Memphis, Tennessee (presently pastored by Dr. Adrian Rogers), said of the printed page:

> Literature can be our most efficient medium of mass communication of the Gospel. Note that I say "most efficient" in terms of the price paid for it, the number of people reached, and the fact that the message can be read over and over again until it is understood. There is no other method that can compare with literature.[7]

Gospel Literature Has No Bad Days

One of the advantages of printed literature is its repeatable nature.

Recently while my wife, Dee, and I were spending a morning of prayer and fellowship in the home of Bill and Vonette Bright, founders of Campus Crusade for Christ, Dr. Bright shared his deep conviction about the printed page.

"If God were to give me miraculous, superhuman strength to go to every family on earth and preach for an hour about Jesus," he said, "or if, on the other hand, He permitted me to take a clear, printed message of salvation to every family on earth, there is no question I would choose the latter."

Dr. Bright added, "If I were to preach an hour to every family, there is no doubt that some days I'd probably not do the best job, and many families might not understand my message the first time through. But anointed literature has no bad days. It can stay for months or years, speaking over and over until the Holy Spirit penetrates the heart of the reader."

Such was the case with Bishnu and his entire family. Before he received the booklet from the Christian workers who visited his village, he was preached to by a dedicated doctor at a medical mission. We cannot discount the impact of that simple encounter, even a full decade later. Nor can we discount the fact that the doctor's medical help may have kept Bishnu alive until he finally received Christ. But it was the printed page, which could be read repeatedly, that finally drew Bishnu, and then his family, into an encounter with Jesus Christ.

Some decision cards to EHC, remarkably, have been mailed years after a campaign has concluded. In one year in Japan, for example, 51 decision cards were processed from a campaign in a particular region that had been completed six years earlier. In Africa a decision card came seventeen years after that specific type of literature and decision card had been used in an area!

Are the Conversions Genuine?

So the printed page, when used in a carefully developed, systematic strategy, is not an inferior or less effective means of communicating the Gospel. But how about the written responses to evangelistic literature? Are they as legitimate as the inquirers who respond at a mass crusade or through other means?

I believe there is no difference, if those who respond to literature are truly searching to know Jesus. Paul made it clear in his letter to the Christians at Rome that he was "not ashamed of the gospel, because it is the power of God for the salvation of everyone who believes" (Romans 1:16). The Good News, even when printed very simply in a booklet, can change a life when it is empowered by God's Spirit.

From almost any culture and context, lasting fruit provides ample evidence that conversions through simple house-to-house literature evangelism do last.

From Mafia to Ministry

A volunteer Sicilian worker, a young pastor, was riding his motorcycle through various villages and visiting each home. He approached the farmhouse of the Paterno family and knocked on the door. Salvatore Paterno, a young son in the family, answered the door but began shouting curses when the young pastor handed him a Gospel booklet and tried to explain why he was there. It was one of those tense moments Christian workers knocking on doors fear the most.

The pastor left and rode away on his motorcycle. But for some reason Salvatore kept the booklet.

A week later the pastor, who had put his address on each Gospel booklet, heard a knock at his door. He was shocked to recognize the same young man standing before him transformed. Gone were the flashing, angry eyes and sneering look. His face seemed to shine with joy.

The pastor invited Salvatore in and heard a remarkable story.

Months earlier, the young man told him, he had left home with one passion—to become as famous as his grandfather, who had worked his way into the high echelons of the Sicilian Mafia. The grandfather was said to have committed at least eighty murders. Even a popular film had been made of the old man's life story.

Young Salvatore wanted to break his grandfather's record and had been attending Mafia training, where he had learned secretive ways to kill an enemy. In fact, he had just returned home from this unusual training when the pastor came to the Paterno farmhouse.

After the visit, Salvatore could not put the small booklet aside. In fact, the moment the pastor sped away, he felt compelled to sit down in a chair and read it. As a result, the conviction of the Holy Spirit was not delayed by a day or even an hour. The youth knew he was a sinner destined for an eternity void of any hope. He sat quietly in his chair and prayed the simple prayer printed on the back page of the booklet. For Salvatore Paterno, the Good News had indeed become "the power of God for . . . salvation."

His parents despised his conversion, actually preferring that he remain with the Mafia. But Salvatore pursued his new life in Jesus with a passion. He attended an evangelical Bible school in Rome and later pastored churches in the towns of Niscemi and Barrafarnca.

It all began with a single "printed" seed!

Bearing Fruit in China

A young woman we will call Yamiko Kurusawa was born on the Buddha's birthday, April 8—an occasion in Japan of great festivity. They call it *Hana-metsuri*, "Flower Festival," and it is as meaningful to Buddhists as Christmas Day is to Christians. So Yamiko was proud of her birthday, feeling her life must have special meaning that would probably lead to some sort of Buddhist mission.

Yamiko's hometown was Hiroshima, a city famous throughout the world because of the devastation of the atomic bomb dropped in 1945. But Hiroshima is also well known in Japan as the religious center of the Buddhist sect Jodo-Sinshu.

Yamiko's family was serious about Buddhist teachings, partly because some of her relatives were temple priests. Yamiko attended the Buddhist equivalent of Sunday school at the community temple every week until she reached the sixth grade. She was rapidly becoming a devout Buddhist, learning from her mother that Buddhist teaching was the one and only truth.

But when Yamiko entered junior high school, she started reading a Communist newspaper called *Akahata*, meaning "Red Flag." It was mailed regularly to her brother, who was 22 and whom the Japanese Communist Party was seeking to enlist. But the young girl read it with even more enthusiasm than her brother.

"As a naïve teenager," she says, "I was fascinated with Communist ideals, and before long I was sharing these concepts in my classroom as well as at home."

Then one day a young follower of Jesus came to the Kurusawa home. Yamiko answered the door and received an eight-page Gospel pamphlet entitled *A Voice Is Calling You*.

"My heart became warm," she says, "as I took the booklet into my hand and began to read words that have never left my memory: 'Come unto me, those of you who are weary and who carry heavy burdens, and I will give you peace.'"

Yamiko wanted desperately to understand more about this Person named Jesus Christ. Who was He and why did He say those beautiful words? Then she noticed that she could fill out a special card and receive something called a Bible correspondence course. Yamiko had never heard of a Bible.

"When I wrote to the office in Japan," she continues, "I was told about a church that distributed the Gospel messages in my community. God soon gave me courage to attend the church. And a year after receiving the Bible lessons, I was baptized in water at this church, making a public confession of my commitment to Christ. This surprised my family, of course, and they tried to stop me. But I knew my life was completely changed. Because of Christ, I had found what I could not find in Buddhism or Communism."

One day Yamiko was reading John 15:16, where Jesus speaks of choosing His disciples "to go and bear fruit—fruit that will last." Yamiko believed she was called to do just that and decided to become an evangelist.

After high school graduation, several years of work, seminary study and six months of special prayer, Yamiko was convinced the

Lord was calling her to China. At that time, 1972, such a mission seemed impossible. China had been a closed door, after all, for many decades. But strangely, within just a few weeks of her call from the Lord, Mao Zedong opened the doors of China to America's President, Richard Nixon.

After years of continuous prayer, Yamiko's church ordained her as their very first missionary to China. Following two years of language training in Hong Kong, Yamiko was recruited by the Teachers University of Xian (pronounced Shian), a major city in China, as a Japanese language teacher. She could live and work in Xian for a year supported by the Chinese government.

As the only Christian among seven foreign teachers on her campus, God began to lead Yamiko to other believers, some of them secret believers because of government oppression. One of these was a peasant girl from the countryside who served the teachers living in the dorm and whose mother led a Christian meeting in her house every Sunday. What joy it gave Yamiko to provide a large box of Chinese Bibles, brought by Christian couriers, for those believers who for years had had nothing but handwritten portions of Scripture!

Later Yamiko received a two-year contract with the 8,000-student Jilin University in Changchun City, Manchuria. At first her attempts to evangelize there met with strong opposition from university authorities. An officer from the notorious Public Security Department, a police agency, even gathered all the foreign students and teachers on campus and warned them not to interfere with government policies regarding religion.

"Please don't forget," he said sternly, "that there is freedom of religion in this country, but not of religious propaganda."

Yamiko Kurusawa knew this spokesman was speaking directly to her. Still, she pursued every possible way to share the Good News with those around her. In December, for example, she decided to hand-deliver Christmas cards to all the Chinese teachers in the Department of Japanese Studies. She was surprised to receive a Christmas card in return from the chairman of the department, and even more surprised to see that he had written a Bible verse inside the card.

Several days later Yamiko visited the professor in his office.

"I went to church for several years when I studied your language in Japan," he explained. "Many times I thought about being baptized." Then he added, "Miss Kurusawa, the Bible is great literature indeed. You should introduce it to your classes. For instance, you could recommend it in your Reading of Japanese Literature class."

Yamiko could not believe what she was hearing. The Public Security official had warned the foreigners that they were forbidden to evangelize, but now she was receiving official permission from the head of her department to use the Bible as a textbook in her classes!

So on Christmas Day Yamiko used her Bible to tell eighty students about the birth of Jesus Christ. She also taught them the Christmas carol "Silent Night." None of the students, representing remote places throughout China, had ever heard "Silent Night," and only four of the eighty had ever heard of Christmas.

Soon Yamiko opened her room for Bible study every Sunday for both Chinese and Japanese students. Many have not only received Christ but have been publicly baptized.

You can see a sparkle in Yamiko Kurusawa's eyes as she refers several decades back to the day a worker from Every Home for Christ came to her doorstep with the Good News. That house call changed her life, and the seed that took root in her heart has indeed produced "fruit that will last."

How did this simple strategy of house calls to the nations begin? Let's take a look at the inspiring answer.

Favor of the Gods

In Haribo's thirtieth rainy season, he stood sacrificing chickens at the famous Kwaio "healing stone." This was a shrine to the gods of his people located high in the interior Kwaio hills of Malaita in the Solomon Islands. The huge stone, they believed, was the key to finding favor with their ancestral gods.

By this time Haribo was well established as a leader in his village. He had learned during his early years to be a faithful young warrior, and had demonstrated to his father an unusual hunger for spiritual things. In his twelfth yam harvest he had undergone the traditional tribal rite of manhood. Now he was becoming a priestly leader of his people who understood the ways of ancestral worship and guided the people to be more faithful to their gods.

Neither he nor his fellow Kwaio tribespeople knew that seeds for a global war—the "Great War," or World War I—were germinating in a far-off place called Europe. Nor did they know that a great revolution was stirring in a place called Russia, where the czar would be put to death and all religion abolished. This would happen in Haribo's thirty-second season of the rains. Modern calendars would show the year as 1917.

How, in this remote volcanic island in the western Pacific Ocean (one of a hundred inhabited islands in a chain east of New Guinea), would the tribal chieftain and his peoples ever hear about the one true God who sent His Son to save them?

A Prairie Fire Commissioning

It was a miracle the young couple survived. Smoke alarms were unheard of in the mid-1940s, and Jack and Hazel McAlister would soon have been suffocated by the dense smoke.

It was December 18, 1946, a freezing night on the prairies of western Canada, when fire swept through the McAlisters' church building. In almost no time the sanctuary was consumed. Smoke billowed unchecked into the modest, two-story residence that had been added onto the church.

Jack and Hazel had spent much of the day signing and sealing almost seven hundred Christmas cards for radio listeners to their three-month-old inspirational program heard throughout western Canada. Jack had also signed a hundred cards for personal friends and family.

That Wednesday evening was the last midweek Bible study before Christmas. The young pastor was just ending a six-week series on the Song of Solomon, the book that beautifully portrays our relationship to Christ. The congregation was not as large as usual; the Christmas rush had taken its toll. But everyone had sung and prayed together, as Christians do all over the world at this special season, and God's presence came in such a special way that many did not leave until 11:30 P.M.

Jack tended the furnace as usual, and he and Hazel retired about midnight, exhausted. They fell instantly into a deep sleep, only to be awakened 35 minutes later—no doubt by divine intervention for the sake of a future that would touch millions of lives.

They woke up in a frenzy, choking in the dense smoke. Their best plan was to jump from the second-floor bedroom window to the roof, then down to the ground. So Jack groped through the blinding smoke, pushed out the storm window and grabbed Hazel, who for some reason had struggled back to bed. He pushed her out the window, then followed.

Now they were on the roof outside the window but still in great danger. Heavy, black smoke was pouring from the bedroom window. Neither could breathe, and it was freezing cold. Jack, who was wearing only summer pajamas himself, wanted something to protect his wife. He reached back through the smoke into the window and pulled a blanket off the bed, which stood nearby.

"Then we had to jump or fall or whatever," Jack says, "and I don't know if I came down head, feet or arms first. I just remember falling, and somehow my little wife came tumbling down on top of me."

Barefoot in the Snow

The couple knew God had protected them as they stood bare-foot in the snow in the church driveway. They were wearing only their nightclothes, with Hazel wrapped in the blanket.

"I can't put into words," Jack said later, "the thoughts that rushed through my mind as I stood there watching the fire blaze and listening to its roar. It was almost deafening. It seemed that all we possessed was about to be destroyed by flames, and all I had between where I stood and heaven was a pair of summer pajamas. It was a strange sensation."

Only ninety seconds had elapsed from the time Jack and Hazel had been awakened. That is all the time it takes (as Jack would often say in later years) for everything to be taken from us—sometimes even less.

Stunned, Jack stood beside his young wife, their lungs and throats burning from the hot smoke. Kind neighbors from across the road rushed to offer assistance and warm clothing. By now firemen had arrived, and Jack told them where the doors, electric switches and stairways were so they could attack the fire more efficiently. Then he just stood there, thanking God tearfully for sparing their lives.

Suddenly Jack realized he did not have his most prized possession, his Bible. It was still upstairs in their bedroom. He was just darting back into the building when a shocked fire chief grabbed him by the arm.

"Where do you think you're going?" he demanded.

Jack explained he had to get his Bible.

"That's out of the question!" the chief said. Then, seeing a determined look in Jack's eyes, he asked a nearby policeman to restrain him.

The policeman soon became distracted, however, and before anyone knew what was happening, Jack bolted through the smoke, rushed up the stairs and grabbed his Bible and "gem book"—a collection of priceless spiritual nuggets he had gathered over several years. Then down the stairs Jack bounded, seemingly oblivious to

47

the flames and smoke, leaping into the street with his cherished possessions.

To Jack, this personal rescue turned the whole night into victory. Later he would say those two simple items were worth more than any dozen buildings in the entire city of Prince Albert, Saskatchewan.

By now the blaze was out of control and heading toward the little back room in the church where Jack had his study. All his books, Bible college notes and miscellaneous clippings and papers would be destroyed. This time Jack dispatched what he would later call a "rush message" to his heavenly Father via God's reliable "wireless" called prayer.

God was already right there anticipating what he was about to pray. Words came to the young man's mind from the apostle Paul on a stormy sea many centuries earlier: "There stood by me this night the angel of God, whose I am, and whom I serve, saying, Fear not" (Acts 27:23–24, KJV). Then, for no apparent reason, the roaring fire stopped dead in its tracks.

It was the second miracle of the night.

Afterward, with the help of two friends, Jack was able to rescue most of his books and personal papers. Some would carry the smell of smoke for years, but much of his library had been spared.

It was an experience Jack and Hazel would never forget. Theirs was a prairie fire commissioning for what lay before them, and it taught the McAlisters early on that possessions mean little. Only people last forever. And Jack was determined from then on to invest everything he had in getting people to heaven.

They would face many fiery trials as God used this young couple to begin a ministry that—through the power of the printed page, saturated with prayer—would probably touch as many people directly with the Gospel as any ministry in the history of the Church. Indeed, five decades later, on May 12, 1995, when Jack and Hazel celebrated their fiftieth wedding anniversary and shared much of this story with me, they remembered those fiery moments and rejoiced in the realization that the ministry they had birthed had been responsible for taking the Good News to nearly one billion homes and as many as 4.5 billion people.[1]

Fiery Trials

The personal trials for Jack McAlister began long before the fire broke out on that cold December night in 1946, destroying their first church and catapulting him and Hazel into a ministry to the nations.

Jack was born in February 1924, and was only twenty months old when his parents learned that he was the first person in all of western Canada to contract poliomyelitis. The word *polio* then was much like the word *cancer* today. Little was known about how to treat this feared disease, and it spelled hopelessness.

The physicians tending to him seemed to do everything backwards—often exactly the opposite of what they should have done, which affected him significantly for life. But God knows exactly what He is doing, as Jack would often testify, and He reminds us powerfully through the pen of Paul "that in all things God works for the good of those who love him, who have been called according to his purpose" (Romans 8:28). Jack was certain he had been called according to God's purpose, and that was enough.

Jack grew up in a home with deeply committed Christian parents. And after his maternal grandmother died, his grandfather moved in with them. Grandpa Manly had retired from teaching after his eyesight failed. But although he could not see very well, he was determined not to let his life go to waste. So he took to the streets almost daily, distributing life-saving printed messages to all who would receive them.

Grandpa Manly bought large quantities of Gospel tracts unfolded because they were cheaper. He would fold hundreds of them at a time while telling his grandson stories of how people responded to "the Good News." These stories made a lasting impact on Jack.

Later in his life Jack was sure that, had he not contracted polio, he would have joined the Royal Canadian Air Force during World

War II. He had a deep passion for flying, and he would have been just the right age to enter the service at the start of the war in 1939. Jack was also sure that, regardless of what might have happened to him in the war, the sport of hockey would have consumed him because of his intensely competitive spirit.

Everyone in Canada, it seemed, played hockey. But not Jack McAlister. He often resented God because he could not skate like the other boys. His earliest memory: sitting high above the skating rink in St. Thomas, Ontario, looking down onto the ice and saying, with tears, "O God, why can't I skate like those other kids? Everyone can do that but me."

But God had a purpose in it. Jack's competitive nature would be redirected. Indeed, he would later be convinced that if an ordinary worker devoted eight hours a day, five days a week, to his job, Jack would work for God at least six days a week and double the working hours each day. This would take its toll, both emotionally and physically, over the years, but it would allow Jack to accomplish far more in half a lifetime than others might in two lifetimes.

When Jack was in his teens, his competitive nature got the better of him. He could not understand what benefit he would gain from courses like Latin and algebra, so he left high school after two years and enrolled in business college. He wanted to change the world and he wanted to do it now.

His early business career—first at a large Canadian candy firm, then at the largest manufacturer of firefighting equipment in Canada—would continue for several years, during which God spoke to Jack and established foundational principles in his heart that would later guide his life.

One day at LeFrance Fire Engine Company, for example, the president said something to which Jack responded, "That's terrible!"

The president said tersely, "Jack, there's only one thing that's terrible in all the world, and that's missing heaven."

Jack was startled. He had not known the president was a believer. But he never forgot those words. And even in his teens, he felt he had to do all he could to keep people from missing heaven.

Living by Faith

When Jack was eighteen, God called him to prepare for full-time Christian ministry. He enrolled in a Bible school in western Canada.

In prayer one day not long after arriving at the college, he committed himself to witness for Christ every single day to someone who did not know Jesus. Jack knew he was in school not just to obtain head knowledge but to learn soulwinning. And, like Grandpa Manly, he would use literature to help him reach this objective.

But the goal was not always easy to achieve. Often he had to board a streetcar and travel the entire circuit several times until he could find at least one person who had never heard about Jesus. He had two Gospel tracts he was especially fond of and always kept a quantity in his pocket. As he began to witness to someone, he would ask the Lord inwardly which of the booklets to give.

During his years at Bible school, God also taught Jack about faith. His parents were careful not to send him money regularly, though they could have. He lived with friends who charged him five dollars a week for room and board—a huge sum at the time, especially when you didn't know where it was coming from!

So through those years, Jack trusted God. Often strangers from thousands of miles away sent the young student money. Relatives he had never met sent him money. More than once he found money on the street. And on several occasions he went out and preached on weekends, for which he received offerings that would cover a few more weeks of rent. He was amazed that people actually paid someone to preach!

Leaders of the Presbyterian Church, who were finding preachers in western Canada in short supply, approached the president of Jack's Bible school. Did he have any talented young students who were good preachers? They would be paid $25 to preach in three towns on a given Sunday.

Because of Jack's strong gifts of communication, he was one of the students selected. He could not believe anyone would pay him $25 to do what he was actually called by God to do! But each weekend of preaching to the Presbyterians covered another five weeks of room and board.

Then Jack was asked to serve as chairman of the Personal Workers Committee and head up its literature effort. Soon he was speaking to students at the college every week about how to win souls through the use of literature.

By the time he finished Bible school three years later, he had led more than two hundred people to Jesus—on the streets, in buses, in parks and wherever he might find them. He had cultivated a passion for souls.

After graduation in May 1946, Jack married Hazel Swanson, the attractive daughter of a prominent pastor in their denomination, and accepted a position as full-time pastor of a small church in Prince Albert, Saskatchewan, where he had filled in during his final summer break. He had just turned 22.

In October Jack and Hazel began a weekly radio program called "Tract Club of the Air" that offered both inspirational encouragement and evangelistic literature. They sent small packets of material to radio listeners who requested it for their own personal evangelism. The listeners, in turn, shared financial gifts, as God enabled them, to help cover the cost of these "paper missionaries" so quantities could be sent to missionaries overseas.

Weeks later, on December 18, fire would sweep through their little church and burn into Jack's heart the conviction that "brick and mortar" means little in the Kingdom of God, while only the soul is eternal. That fire "commissioned" Jack and Hazel McAlister to a much greater mission—one that would touch the world.

Souls Are Eternal

During the earliest weeks of their new vision, Jack became convinced even more of the significance of the printed page in evangelism. A missionary from Africa, Austin Chawner, visited Prince Albert and saw the literature Jack was offering over the radio. This was exactly what was needed in Africa, Austin told him. In fact, he had just purchased a small, manual printing press in Africa, but lacked the paper to print the needed messages.

Then Austin recounted a remarkable story that affected the young preacher deeply.

An illiterate old man from a remote African village had found a small Gospel pamphlet and walked an astounding two hundred miles to find someone who could read the message to him in his language. When he found that person, he asked him to read it slowly for him. The man obliged. Then he said, "Read it one more time." The man read it over and over.

Suddenly the old man grabbed the paper out of the reader's hands, thanked him for taking so much time to read him the message and headed back two hundred miles to his village deep in the bush.

Once there, the old man held up the same Gospel booklet (perhaps upside-down!) and began to "read" the message he had memorized from repeated hearings. A crowd gathered to listen. The village was illiterate but had heard about the gift of reading and believed that whatever was printed on paper must be true. Many professed Christ, including the old man, as a result of the Gospel pamphlet.

When Jack heard this testimony and recalled his own experiences of using Gospel literature to win two hundred souls to Jesus in Bible school, he became convinced God would use the printed page to win multitudes to Jesus.

Months later Jack traveled to Africa and confirmed Austin Chawner's testimony about the belief of illiterate Africans in the authority of what was printed on paper. Farmers there would do anything they could to obtain a piece of literature. Then they would cut it into pieces, attach various pieces to sticks, and place a stick in the corners of their fields to ward off evil spirits. Villagers were convinced that the words on these pages, even if they could not read them, held that kind of power.

By then, during the late 1940s, literacy was spreading rapidly across Africa. It was only a matter of time, Jack realized, before there would be at least one reader in each of these African homes.

And when that happened, people would truly be ripe for the harvest. They could be reached right where they lived.

The Families of the Earth

Following several years of fruitful ministry in Canada, a Baptist pastor in southern California invited Jack to help launch "The Tract Club of the Air" on what was then one of the largest radio stations, Christian or secular, in the United States. Jack and Hazel prayed about what to do.

Then the Lord spoke to Jack in an unusual way. It was a warm day in the summer of 1951. Jack was meditating on Genesis 12, in which God told Abraham:

> "Get thee out of thy country, and from thy kindred, and from thy father's house, unto a land that I will show thee: And I will make of thee a great nation, and I will bless thee . . . and in thee shall all families of the earth be blessed."
>
> Genesis 12:1–3, KJV

Jack was consumed with the passage. Each time he read it, it seemed the message was for him. God was speaking to him directly through Scripture.

So after much prayer, Jack and Hazel were sure God wanted them to move. Within weeks they were on their way, and soon Jack began the weekly radio program in America.

As "The Tract Club of the Air" grew in popularity, Jack's vision for touching the whole world also grew. But there was something special about God's promise to Abraham that Jack could not erase from his mind: *And in thee shall all families of the earth be blessed.* Somehow he was sure this was a promise directly to him. The words *all* and *families* especially intrigued him. He sensed God had a clear plan that soon would unfold, and its focus would be "all families of the earth."

54

Reaching Every Home

Jack mobilized his radio listeners to send a million Gospel messages to France, another million to Germany and yet another million to Italy. (Friends would say jokingly of Jack that the smallest number he knew was a million.) It wasn't long before "The Tract Club of the Air" outgrew its name and became a much larger vision called World Literature Crusade.

Early in 1953 Jack's brother, Bob, joined him in the WLC work. A new radio program was launched called "Oriental Opportunity," focused on mobilizing the Church in North America to help evangelize the Orient. Bob was to travel to the Orient to meet with missionaries and see the need firsthand. But days before the planned trip, Bob told Jack he felt checked in going. He sensed he should stay home and develop the ministry there.

Jack was confused. He felt certain Bob was to go. But that night Jack and Bob attended a missionary rally in California at which the Reverend Paul Pipkin preached what Jack later would describe as one of the greatest missionary messages he had ever heard.

He wept for the lost that night as never before. And he heard God's voice clearly: *You are the one I want to go to Japan.*

When Jack arrived in Tokyo in early 1953, it was one of the largest cities in the world. Japan was a vast, unevangelized nation of 83 million people. And two out of every three persons on earth lived in Asia.

Jack met Ken McVety, a respected fellow Canadian he knew only by reputation who had gone to Japan as a missionary two years earlier. Already Ken had learned to speak Japanese fluently. Together they walked out onto a busy street to ask people if they knew about Jesus.

The first man they spoke with had never heard Jesus' name. Another said he had read about Him in a history book once when he was in the university, but that was all he remembered. An old man wanted to know where this man called Jesus lived.

"We didn't find a single person who knew anything meaningful about Christ!" Jack recalls. Yet this was a country as literate then as the United States or Canada. It was possible to reach the people, Jack was convinced, but he knew it had to be done systematically, family by family, or else millions of people would be missed.

That night Jack and Ken met at Ken's new office flat at 346 Eifu Cho Sugiwami in Tokyo. There they placed a large map of the city on a typical Japanese *tatami* mat and prayed about a plan to reach every person with the Gospel in Tokyo, as well as in all of Japan. They agreed that if they were to take a Gospel message systematically to every family, it would be necessary to divide the city (and eventually the country) into manageable areas and assign each area to a church. Reaching every home, they were convinced, was the only way to make sure the job got done. It was the only way to measure the results. They also decided that because God loves children, they should print an extra message for each home designed specifically for boys and girls.

As the details of the vision unfolded, excitement filled the hearts of the two dreamers. Ken McVety was consumed with the dream to reach all of Japan with the printed Gospel, since there was a dearth of Christian literature at the time in that nation. A collection of the evangelical books he knew of available in the Japanese language could fit onto a shelf just thirteen inches long!

Questions surfaced that night about follow-up. They decided that a decision card should be included with each piece of literature, so all who responded could be sent some kind of follow-up Bible course.

By midnight the dream of what they called the "Every Home Crusade" was firmly planted in these two hopeful hearts. And how that dream would come to reality! Within five years every home not only in Tokyo but in all of Japan would be visited.

Today three additional coverages of the nation have been led by the Japanese Church. More than 392,849 Japanese seekers have sent in response cards indicating they have received Christ or that they want to know more about what it means to be a Christian.

In East Asia, carefully tabulated records from Every Home for Christ indicate that 411,210,994 "paper missionaries" have been distributed, the vast majority house to house. If South Asia is added (which includes the vast subcontinent of India), that number swells to an incredible 870,952,129 Gospel messages, or almost one billion. And since the vision has spread elsewhere—to Africa, Latin America, Europe and the Pacific—nearly two billion "paper missionaries" have been sent out to every country on earth.

What Jack saw as he prayed over the map of Tokyo with Ken McVety, less than seven years after his prairie fire commissioning, was really a simple plan. But if carried to its fulfillment, it could be one of God's key strategies to reach the world for Jesus. The next few decades and some extraordinary miracles (which we will look at in Part 2 of this book) would prove the job could be done.

Does it take super-Christians to reach the ends of the earth with the Good News? Or can ordinary believers like you and me help accomplish it?

4

The Face of Coconut Meat

There was a strange whistling sound in the skies, followed by a horrendous explosion. The Kwaio, a people of spears and machetes, had neither heard nor seen anything like it. Villagers everywhere lay dead or wounded. Another blast came, then another. It was hard to count the dead.

Weeks earlier a British government officer, a man with a face the color of coconut meat, had come to their island conducting a government survey. Malaita and the three other main islands in the Solomons—Marovo, San Cristoval and Guadalcanal—had served as a British crown colony since 1893. But coastal Kwaios had misunderstood the intrusion, and a few angry tribesmen had bludgeoned the official to death with their machetes, along with his party of police officers. Now the friends of the man with the face of coconut meat had come back to retaliate.

The explosions came from a British naval vessel commissioned from Australia to the waters off the coast of Malaita. Outsiders called the year 1927. Haribo knew it as his forty-second season of yam harvests.

As the shelling stopped and the battleship departed, Haribo wondered why all this hatred had been directed at his people. Fear filled his heart about the amazing power these enemies had. He knew they could return anytime and easily kill all the Kwaio.

Not only fear but hatred began to develop among the Kwaio for all outsiders. In fact, for the next half-century, visitors and even government officials would not be welcome to the interior of their island. Several Christian missionaries would try to penetrate the region and be martyred. Others would attempt to preach the Gospel, but the seed would fall on infertile soil.

As for Haribo, his fear would linger for many more yam harvests—in fact, for at least 63 of them—before he would meet an angel, quite literally, to escort him to a place where all his fears would flee forever.

Vanguards with a Vision

Remi Crespin's final letter to the Every Home for Christ office in France began with an urgent plea: "sos . . . Need more literature!" The letter came on June 13, 1993, just a few days before Remi died of cancer at age 56.

As a retired schoolteacher, Remi Crespin had taken on what seemed to be a one-man crusade to reach the lost throughout France. Since 1979 he had walked literally hundreds of miles through eight different regions of France, distributing messages of salvation to nearly one hundred thousand families.

During those years Remi asked only three things of the EHC office in Paris: a compass, a pair of binoculars and Gospel booklets to distribute home to home. He needed a compass, he said, to know where he was. And he needed the binoculars to spot distant villages that sometimes lay hidden in the French countryside.

Remi's efforts of evangelism are legendary in France. They serve as an example and blessing to many of his fellow Christians. But they also drew the attention of the enemy, and Remi was stricken with a deadly cancer. After three operations, he refused to give up. He told Pierre Clément, the EHC director in France, "I often return home from my trips exhausted, discouraged, frozen and soaked to the bone. But there is still only one thought on my mind: When is the next campaign?"

The last line of Remi's final letter to EHC reinforced his plea: "I have no Gospel literature left to distribute in the villages of Flers and Aubusson. Please send more."

Since the birth of the Every Home Crusade strategy in 1953, as I described in the last chapter, thousands of similar city, village and rural campaigns sponsored by Every Home for Christ have been spearheaded throughout the world in at least 177 nations. In France, for example, Remi was participating in a campaign called "Operation Villages." Because there are an estimated thirty thousand small towns and villages in France of some five hundred people each, Christians who want to be on the cutting edge of evangelism are encouraged to volunteer and visit one or more of these villages during their summer vacations. Many hundreds like Remi have enlisted in recent years. They are not full-time workers, not super-Christians, but ordinary believers who collectively reach millions of people with the Gospel as they visit families that might otherwise be overlooked.

There is Madame Mollier, a French widow in her seventies. In 1994 she sent the EHC office in Paris a lengthy list of villages she planned to reach house to house with Gospel messages that coming summer. Several months later, after the summer had passed, she sent a report listing the names of not only the villages she had promised to reach, but additional ones as well.

"I took the liberty of covering these 32 other hamlets in addition to the villages already assigned," she reported. "These added villages were well hidden in the French mountains, and I thought they risked being forgotten."

Madame Mollier had gone to every single home.

Growing Up and Going Out

The examples of Remi Crespin and Madame Mollier remind us how the early Church engaged in their strategies of evangelism. As New Testament believers (ordinary fishermen or tax collectors or people in business) grew up in Jesus, they went out with the message of His love and became vanguards with a vision, cutting-edge believers on the front lines of the battle for souls.

Growing up and going out—here is the challenge all believers ought to embrace.

Let's look at the early pages of Acts to see what made this emerging body of first-century believers so successful. We will discover some clearly defined patterns of early Church evangelism. And as we read through the whole of the book of Acts, we see those early models continually being refined and strengthened as the Church reached out to evangelize the world.

In particular, we find three foundational passages that paint a picture of how the Church grew up in Christ so she could go out with the Gospel. A careful look at these passages will guide us in how we might ultimately reach our cities—and the world—for Jesus in our generation.

First let's note Luke's description of the early Church immediately following the outpouring of the Holy Spirit. He pictures a Church being strengthened and sustained in her process of maturing:

> So continuing daily with one accord in the temple, and breaking bread from house to house, they ate their food with gladness and simplicity of

heart, praising God and having favor with all the people. And the Lord added to the church daily those who were being saved.

Acts 2:46–47, NKJV

Another foundational passage essential to our understanding of the growth and extension of the early Church is Acts 5:42:

Day after day, in the temple courts and from house to house, they never stopped teaching and proclaiming the good news that Jesus is the Christ.

A third foundational passage that will help us understand the heart of early Church evangelism is from Paul's departing exhortation to the Ephesian elders:

"I kept back nothing that was helpful, but proclaimed it to you, and taught you publicly and from house to house."

Acts 20:20, NKJV

From these three passages, a unique variety of interesting patterns emerges concerning the growth and outreach of the early Church. Together they constitute what we might see as the primary ingredients of a believer who "grows up in Jesus" so he or she can ultimately "go out for Jesus"! Do these ingredients characterize you and me?

A Persistent People

First we discover that the early Church refused to give up in her dual task of growing in Jesus and telling others about Him. We make this discovery almost in passing as we read in the first foundational passage the phrase *so continuing daily* (Acts 2:46, NKJV). The key word is *continuing*. It suggests that the early Church comprised a persistent people.

Persistence is "the quality of continuing in a task until its completion, no matter the obstacles." Consider the famous American inventor Thomas Edison. He personified persistence. It is said that Edison attempted some ten thousand separate experiments before discovering the secret to making a successful storage battery. Someone asked him later what it felt like to experience ten thousand failures. He replied, almost incredulously, "I didn't fail ten thousand times. I simply found ten thousand ways that wouldn't work."

At the heart of persistence is a spirit of determination. And the key to determination is purpose. Sadly, some believers seem to lack purpose in their lives. Many have never set goals for evangelizing the lost, for example, or considered the possibility that they might reach tens of thousands of families, as Remi Crespin and Mrs. Mollier did. These French volunteers were ordinary people who simply made themselves available for the task and demonstrated persistence while doing it.

Paul described his own spirit of persistence and determination when he told the Corinthians, "I run straight to the goal with purpose in every step" (1 Corinthians 9:26, TLB).

If we hope to complete the task of evangelizing the world in our generation by reaching every person in our cities, towns and villages with the Gospel, we will need a spirit of persistence.

A Consistent People

The early Church also manifested a quality of consistency. Look again at our first foundational passage, Acts 2:46–47, and notice the word *daily*. The New Testament believers were not involved merely on a particular day of the week, like the Sabbath or Sunday. They lived out their Christianity daily. They worshiped daily, evangelized daily, fellowshiped daily.

Daily is a word essential to our study. In fact, either *daily* or *day after day* is used three times in our first two foundational passages, suggesting that New Testament Christians were faithful and regular in their patterns of worship and service. Simply stated, they were a consistent people.

63

Consistency is "the quality of remaining constant." It speaks of maturity. Early Church believers were more than Sunday Christians. They demonstrated their discipleship constantly—in fact, daily.

Later Paul would write to the Galatian believers regarding the fruit of the Spirit called faithfulness (Galatians 5:22). In the days after the birth of the early Church, we see this fruit clearly evident. Surely this quality was the outflow of the enduing with power by the Holy Spirit that came on the Day of Pentecost. It tells us that Spirit-filled people will be consistent in their walk as well as in their work. Mature people always manifest a spirit of consistency.

A United People

Next we discover that the early Church served the Lord "with one accord" (Acts 2:46). *With one accord* is an expression that appears several times in the early verses of Acts (see also Acts 1:14 and 2:1, NKJV). It speaks of a united people.

Note the report from Acts 2:44 that "all who believed were together, and had all things in common" (NKJV). A church will never grow if its congregation is divided. Further, the Body of Christ at large will never have an impact on any community, much less the world, until it is united. As Ed Silvoso points out in his book *That None Should Perish* (Regal Books, 1994), unity is essential for developing a strategy to affect our cities significantly for Christ. Ed refers to the churches in Stockton, California, where pastors who met together regularly for prayer finally agreed they would no longer refer in their evangelism efforts to their individual churches, but tell the unsaved they represented simply "the Church in Stockton."

The key to unity, of course, is a spirit of cooperation—a quality clearly evidenced in the early Church. One thing is certain: No matter how pure a people may appear in proclaiming their doctrine, if they do not cooperate with others in strategies to win the lost for Jesus, they do not measure up to the unity of the early Church.

A Loyal People

We also find that the early Church was composed of a loyal people. We infer this from the fact that they met "daily . . . in the temple" (Acts 2:46, NKJV). First-century believers not only gathered in their homes but recognized the importance of coming together corporately. This suggests an attitude of loyalty toward the group. Early Church believers were committed to one another.

So in addition to unity, the Church needs loyalty. This loyalty must begin with a focus on and toward the local church. No church will ever grow beyond its walls to touch its community and the world meaningfully if it is divided and uncommitted. Thus, a spirit of commitment, which is at the heart of loyalty, is essential if we are to be a cutting-edge people.

Are we truly loyal to our local congregations?

A Giving People

Our first foundational text, Acts 2:46–47, next describes a church committed to "breaking bread," which pictures a giving people. Something in the expression *breaking bread* suggests a loving spirit of generosity and hospitality. Early believers gave of themselves as well as of their possessions. Such an attitude of servanthood is vital because Jesus said the world will know we are His disciples if we love one another (see John 13:35). And at the heart of loving is giving.

Jesus also said, "It is more blessed to give than to receive" (Acts 20:35). To break bread meant that early believers went out of their way to minister the love of Jesus generously to everybody, everywhere. A growing church is a loving, giving church—a church marked by a spirit of generosity.

A Going People

And from this spirit of giving will emerge a desire to be "going"! Note specifically where the disciples broke bread: "from house to house." This reveals a caring, concerned people who involved themselves willingly beyond the confines of their own spheres of comfort.

This pictures a "going" people. No church will ever grow simply by waiting for the community to come to it. Such would be impossible anyhow in the vast majority of villages and towns in the developing world, where not a single church exists. (More than ninety percent of India's towns and villages, for instance, have no church of any kind.) Thus, if we are to develop a growing church, we must develop "going" Christians willing to step out of the confines of their own congregation to touch a hurting, waiting world—house to house!

Remember how Jesus "went about doing good, and healing all that were oppressed" (Acts 10:38, KJV). Notice, He "went about"! God wants His children to get out and minister the love of Christ wherever people are hurting. Like the good Samaritan who went out of his way to minister to the man who had been severely beaten (see Luke 10:30–35), we must go out of our way to touch our neighbors.

Compassion becomes the key to a going people. We must be so flooded with Christ's love that it overflows into involvement. As Oswald J. Smith often preached, "Compassion is not pity. It is love in action."

A Happy People

There is more to be discovered about the early Church and her patterns for maturity and growth. The early believers not only broke bread from house to house, but they did so "with gladness . . . of heart" (Acts 2:46, NKJV). Gladness of heart pictures a joyous, happy people. The joy of the Lord is essential to a growing, vibrant church.

Joy is a fruit of the Spirit produced in and through believers who learn to walk in the Spirit (see Galatians 5:16, 22).

Joy also produces healthy, radiant, "reproducing" church members. Proverbs 15:13 declares, "A merry heart maketh a cheerful countenance" (KJV), and Proverbs 17:22 says, "A merry heart doeth good like a medicine" (KJV). Indeed, a happy church is a healthy church. And for a church to be truly happy, it must be involved in the evangelization of the lost. Jesus told His disciples there is joy in heaven over even a single soul who repents (see Luke 15:7, 10).

A Steadfast People

Equally significant in these patterns of early Church growth was the Church's obvious stability. The King James Version says they carried out their ministry not only with "gladness" but with "singleness of heart." This suggests they were a steadfast people firm in their convictions. Like the psalmist they could declare boldly, "My heart is steadfast, O God, my heart is steadfast" (Psalm 57:7, NASB). They were particularly steadfast to a simple, three-word doctrine—Jesus is Lord!

Intensity of conviction is foundational to the health and growth of any congregation. It is also essential for the personal growth of the believer. I am not speaking of dogmatic, misguided allegiance to certain nonessentials of salvation, but of singleness of heart to the conviction that Jesus must be Lord in all we do. Indeed, if Jesus is Lord of (and in) all we do, everything else necessary for growth and productivity will swiftly fall into place.

A Praising People

Worship was at the heart of the early Church. The New Testament believers were clearly a praising people. When the early verses of Acts say the infant Church was "praising God" (see Acts 2:47), we can picture a people constantly in praise.

67

Indeed, it was in a spirit of praise that the early Church was born. Their divine empowerment in the Upper Room (see Acts 2:1–13) was accompanied by supernaturally inspired adoration and praise of God, which numerous visitors to Jerusalem heard in their very own languages. Now, perhaps weeks or months later, we see this spirit of praise continuing.

The simple words *praising God* suggest that praise permeated everything God's people undertook. They broke bread house to house praising God. They continued in the temple praising God. Worship was at the heart of every function in the early Church. It was more than an act; it was a lifestyle—a lifestyle that flowed out of a deep reverence for God.

A Humble People

And out of this spirit of reverence we see a truly humble people.

Luke tells us the early Church was continually "having favor with all the people" (Acts 2:47, NKJV) even as they spread the Gospel. This suggests that the non-Christian community respected these believers, presumably because of the servant attitude they demonstrated wherever they went. Only a humble, serving people could have this kind of impact for Christ on a community.

And what was so needed twenty centuries ago is even more essential today. Before we can reach our cities *for* Jesus, we must love our cities *in* Jesus. And before we can love our cities in Jesus, we must ask the Lord to baptize us with a special measure of humility.

A Trained People

The early Church was well trained for the task before them. We find this quality, as well as the remaining qualities on our list, in the two additional passages of Acts I cited earlier (Acts 5:42 and Acts 20:20). Note Luke's description of the early Church in Acts 5:42 (NKJV):

And daily in the temple, and in every house, they did not cease teaching and preaching Jesus as the Christ.

The narrator, Dr. Luke, is referring to teaching about Jesus, as well as preaching the message of Jesus. Teaching, of course, concerns training. The suggestion here is that new converts as well as inquirers were taught all that was necessary for growth and discipleship in Christ. Early believers knew the doctrines of Christ well enough to communicate them to others. They were prepared for the challenge.

A growing church, then, requires a people well trained in Jesus.

A Bold People

We see in the same verse, Acts 5:42, that the early apostles not only taught Jesus but preached His message of salvation. This was the proclamation focus of their ministry. They proclaimed the message of salvation in Christ daily. And they carried out this dual commitment (to teach and preach Jesus) in the temple as well as in every house—and they did it boldly.

Note the scope and totality of their ministry. These first-century apostles not only trained the early Church but exhorted them to action, and they did so in public gatherings as well as systematically, house to house. They knew this was the only way to literally fulfill Christ's Great Commission.

A Vanguard People

At the heart of the vision of the early Church to reach everyone with the Good News was their pioneering spirit. They were, quite simply, vanguards. A vanguard represents "the foremost position in an army." The term speaks of those on the cutting edge.

Later in the book of Acts, physician Luke would describe this quality in Paul, whom he quotes as saying, "[I] have showed you, and have taught you publicly, and from house to house" (Acts 20:20, KJV). This suggests that Paul demonstrated his experience by stepping out as an example. He led the way onto the front lines of battle.

And that is precisely what a vanguard does—like our brother Remi Crespin, the brave French schoolteacher with his compass, binoculars and booklets about Jesus; or the courage and commitment of Madame Mollier to go deep into the French countryside to reach families in villages that otherwise might never hear about Jesus. Neither was a full-time Christian worker. Neither had been ordained by any denomination or missionary society. They were just vanguards who loved Jesus and wanted everyone to experience His grace.

Not all vanguards use their feet to step out into the battlefield for lost souls. Some use folded hands in prayer. Others use open hands in giving. But all vanguard believers do *something* to help evangelize the lost. They are consumed with a spirit of intensity.

Intensity comes from the Latin word *tensus*, which means "to be stretched tight." Vanguard believers become uptight, in a sense, about the vast numbers of people who do not know Jesus. And this intensity drives them—through their praying, giving and going— to the front lines of warfare for lost souls.

A Productive People

And all this leads to fruit. The foregoing qualities, when combined, bring results. Simply stated, the early Church was a productive people.

We discover this quality in the concluding words of our first Scripture passage: "The Lord added to the church daily those who were being saved" (Acts 2:47). Note again the word *daily*. The number of believers did not multiply through mass rallies on weekends or powerful Sunday services in mega-churches. Healthy early Church believers reproduced additional healthy new believers, who themselves began reproducing. And all this happened daily because they were proclaiming the Gospel "daily" both "in the temple" (the public arena) as well as "in every house" (Acts 5:42, NKJV).

Vital to our study is how all these qualities build on one another to establish a reproducing body of believers. Early Christians were taught to live out their Christian experience in such a way as to produce fruit daily.

Their persistence, for example, caused them to continue in the task of reaching out with the Good News. Their consistency led to souls finding Christ daily. Their unity and loyalty bore fruit in the form of new converts—daily. The same could be said of the generosity they demonstrated, as well as their compassionate involvement, joyfulness, steadfastness, worship, humility, training and boldness. *Because the early Church manifested these qualities daily, the Church multiplied itself daily.* Early believers simply lived out the life of Christ every day in the fullness of His power, and He made them fruitful every day as a result.

Ordinary People

New Testament believers, then—ordinary people, all of them—grew up in Jesus and went out with His message of love. They were vanguards with a vision.

Today Remi Crespin is with Jesus and needs neither binoculars nor compass to see where he is going or how to get there. But if he could speak with us from heaven, I know he would share the joy of being a vanguard with a vision. And I am sure that before the conversation was over, anyone who talked with him would become a vanguard, too.

5

The Wisdom of Haribo

It was known as "Black Monday" in a land more than five thousand miles from the mountainous rain forest of the Kwaio people living in the Solomon Islands. Haribo had just seen his forty-fourth yam harvest. The year was 1929, a tragic period for the prosperous land of America. That land, one Haribo knew nothing of, was entering a period that forever would be known as the Great Depression.

In Kwaio territory, by contrast, currency would never fail, and the concept of a bank failure, not to mention a bank, was unfathomable. For currency Haribo and his fellow warriors traded food—yams, pigs, chickens and sometimes rare, finely polished seashells from the coast that were beaded on twine. A wealthy family had several pigs and perhaps even a few chickens. But only a priestly chief like Haribo had beaded strings of seashells.

Haribo's family, which also had many pigs and chickens, was gaining stature throughout the region. Haribo himself had become a respected spiritual leader. Wisdom flowed from his lips as he guided fellow Kwaio tribesmen in matters of their spirit gods.

To have survived 44 seasons of the rain made Haribo relatively old. Many Kwaio adult males had died by this age. But Haribo was not even halfway through his earthly journey. He would see at least sixty more yam harvests before becoming a key part of another harvest—history's greatest harvest of people finding Jesus.

Feet with a Mission

There are no easy roads to Isampalli, a tiny village in the Warangal district of Andhra Pradesh, a large state in south India. Anyone wanting to visit that village has to journey many miles from a main road through rugged fields. The region surrounding the tiny town has lost countless lives to famine over many generations. The weather is always hot and water is in scarce supply. The inhabitants of the region are backward socially and economically.

Such was the life Kancha Narasayya was born into 35 years ago. Kancha, the firstborn son, had six brothers and sisters. Raised a strict Hindu, he worshiped trees, animals and snakes. His family's livelihood depended on the constant cultivation of a tiny piece of land. Poverty was their way of life.

The village of Isampalli was located in a district owned by a rich man who ruled like a ruthless king. He treated the villagers as slaves; they rarely tasted the fruits of freedom enjoyed in neighboring regions. But Kancha's parents desperately wanted a better life for their son, so they sacrificed everything to send him to a school in a nearby city. There this Hindu teenager was one of the first people of Isampalli to learn to read and write.

Kancha sought housing at a state-run government hostel. Because he was poor, he received special government grants for his education. In a few years, though he had had no early years of education, he finished high school. But in his classes he was exposed to a variety of philosophies that reminded him of his struggling parents still enslaved by the wealthy landowner of his home district.

Communism soon became the prevailing philosophy of the school, and its influence swept through the region. Eighteen-year-old Kancha was caught up in a radical Communist group known as the Naxalites, a movement begun by university students in a village called Naxalbari in North Bengal, India. Influenced by the philosophy of China's Mao Zedong, Naxalites taught common people that they had to eradicate the rich to become truly free. These Communist radicals carried out raids at night against wealthy people, robbing and killing to achieve their ends.

When Kancha finished school, he was full of enthusiasm and embraced the movement. He agreed to follow its doctrines and spread its vision passionately. Like all good Communists, Kancha declared himself an atheist, decrying the injustices done to the poor as the rich got richer.

In time Kancha moved into the ranks of the junior leadership of the movement. He followed his senior leaders everywhere and learned all he could about effective leadership. A rising star among the Naxalites, Kancha found great satisfaction in serving what he saw as a cause worth dying for.

Before long the impact of the movement intensified. The densely forested hills around Isampalli, where Kancha lived once again with his parents, provided ideal hiding places for young Naxalite rebels mobilized to help in the struggle. Soldiers of the Indian military were sent into the area to arrest those identified as Naxalites.

Kancha's parents heard about the military presence in the area and were afraid Kancha would be arrested. One night they refused to let him leave home. That very night various rebel hideouts were discovered and many of the radicals captured, including most of Kancha's friends. Some were beaten; several were killed. Kancha knew that if he was identified as a leader of the group, he faced a similar fate at the hands of Indian soldiers.

Finding a New Friend

A few days later, two young men visited Isampalli. They were evangelists sharing Gospel literature from house to house, giving one booklet to adults and another to younger readers.

Kancha's illiterate parents had no idea what the messages contained. Had these Hindus known the literature was Christian, they would have destroyed it. But the Holy Spirit was at work, and the Narasayyas sensed it was something their son should read.

That night when the young rebel returned home, he read both booklets carefully, but it was difficult for him to grasp the truth of the messages. A war for his soul began to rage. Kancha tossed the booklets aside, determined not to read them again.

The following day his father asked, "What is written on those papers you read last night?"

"Information about a new kind of god," Kancha replied.

"Where is this new god?" asked his father. He thought Kancha meant another Hindu god, of which there were millions.

"I can't really say," said Kancha, and left the house hastily.

He had no idea the Spirit of the one true God was at work in his heart.

The next day the youth heard that a close friend of his, another Naxalite, had been killed by soldiers. A large memorial service was held in remembrance of the young man, whose body was cremated Hindu-style amid burning sticks. Kancha had considered his friend wise, well educated and morally upright, and he returned home that night deeply depressed and unable to sleep. Emptiness flooded his heart. Slumped on a chair, he thought about the problems of life and the seeming lack of solutions to human suffering.

Suddenly Kancha glimpsed the two Gospel booklets resting on a table across the room. He made his way to the table, staring intently at their titles: *From Darkness to Light* and *Do You Want a Good Friend?* The booklet about finding a good friend, in the wake of the death of Kancha's close friend, captured his interest. He had read it several times two days earlier. But he could not grasp how this Person called Jesus Christ, who lived so long ago, could be his special Friend.

Even so, he filled out the accompanying response card and sent it to the Every Home Crusade office in Secunderabad. In less than two weeks Kancha received four Bible lessons, which he soon finished, and received a graduation certificate, along with a New Testament.

He set the Bible aside without reading it. He still had many unanswered questions about life and a continuing sense of emptiness.

The battle for Kancha's soul continued for six months. The two EHC field workers who had first come to his village continued to visit regularly to talk with this young man—the only person from Isampalli to respond to the Gospel. In fact, no Hindu in any village in the region was known to have accepted Jesus. Still, the Christian workers counseled Kancha about life, death and salvation through Jesus Christ. Once, they stayed for several days, talking to him continually about the ways of God.

Victory finally dawned on the battlefield of Kancha's heart. The young Communist leader opened his heart to Jesus and received Him as his Lord and Savior.

The process of conversion had been slow in Kancha's life, but the change was dramatic. He could not contain his joy. Soon each member of his family surrendered to Jesus Christ. The Narasayya home became a center for evangelism for the village (the first village in the region known to have had a Hindu accept salvation in Christ) and the surrounding area. Many in Isampalli found Jesus as Lord and Savior.

As Kancha studied God's Word, he recognized his need to be baptized. He also wanted to change his name, feeling it had too many ties to his Hindu past. He had read in the Gospels about Christ's disciple named Nathanael and wanted to be like him. When the day of his baptism arrived, he invited other recent converts to join him, and 25 villagers responded. He entered the waters of baptism as Kancha Narasayya but came up shouting, "I will be Nathanael!"

Soon Nathanael set about to visit every home in hundreds of villages dotting the countryside around Isampalli, and throughout the vast Indian state of Andhra Pradesh, sharing how they, too, could meet his good Friend. He felt as if God had given him "feet with a mission." Every step he took seemed to be driven by the words of Scripture:

"How beautiful are the feet of those who bring good news!"

Romans 10:15

Crusaders for Christ

The Christian workers who took the Gospel to Isampalli are two of the "vanguards with a vision" that we described in the last chapter—twentieth-century soldiers on the front line of the battle for souls. The work of reaching every home with the Gospel in remote areas would be impossible without such footsoldiers willing to take the Good News where others have not been. The conversion of Nathanael, who himself became a vanguard with a vision, took place only because two other young men were bold enough to enter his troubled region. Nor did they stop after one visit. They came again and again.

Although most systematic, home-to-home EHC evangelism initiatives use Christian volunteers, it became clear in the early years of the ministry that carefully trained, full-time crusaders would be essential to reach remote places where volunteers simply cannot go. Often these "pioneer crusaders," as they came to be called, face beatings or even death as they spread the good news of Jesus. These workers, especially in Hindu or Muslim lands, may have their literature seized and burned while their luggage or backpacks are thrown down steep mountainsides or into raging rivers.

Not long before Nathanael came to Christ, one of the field workers evangelizing in his area was stripped naked and tied to a tree for almost a day. Only God's protection kept deadly animals away. Late that night he was brutally beaten and finally released.

A postman in nearby Karnataka, India, observed about these crusaders for Christ: "I am amazed at the faithfulness and sincerity with which these young men go about their work. I have been assigned just three villages in the area, and sometimes I'm not even faithful in taking the mail to all of them. But these young men go to many more villages than I do, and they do so with great joy."

Pioneer crusaders are full-time personal evangelists who visit literally hundreds of homes in an average week. They are usually young men, although young women are permitted to participate in areas where it is acceptable culturally and where they will not be endangered. A crusader must be in good health because of the tremendous physical hazards associated with the work. He or she must possess above-average knowledge of the Bible and must often counsel new converts in unusually remote areas where no churches have ever existed. The average pioneer crusader preparing for Every Home for Christ initiatives undergoes four to six weeks of intensive training to become familiar with the overall work of the ministry and to be equipped spiritually for the task.

Each crusader carries only enough equipment for basic needs like eating and sleeping. Often he cooks his nightly meals over a campfire alone or with his partner. Usually he is equipped with a bicycle. (In many countries very few other forms of transportation are reasonably available.) It is not uncommon in some nations to see a pioneer crusader carrying his bicycle on his shoulders while crossing a river or traversing a rugged hill.

An average pioneer crusader can reach as many as two hundred families in a single day. But I have met crusaders in the South Pacific who traveled by boat two or three weeks over rugged seas just to visit a tiny island with only eleven families. In other regions, where the population is more dense, a pioneer crusader may visit considerably more families per day. They work faithfully five or six days a week to make sure no home is missed. In the Mount Everest region of Nepal, teams of crusaders were flown in by helicopter and left for days to visit Sherpa villages before being picked up and flown out again. No known village was missed.

Many EHC pioneer crusaders, like Nathanael, are converts of the very ministry they now serve full time. They recognize the need to go to the most remote places. After all, if someone had not bravely come to them, they might never have known of Christ's love.

Pedaling for Jesus

Joseph Gambo, who lives in the Rift Valley of Kenya, is an example. He came to know Christ through a simple printed Gospel message when workers visited his remote village more than two decades ago. The young African picked up the booklet titled *He Wants to Be Your Friend* and read about Christ for the first time. That very day he gave his heart to Jesus.

Joseph soon felt a passionate desire to tell others about Jesus. So he wrote the distant EHC office in Kenya asking for quantities of literature, which he promised to distribute systematically from home to home in surrounding villages. Soon Joseph became an unofficial pioneer crusader. He rode his bicycle over rough roads, through heavy rains and under the scorching African sun—sometimes pedaling for Jesus more than two hundred miles in a given month.

Because Joseph was the only known Christian evangelist working in the entire area, it became clear that the amazing spiritual fruit growing throughout the region was the result of Joseph's labors. In just 36 months an estimated 17,000 Africans came to faith in Christ in Joseph's region as a direct result of his efforts.

Like Nathanael, he had feet with a mission.

Walking Around His World

Daniel Soeharto from Central Java, Indonesia, converted from Islam after reading a single, twelve-page Gospel booklet. He joined a group of seven believers in his small village, then entered an EHC training program to become a full-time church planter. Finally Daniel began a remarkable ministry that, by the time I met him on a memorable journey to Central Java in June 1995, had touched literally hundreds of thousands of families.

For fourteen years Daniel distributed Gospel literature home to home averaging one village a day, five to six days a week, 48 weeks a year. He has evangelized more families than any worker I have ever met.

Daniel kept written records for every village he visited. These records show that with an average of three hundred homes per village and five persons per home, Daniel has provided reasonable access of the Gospel to about 1,500 people a day, or 360,000 people each year (counting 240 days of ministry). Multiply this total by fourteen years of service, and you can see that this dedicated crusader may have taken the message of Jesus Christ to an astounding 5,040,000 people (in about a million households).

And because the EHC ministry in Indonesia yields about a three percent harvest of decision cards per home from its home-to-home initiatives (double or triple that of many parts of the world), Daniel may be responsible for more than 30,000 people pursuing a knowledge of Christ out of the 1,008,000 Indonesian households he visited. (Further, because these cards often represent more than one decision per household, the actual number of individual decisions may be much higher.)

To accomplish this incredible task, Daniel trekked to distant and remote areas of Central Java. Sometimes buses were available to transport him to certain areas, but he traveled mostly by foot or bicycle. He walked an estimated seven miles a day, or a minimum of 35 miles a week. So we can calculate that, traveling 48 weeks per year, he walked an amazing 23,520 miles in fourteen years. That is equivalent to walking completely around the world at least once in order to tell others about Jesus.

Talk about feet with a mission!

Feet of Courage

Often new converts won through systematic, home-to-home evangelism become powerful pioneer evangelists penetrating unreached areas of their own cultures. Such was the case with a young Muslim couple from northern Côte d'Ivoire (Ivory Coast, in western Africa) whom we will call Mahil and Kara Lomes.

Sponsored by Mahil's wealthy parents, the Lomes set out for Riyadh, Saudi Arabia, to participate in the *hadj*—a journey to Mecca that all healthy Muslims are required to make at least once in their lifetimes. Their plans called for travel by train to the capital city of Yamoussoukro, where they would catch a flight to Saudi Arabia. On the way Mahil and Kara decided to spend two days with close friends in the city of Duékoué.

On the second day of the visit, while their friends were at work, evangelists came to the door. Mahil and Kara had arrived during the Every Home Crusade in Duékoué. Kara accepted the literature politely, unaware that it bore a Christian message. She put it into her purse, intending to give it to her friends when they arrived home—but she forgot.

The next day the Lomes left for Yamoussoukro. As the train pulled away from the station and Mahil settled back into his seat for a nap, Kara reached into her purse and discovered the Gospel literature.

Maybe this will make interesting reading, she thought as she opened the small booklet.

81

Within minutes the Holy Spirit began to work in Kara's heart. Mahil dozed quietly as his wife read with fascination each new sentence that spoke of a Savior who came to redeem the world.

By the time Kara finished reading the booklet, something had happened in her heart. She was convinced the message was true. Jesus Christ was indeed the Savior of the world. Quietly she asked Him into her heart, praying the simple prayer of repentance printed on the last page of the booklet. Then she woke her husband and told him what had happened.

Instead of being angry, Mahil read the message and felt the same power of God's presence. In moments he, too, had given his life to Christ. And the train had not even arrived at Yamoussoukro.

So dramatic were the conversions of Mahil and Kara that they decided to terminate their pilgrimage to Mecca. They called Mahil's father and explained what had happened. The old man rebuked them angrily over the phone, telling them they were no longer welcome in the family. But the young couple knew they had found eternal truth. They returned to Duékoué and sought help from the EHC office there, where they were nurtured in the Lord and encouraged to begin sharing with others what had happened in their lives.

Eventually Mahil and Kara became full-time EHC workers in Côte d'Ivoire. They have since moved to another large city where they have launched its first systematic, house-to-house evangelism program. Already several Muslims have professed Christ as Savior because of the "courageous feet" of Mahil and Kara Lomes.

Courage is indeed a prerequisite for many of these warriors, who often find themselves facing tense situations that easily could cost them their lives.

Julio Flores, for example, was returning home from an EHC assignment in the Nicaraguan town of Rio Blanco during the days of bitter civil war in that troubled Central American nation. He was stopped on the road and taken prisoner by a group of armed guerrillas preparing to do battle with a rival rebel command. The guerrillas accused Flores of being an "infiltrating CIA journalist" and sentenced him to death. Then, just before the battle began, a rebel officer appeared from nowhere and released him, telling him to run as fast as he could. Julio knew someone's prayers had been answered.

His "beautiful feet" took him to the edge of the battlefield as he ran with all his might—much to the shock of a group of villagers, who told him excitedly that he had just run through an active minefield. A woman in the village, they explained, had lost both arms to an exploding can of talcum powder, a mine in disguise that she had picked up only a short time earlier in that very field.

Feet of Faith and Joy

Often these "feet with a mission" find themselves taking unusual steps of faith that produce much joy. Recently, for example, an EHC Solomon Island worker named Sakiusa prepared a list of supplies that the EHC base on their remote island needed to sustain its outreach. The list included office stationery, kitchen utensils, household items and various hard-to-find farming implements. The total cost: two thousand dollars. Sakiusa took a boat to the distant capital city of Honiara on Guadalcanal Island, trusting God would meet their needs—though he had no idea how. He had spent his last dollar for his boat fare.

When he arrived at the wharf, a young man in a government van who had heard Sakiusa was coming was waiting for him. Having no idea about the list of needed items, he informed Sakiusa that he had brought several pieces of equipment for the base that he thought Sakiusa might need. They compared lists and found that about half of the items needed so desperately had already been purchased and were already waiting in the van! Then the young man drove Sakiusa to where he was to lodge for the evening. It was at an inn owned by Christians who provided him free lodging.

That night Sakiusa received a surprise gift from a foreign visitor of twelve hundred dollars in cash. It was exactly what he needed. He did the rest of the shopping the next day, obtaining every item on the list. He was even able to buy a large rug for the floor of the base office and purchase airfare back to his home island.

Sakiusa had set out for Honiara with only a list of needs and a heart of faith. Now he was returning with boxes of blessings and a heart of joy.

Similar was the joy experienced by a young EHC worker in Fiji traveling to a distant city to fulfill that day's assignment. The bus fare was $2.05, but he lacked even a single cent for the journey.

Lord, he prayed, *touch one of Your children who is here in town to bring my bus fare to me.*

He even told God the exact amount. Then he waited and watched. No one came.

He waited a little longer. Then he sensed the Lord speaking: *When do you really need the money—now or when you board the bus?*

The answer was obvious. He did not need the money until he boarded the bus. So the worker promptly headed for the central bus station. He hoped another believer would see him as he walked along and ask if he had any needs.

But he soon arrived at the bus terminal, still with no fare. Passengers were already boarding, though the bus driver had not yet come.

Another thought came to him: *Exactly when do you need the fare— now or when the driver gets on the bus?*

Again the answer was obvious. He did not need the $2.05 until the bus driver arrived. So he boarded the bus and made his way to a seat near the back. He knew the bus driver would get on shortly and begin collecting the fares.

So he prayed once again, *Lord, I'm on the bus now, and soon the driver will come to start collecting the fares. I am still waiting for my bus fare. Please send someone soon to bring me the money.*

Several minutes passed while the worker sat anxiously by the window. In a moment the bus driver boarded and started the engine to move the bus forward to allow another bus to depart.

Suddenly it happened. Just as the bus began moving, someone called the evangelist's name through the open window. A Christian brother had seen his old friend from the other side of the street and dashed over to ask him where he was going. The evangelist explained he was heading to a particular city for ministry.

Quickly the friend reached into his pocket, pulled out a two-dollar Fijian note and handed it to the young worker.

"Here," he said, "buy yourself something to eat along the way."

The worker's heart was flooded with joy, although he was still five cents short.

"My brother, God has brought you here at this exact moment to help provide my fare," he responded joyfully. "I've been asking God to provide a miracle because I had no money when I got on the bus."

"How much is the total fare?"

Only then did the evangelist admit he still lacked a nickel; whereupon his friend, God's special agent, took an additional dollar note from his pocket and handed it to this faith-traveler.

"Here," he shouted over the roar of the bus engine. "This will help pay the rest of your fare."

Another mission—another miracle. And oh, the joy of it all! The Fijian worker's faith and his feet with a mission were facilitating the spread of the good news of Jesus Christ across that island nation of the Pacific Ocean.

And especially exciting: This crusader knew that the end result of his steps of faith would mean the planting of many new churches—a vital fruit of this home-by-home strategy that we will read about next.

Weapons of Fire

Haribo, now considered an elder of the Kwaio people, had lived through 57 rainy seasons and gathered in as many yam harvests. The Kwaio people on the rugged island of Malaita in the Solomons had no idea another "great war" was being waged globally. But not only was the second World War underway; it was moving closer to their remote island chain.

Hardly fifty miles away, though it might have been a thousand, the Solomons' largest island, Guadalcanal, rose from the azure Pacific. Several full moons earlier, a people speaking a strange tongue, short in stature but bearing powerful weapons of fire, had invaded Guadalcanal. The outside world, in this year of 1942, knew these people to be Japanese soldiers who were moving relentlessly through the South Pacific capturing island after island.

By late summer the fires of the spirit gods were unleashed in the Solomons. American Marines landed on Guadalcanal in the first of their amphibious assaults against the Japanese-held positions in the Pacific. The Marines seized Henderson Field in Honiara, the capital of Guadalcanal, after fierce ground, sea and air attacks. Later that fall, the skies not far from Malaita were lit up for three days and nights. History would call it the Naval Battle of Guadalcanal, in which an amazing 28 Japanese vessels were sunk in three days.

Haribo and his people tended their pigs and harvested their yams through the sound of distant artillery fire—something Haribo and his people had not heard since the British warship attacked their island fifteen rainy seasons earlier. This time, however, the guns were firing in the distance. Haribo's people saw little of this great war, and no signs of either Japanese or Americans in the interior of Kwaio. Incredibly, Haribo would wait still another fifty seasons of the rain before outsiders would finally come to their remote region.

But then they would come in peace—and bring with them a miracle.

Graveyard of Siberia

Olga rubbed her tired eyes and pondered her next words in answering the essay question about the early days of the Bolshevik Revolution. The exam had just begun, but already her mind was wandering. She had traveled many hours from the remote Siberian city of Magadan, on Russia's far eastern coast, where she had served for several years as a professor of Marxist philosophy at the University of Magadan.

Magadan, a city of one hundred thousand, is known to Russians as a graveyard for more than nineteen million Soviet citizens. It was here that Stalin and other Soviet leaders most often sent dissidents, criminals and other perceived troublemakers for a life of exile or, not infrequently, execution. Magadan is also called the Siberia of Siberias, because for half the year the city is almost completely isolated by Arctic winter. Even planes cannot fly in because of the severe winter weather, and the sea between Magadan's coast and northern Japan freezes over, making shipping impossible.

Olga had come to accept life in Magadan, however, and had proven a gifted professor of Marxist-Leninist philosophy at the university. Now, as required by her school, she had flown across the Sea of Okhotsk, over Sakhalin Island, to the city of Khabarovsk to take an exam that would upgrade her credentials. She had no idea of the dramatic, even supernatural change that was about to take place in her life.

The young philosophy professor picked up her pencil and tried to write another sentence. Suddenly, for apparently no reason, a strange thought flooded her mind: *I have to find God.* Atheists usually do not think such thoughts, and Olga had been an atheist all her life.

She tried to write another sentence, but her urge to find God only increased. Soon this unusual feeling was accompanied by a sense of anxiety. Olga had to do it *now*. The urge simply would not wait.

Her heart raced. The feeling turned to near-panic. She could not explain it, but she laid her pencil on the test pages and jumped to her feet. Before the startled presiding instructor could open his mouth, Olga dashed from the room, rushed down the stairs and into the street.

I must find God.

The one place Olga thought to go was to the Orthodox church in the center of Khabarovsk. She had heard only negative stories about the Church in Russia, but it was the only place she knew she might find God.

88

She found the church quickly with its traditional, onion-shaped dome rising high against the gray Russian sky. Darting into the ornate sanctuary, its walls adorned with glistening icons, she was met by an Orthodox priest.

"I must find God!" she burst out.

The priest stared at her stoically, then handed the obviously distraught woman several candles.

"Light these," he said, "then kiss some of the icons hanging along the walls."

Olga knew instinctively this was not the answer she sought.

"No," she informed the priest abruptly. "I didn't come to find religion. I came to find God."

With that she turned and rushed from the church.

A few minutes later, out on the street, she saw, to her amazement, a large poster attached to a decaying brick wall. It said in Russian that an American "evangelist" (a new word to her) was in Khabarovsk that week to tell people how they might find God. The poster included the address and times of the meetings. Unbelievable!

That night the young professor located the old Communist hall rented for the evangelistic meetings. Every aspect of the service fascinated her, including the lively singing and well-prepared message about what it meant to be a follower of Jesus Christ. She was one of the first to respond to an invitation to receive Jesus as Lord and Savior.

Olga never returned to the exam room to finish her test. So startling was her transformation, in fact, that she knew she could never teach Marxist philosophy again.

When she arrived back in Magadan several days later, she went to the head of her department at the university intending to resign.

"I can no longer teach Marxist-Leninist philosophy," she announced.

"Why not?" the department head asked tersely.

Olga recounted her unusual experience in Khabarovsk and explained that she had found God.

"It's not necessary for you to cease teaching Marxist-Leninism," he objected.

"But I cannot teach something I don't believe in."

Then he explained that there was such a shortage of teachers of her caliber in Magadan that he simply did not want to lose her. She insisted she could no longer teach Marxism.

"What would you be willing to teach?" he asked.

"I can teach the Bible as philosophy," she answered haltingly. "That I can believe in."

To Olga's amazement her supervisor agreed.

"That will be fine," he said. "You may teach the Bible as philosophy, as long as you stay in the university."

Thus began a remarkable chain of events in the teaching career of this young philosophy professor. Within six months Olga had led sixty of her students to Jesus Christ and, in addition to conducting her usual classes, met with them in weekly Bible teaching sessions.

Soon several of Olga's students came to her.

"We need a full-time pastor," they said.

"I'll try to find someone suitable," she replied.

"Our group has already discussed it," said the students. "We all agree you should be our pastor."

After considerable encouragement, Olga finally agreed, and a church was born.

Interestingly, only a few months later, Paul Iliyn, regional director of Every Home for Christ for the Commonwealth of Independent States (CIS), visited Magadan and heard Olga's unusual testimony. He had come to begin an every-home evangelism and church-planting campaign in far eastern Siberia and needed a place to begin a Bible school to train young church planters. Olga quickly volunteered her church, and within six months 26 students had enrolled full-time in the training center.

Filling Up Their Town

The Bible school in Magadan was a sister school to one Paul Iliyn had established in Kiev, Ukraine, not long after the breakup of the

Soviet Union. The need for trained leaders was especially strong in the old Soviet republics. For seventy years they had been bound in atheism, with seminaries and Bible schools closed and sometimes destroyed. The result: a tremendous shortage of qualified church leaders, and thousands of smaller towns and villages with no evangelical church of any kind. Carefully equipped men and women were needed to go into these towns, reach every family with the Gospel and plant churches with those who responded. Paul knew that for this to happen, they needed Bible training schools to produce able church planters.

By 1993 the training center in Kiev, called St. James Bible College, had (with the assistance of Paul Iliyn's home church, The Church of the Highlands, in San Bruno, California, and Kay Arthur and her Precept Ministries staff of Chattanooga, Tennessee) established two hundred young men and women deep in God's Word and trained them to become evangelists, pastors and church planters.

In 1995 the second training center was established in Olga's church in Magadan (also with the help of The Church of the Highlands and Precept Ministries).

One of the very first church planters from St. James Bible College was Vasily Dektorenko. Barely in his twenties, Vasily was convinced that he and his brother, Alex, who lived not far from Kiev, could "fill up" their town with the Gospel, house to house on weekends, even while Vasily continued his studies at the Bible college on weekdays. So he approached the school administrator.

"Sir, do I need to complete an entire year of training before I can start reaching people with the Gospel in my hometown?"

"It is essential that you complete your training," the director explained, "if you are to become an effective pastor. But there's nothing wrong with putting into practice now what you have already learned."

So Vasily and Alex began an every-home evangelism campaign the very next weekend in their hometown of Zhitomir. Soon they were on their way to sharing the good news of Jesus with every home in Zhitomir. With the help of a few volunteers, the brothers

91

visited more than 25,000 families over the first few weeks. Each family was given not only a Gospel message and response card, but a special invitation to attend a new church being started in the city.

On the day of the first church service, the two young brothers were astonished to find nearly four hundred people gathered from throughout the city. The former Communist hall they had rented was packed. There were no deacons, elders or ushers, and the people present had never attended a church in their lives. Vasily began by asking how many had come to the meeting to learn more about Jesus Christ. Everyone raised his or her hand. Then Vasily asked how many wanted a New Testament. Again, every hand went up.

Thankfully, about a month before the first meeting, a shipment of New Testaments in their language had arrived from International Bible Society in America. Praise God! Everyone was given his or her own New Testament. It was an instant church of four hundred new believers.

But the growth had just begun. Within two years the congregation consisted of 46 separate discipleship groups, called Christ Groups, with a total membership of at least three thousand.

The concept of a Christ Group had grown out of necessity many years earlier in the ministry of Every Home for Christ, when new believers were coming to Christ in areas with no churches of any kind.

The Christ Group Phenomenon

Christ Groups like the ones in Zhitomir, Ukraine, represent the answer to a significant challenge Every Home for Christ faced in 1975.

That year EHC completed its first nationwide every-home coverage of the vast nation of India, then with an estimated 550,000 villages. The ten-year task had involved as many as eight hundred full-time evangelists and many thousands of volunteer workers during any given month. The fruit was encouraging: 1,250,258 Indians, mostly Hindu and Muslim, sent in decision cards—the vast majority of which (about 67 percent) indicated that the senders had prayed to receive Jesus Christ as Lord and Savior. The remaining 33 percent wanted additional information about what it meant to receive Christ.

But the process of discipling so great a number seemed almost impossible, even though every person responding was already enrolled in a well-prepared, four-lesson Bible correspondence course. About ninety percent of the responses came from people who lived in tiny villages, hamlets and even moderate-sized towns with no Christian church of any kind to provide adequate nurturing and fellowship. What would happen to these new believers, EHC workers wondered, even if they completed the Bible correspondence course successfully? It seemed almost criminal, spiritually speaking, not to provide some means of ongoing follow-up to assure that these new converts would become functioning members of a local church. But how could that happen in places where no organized group of believers existed?

The answer came as the result of hundreds of hours of prayer and discussion regarding the preservation of the harvest.

The Christ Group Defined

Christ Groups—such as the ones begun by Vasily and Alex Dektorenko in the brand-new church in Zhitomir—are small cells of new believers formed as a result of home-by-home evangelism and established primarily in areas with no Bible-believing congregations.

The concept of a Christ Group is based on a pattern originated by Jesus—"Where two or three are gathered together in My name, I am there in the midst of them" (Matthew 18:20, NKJV)—and implemented by Paul in his relentless missionary travels. Paul sought to form and sustain cells of new believers right where they lived so they could communicate with one another and enjoy fellowship in prayer and Bible study (see Romans 16:5 and 1 Corinthians 16:19).

Dr. Jim Montgomery, writing in his book *DAWN 2010: A Strategy for the End of the Age,* strongly affirms the need for Christ Groups. The leader of the DAWN strategy (to "Disciple A Whole Nation" through

93

saturation church planting), Montgomery refers to Paul's explanation of the process involved in proclaiming the Gospel: "We proclaim [Christ], admonishing and teaching everyone with all wisdom, so that we may present everyone perfect in Christ" (Colossians 1:28).

Believers with a heart for the lost, says Dr. Montgomery, realize we must proclaim the Gospel to everyone by every means available. But, the missiologist adds:

> According to this verse [Colossians 1:28], we also want to admonish and teach *everyone* so that *each* may be presented perfect in Christ. This can happen only when new believers are gathered in a teaching, growing, worshiping, discipling environment: a church. And only when there are churches *everywhere* in a nation and people group can such a setting be made available for *everyone*.[1]

The Christ Group Purpose

Where there are already solid evangelical churches in an area, EHC workers always encourage new believers to join one. They also ask the local churches to visit and nurture the new believers. But they organize Christ Groups for new believers in places where no churches exist to nurture them.

Each local EHC office has some idea of how far along a new believer is spiritually by his or her response to the Bible lessons or by letters he or she has written. Then a field evangelist is sent to an area where these new believers live and uses this information while meeting with them to designate initial leaders for each group.

Although the primary purpose of a Christ Group is to provide nurturing where otherwise it is unavailable, groups are also formed in some places like the old Soviet Union where some evangelical churches, because of legalism or traditionalism, do not welcome new believers.

The Christ Group Plan

Each Christ Group meets once or twice a week in various members' homes, spending about two hours at each meeting. The first forty minutes are devoted to Bible study, the next forty minutes to sharing victories and problems of various members, and the final forty minutes to prayer.

Critical to a group's success is the careful attention by the field evangelist who first formed the group. Ideally, twice each month the worker visits each Christ Group in his or her assigned region, meeting first privately with the leader of the group, then with the entire membership (depending on each local situation). The purpose: to guide or offer help in situations beyond the spiritual understanding of these relatively new believers.

After twelve months of intensive, twice-monthly follow-up, the Christ Group begins to function on its own. If it grows into a sizable congregation, it is encouraged to affiliate with a larger evangelical denomination. (Many Christ Groups, such as ones in Indonesia and Fiji, have grown into sizable independent local churches that later chose to form their own fellowship of churches.)

Surviving Persecution

Wherever the Christ Group plan has been implemented faithfully in the years since the initial launching of the concept, the result has been substantial personal growth.

But not all Christ Groups have been planted as the result of a single evangelism coverage of an unchurched area. Perhaps the one that took the longest to establish in the nation of India was the Christ Group formed in the village of Doodi Halli in the state of Karnataka. It was a group that was to experience wave after wave of persecution.

Jaya Prabhu, an EHC field worker, was the first Christian to visit the village of Doodi Halli in 1976. Not a single person responded to the home-by-home contacts—not even a request for additional literature. But Jaya continued to visit this village at least twice a year, leaving free Gospel booklets for adults and children at each home and speaking with the people to whom he had given literature. Whenever possible, Jaya sought to engage villagers in conversations about Jesus.

Finally, after nine years of Jaya's regular visits to the village, a young college student named Chandrashekar opened his heart to Jesus Christ in 1985. He completed a Bible correspondence course and began to visit families in Doodi Halli and the surrounding area. Because he was from the village, people knew him and began to respond. Many more gave their hearts to Jesus. Sixteen months later Chandrashekar sensed a call to full-time ministry, and in the fall of 1986 he left for the much larger city of Yavatmal, in the state of Maharashtra, where he would pursue two years of missionary training at a respected Bible institute.

As soon as Chandrashekar left, a wave of intense persecution against the young believers of Doodi Halli was launched by a Hindu guru, who represented political authority in the village. Persecutors actually entered the house of every believer, forcibly carrying away their Bibles and other Christian literature and burning the confiscated materials in a public bonfire in the village square.

Three months later came a second wave of persecution. The Hindu guru fined the believers and gave all the villagers an ultimatum: "If you want to follow Jesus, you have no place here. You must leave Doodi Halli. If you wish to remain, you must renounce Christ."

The persecution was too much for a few, who stumbled spiritually and turned their backs on their faith. Those who stood firm were persecuted even more severely. They were not allowed to draw water from the village well and had to travel great distances for even small amounts of water. They were also prohibited from purchasing items from village shops, even for necessities like food. Other villagers were forbidden to speak with these believers, and if they did they were fined.

The persecution subsided for a few months. Then a third and much more intense wave came. The crops growing in believers' fields were either stolen or destroyed. The anti-Christian group entered the houses of believers, looted most of their belongings, beat them severely and dragged them into the village square for public humiliation. Christians were pushed to their knees and commanded to worship Hindu idols. Some lost their homes.

Some of the newer believers who wanted to remain faithful to Christ contemplated suicide. They were young in their faith and saw no way out of their dilemma. One actually prepared a broth mixed with poison, which some of his fellow believers were going to drink, when a knock came at the door. It was the chief of a nearby village who, although not a Christian, had come to console them.

"If you have such steadfast faith in your God," he told them, "surely He will save you."

It was enough of a message from God to tell them not to take their lives.

So the Christ Group at Doodi Halli survived and grew, and the persecution stopped. One year later, in October 1987, a Christ Group member named Venkatesh, a graduate in commerce from a nearby university, announced that he, too, planned to become a full-time minister in the Lord's work. His mother, Seethamma, had been one of those most humiliated publicly by the village guru.

In the following 24 months, the Christ Group prospered even more. Several additional young men and women committed their lives to full-time Christian service. God was now prospering the believers. All who had lost their homes and belongings during the period of persecution were able to rebuild. By July 1993 three more young men from the Doodi Halli Christ Group enrolled in the same missionary training course that the first Christ Group convert, Chandrashekar, had finished several years earlier.

By now this one Christ Group in Doodi Halli had commissioned eight full-time workers for Christian ministry—and all because a committed Christian evangelist made regular visits at least twice a year for nine years in the same village before he saw a single convert.

The Gospel in Gomolong

But can house-to-house evangelism using Gospel literature actually result in the planting of churches? I sought the answer to this question firsthand in the world's most populated Muslim land, Indonesia, when I visited there in 1995.

My adventure began with a 24-hour, 12,000-mile journey by jumbo jet to the other side of the world, followed by a long, bumpy ride over the rocky, hilly terrain of Central Java with our director for Indonesia Every Home Contact, Romy Romulo. I had made the journey to see with my own eyes the unusual fruit of a single Gospel booklet that had begun a chain reaction resulting in the planting of the only church in this remote Muslim area.

Romy and I found ourselves in a town called Somondomore about fifty miles outside the city of Yogyakarta. Somondomore is an Islamic community of about 3,500 people, their houses scattered across the rugged, mountainous region.

High on the hillside before us, for everyone in the village to see, stood a beautiful church building constructed by the new Christians who now worshiped there. Standing beside Romy and me was a young pastor and EHC field evangelist, Daniel Soeharto, the convert from Islam I described in the last chapter who walked an amazing 23,520 miles in fourteen years (the equivalent of walking completely around the world at least once) in order to tell other Indonesians about Jesus.

Soon I would be addressing the modest but growing congregation of that church, explaining why I had journeyed from half a world away just to see what God was doing in their village. I saw their joy and realized I was witnessing the amazing results of what can happen in "the uttermost parts of the earth" when someone is courageous enough to take the Gospel where others have never gone.

But first I asked Romy how this church came to be. He smiled and explained that it had actually begun about fifteen years earlier. That was when Daniel Soeharto lived in a distant village called Gomolong.

He had been visited there by two young Christian evangelists making Gospel house calls throughout the region. They visited every home in Gomolong that day giving out simple Gospel presentations for adults and children. Neither of the two booklets was more than twelve pages long.

Nineteen-year-old Daniel read both messages with careful intensity. Although he had grown up in a strict Islamic culture, he was fascinated by these messages. In fact, it seemed to him that a brilliant light shone on each word as he read. When he finished, he prayed the brief prayer suggested at the end of the booklet and received Jesus Christ, the only Son of God, as his Lord and Savior.

Many others in Daniel's small village were reading the same messages that day. In fact, by the time Daniel finished filling out the decision card accompanying the booklet, at least seven others in his village had done the same. The Gospel had come to Gomolong.

Within a few days the Every Home for Christ office in Jakarta received those decision cards and followed them up by sending the first of a four-part Bible correspondence course. After Daniel finished the fourth lesson in the course, he wrote the EHC office for additional help and was told that a Christ Group would be forming in his village. Daniel joined the group for its very first meeting.

Several months later he heard about a newly formed Christ Group training center in his region of Central Java, where people who had received Christ in the village campaigns were being trained as full-time workers to reach even more villages. In spite of the objections of his Muslim family, and despite the rejection he had experienced from his friends and community, Daniel applied for training at the center and was accepted. The year was 1981.

In the months that followed, Daniel led the members of his family one by one to Christ—the two Gospel booklets delivered to his home producing even more fruit.

Following a year of training, Daniel became a full-time Christian worker with the Indonesia Every Home Contact outreach. He knew that all the villages he would visit in the days ahead were Muslim. He also knew the opposition that a Muslim faced who became a Christian. But Daniel had great hope in his heart because he now knew the power of God for salvation.

Little did he realize how much of Central Java he would visit, sharing the good news of Jesus Christ with as many as five million people over the following decade and a half.

A Tale of Two Seeds

Years later I stood with our director, Romy, and Daniel looking at the beautiful church in Somondomore. It touched me that Daniel could still remember the titles of the two booklets that had brought the Gospel to him: *He Wants to Be Your Friend* and *How to Enjoy Life to the Fullest*. And his story made me consider the power of the printed page to change lives.

How, I asked Romy, had Daniel come to be the pastor of this church? And had he actually planted it himself while continuing the work of taking the Gospel to so many of the neighboring villages?

Then I heard the rest of the story. A full six years before Daniel received the seed of the Gospel at his home in Gomolong, another EHC evangelist was distributing identical seeds in Central Java. Because no village was to be missed, he eventually reached the Muslim village of Somondomore—the village in which we now stood—where, to his knowledge, no Christian witness had ever come. He distributed the good news of Jesus to every home and, whenever possible, gave a personal witness, although no one showed any interest.

But one old man in the village had been touched by the simple message. Mr. Huparman read his booklet repeatedly. Then one night, with great courage, he filled out the decision card and mailed it to the EHC office in Jakarta. Mr. Huparman was the only person in the entire village to respond.

Soon he received the first lesson of a Bible correspondence course titled *The Way to a Happy Life* and completed it. A second lesson came, then a third. By the fourth and final lesson, Mr. Huparman (but not his wife) opened his heart to Christ. Upon finishing the course, the old man wrote a beautiful testimony describing how Jesus had changed his life.

For several years he continued to be the lone Christian in the village, worshiping Jesus secretly. But a desire for fellowship with other believers flooded his heart, so he wrote the EHC office asking if someone could come to his village and help him grow in Jesus as well as tell others about Him. Daniel Soeharto, who by then had found Christ in Gomolong and finished his Christ Group training, was assigned by the EHC office to visit the village.

When Daniel arrived in Somondomore, Mr. Huparman met him with great enthusiasm. Although he was the only convert in the village, they decided to begin a Christ Group. Mr. Huparman invited one other person, a man named Warsito who was sympathetic to Christianity because of the changes he had seen in Huparman's life.

Within days Warsito gave his heart to Christ, and a tiny Christ Group of just two people (three when Daniel was present) began. For many weeks the number stayed the same. Meanwhile, Daniel continued to visit towns and villages throughout the area, with periodic stops at Somondomore.

More than a year passed. Then they decided to hold an Easter Sunday meeting and invite everyone in the village. Amazingly, scores of villagers came and several received Christ as Lord. Soon the number of converts grew to almost fifty adults and seventeen children. Mr. Huparman's wife became a believer. The church was well established, and soon the offerings of many members of the Christ Group enabled them to build a new sanctuary to adorn the highest hill overlooking Somondomore.

When I visited, the Somondomore congregation had a missionary vision to reproduce themselves in other villages of the region. Members proudly showed me their maps and five-year plan to plant at least two churches a year for the next five years in neighboring villages.

I marveled at the grace of God and how this church had begun out of two simple printed Gospel seeds—one planted in the heart of Daniel Soeharto years earlier in the distant village of Gomolong, and one in the heart of Mr. Huparman in Somondomore. God was clearly at work among the previously unreached peoples of Central Java.

Down from the Mountain

My visit to Somondomore was a mountaintop experience both literally and figuratively. But coming down from that Central Java hilltop and journeying to one final destination before heading home would confirm my already strong belief as a missions strategist that systematic, house-to-house evangelism is one of the most effective methods in the world today for church planting, especially in areas where the Gospel has never gone or has never effectively taken root. Churches do indeed result from simply going home to home with the Gospel.

Following our bumpy descent from the mountains surrounding Somondomore, Romy Romulo and I traveled about 25 miles beyond the metropolis of Yogyakarta to the small village of Ngrombo. Our plan was to visit one final village church that Romy knew had resulted entirely from house-to-house evangelism conducted in the region more than a decade earlier.

That night I stood before a packed congregation of believers who now made up The Church of Christ of Ngrombo. It was born entirely out of home-to-home evangelism in the village where no church had previously existed.

Following a lively meeting, I spoke with a man named Mr. Suwandi who was visiting that night, a deacon from a Reformed Church in a neighboring village and the political head (equivalent of a regional mayor) of the entire area. As we talked, I discovered something amazing. His Reformed church about ten miles from Ngrombo was born out of the same regional house-to-house evangelism campaign that gave birth to The Church of Christ in Ngrombo ten years earlier!

I told "Mayor" Suwandi how amazed I was that two churches of such diverse worship styles (and even theological traditions) could be born out of the same simple evangelistic outreach.

He smiled and added, "Oh, but there is yet a third church born from the same campaign. It is the Bethel Church of the Assemblies of God."

A Pentecostal church thriving in the community of Pujuk about ten miles in the opposite direction! My heart rejoiced as I realized that in an area of little more than thirty square miles, perhaps less, three thriving village churches had all been planted as a result of the same house-to-house evangelistic activity a decade earlier. Equally amazing to me was the fact that each of the three congregations had chosen to become identified with a different evangelical denomination, all of which had participated in the initial every-home campaign in the region and later benefited directly from the resulting fruit.

"Mayor" Suwandi went on to tell me that these congregations were already reproducing themselves in Central Java. From this Church of Christ congregation alone, he said, seven converts had already departed for seminary, each planning to plant a church in his home province after finishing training.

As Romy Romulo and I drove later that night through the darkened village streets of Ngrombo, he told me with pleasure that since the beginning of the every-home strategy in Indonesia in the 1970s, more than 3,460 similar Christ Groups had been born.

And then I realized the full significance of a systematic, New Testament, house-to-house evangelism strategy. It involves even more than providing everyone in a nation in a measurable way reasonable access to the good news of Jesus. It is also one of the most practical ways to plant growing, reproducible, New Testament churches.

PART 2

Harvest Scope

The Totality Factor in Reaching Our World for Jesus

When I described to a friend the concept of this book in its early stages, he suggested I title it *All and Every—God's Two Favorite Words!* The Great Commission of Christ to His disciples was indeed not merely to reach "much" of the world with the Gospel and "most" of its inhabitants, but "all the world" and "every creature" (see Mark 16:15, KJV).

Earlier Jesus described to His disciples what might be called His "must-bring" mandate when He spoke in John 10:16 of "other sheep" that had to be brought to His fold, suggesting the far-reaching scope of the harvest. Today that "range" or "extent of action" (as *scope* is defined) includes every potentially neglected pocket or sphere of forgotten humanity.

In this section we will better understand how rapidly we are moving toward the ultimate evangelization of these other sheep and the literal fulfillment of Isaiah's sweeping prophecy: "The earth will be full of the knowledge of the LORD as the waters cover the sea" (Isaiah 11:9).

A Miraculous Discovery

Haribo felt sharp pains in his back as he gathered yams from his garden. Few in Haribo's village—or throughout the entire region of East Kwaio, for that matter—were older than Chief Haribo. He had lived to see yet another yam harvest, his seventieth—or was it eighty? It was getting hard to remember.

For the outside world it would soon be the decade of the 1960s. But neither Haribo nor his people knew anything of the turmoil raging throughout the world—the upheaval of Mao Zedong's devastating Cultural Revolution in China, with its execution and starvation of millions, or the tension created between the world's two great superpowers, the United States and the Soviet Union, over nuclear missiles on a small island nation south of America's East Coast called Cuba. It was the same place Americans had fought the Spanish more than sixty yam harvests earlier, when Haribo was a youth. Nor did Haribo's people know the world had entered the age of space exploration after the Soviet government launched a man-made satellite called Sputnik in 1957—even though they had spotted a strange, dimly lit, flickering star they had never seen before moving in the distant midnight sky.

Twelve harvest seasons later a man would walk on the moon, while Haribo would still be here waiting to take his own journey into the heavenlies—a journey from which, amazingly, he would return to his people, to recount in vivid detail a most miraculous discovery.

Captives for Christ

Ramudu of Tumella, India, was an untouchable, but not because he fell into that particular Indian caste. Ramudu was an untouchable because, like many others in various nations who are put into prison, he fell into a unique category of the unreached.

Ramudu is six feet three inches tall and weighs 170 pounds—an exceptional physique for an Asian. He terrorized the villagers of Tumella. Officially he murdered five people; unofficially, nobody knows—nobody dares to say.

He was known to fly into a rage and grab a man by his legs, turn him upside-down and smash his head on the rocky ground until he was dead. Over the years Ramudu was incarcerated various times for his crimes and became a terror even within the prison walls. He was motivated by hatred, anger and vengeance.

While serving a prison term for murder (for which he had somehow escaped the death sentence), Ramudu was visited by two field evangelists who were calling on every dwelling in the area and sharing a printed introduction to Jesus as Savior. The prison warden granted permission for these workers to visit every cell and give every inmate a Gospel message.

But Ramudu did not read the booklet.

On his release Ramudu was charged with another murder and sent to a prison in South Central India near the city of Hyderabad. This time it appeared there was no avoiding the death sentence.

This prison, interestingly, was visited by one of the same Christian workers Ramudu had seen a year earlier. This amazed him. He was impressed by the persistence and compassion of these people. No one else had come even once to encourage him or offer hope, while this worker had visited twice—and even managed to find him in a different prison.

Ramudu listened intently as the plan of salvation was explained through his prison bars. And he agreed to receive the printed Gospel booklet. God had begun to work in the killer's heart.

For days Ramudu read the booklet, perhaps a half-dozen times a day. The simplicity of the message touched him.

In the meantime, perhaps because of the fear of those who had brought charges against him, Ramudu was acquitted of the most recent murder. The criminal was once again released and headed for home.

Back in familiar surroundings, Ramudu quickly lost interest in the Gospel. He rejoined old gang members and before long was again terrorizing small villages in the region. It was almost as if he was driven by demons.

Still, the message he had read so often in prison was now committed to memory and seemed to haunt him in the night.

A New Creation

Not long after Ramudu returned to his village, a frail young evangelist we will call Samuel left the Every Home Crusade office in the same region of India to continue systematic village campaigns, conducting follow-up where other workers had visited months earlier. Where there had been multiple converts in a village with no church, he sought to plant a Christ Group. One of the villages Samuel was scheduled to visit was Tumella on the Krishna River—an arduous journey of 25 miles, all of which he traveled by foot.

By nightfall Samuel reached the west bank of the river, but he decided not to cross it in the dark. Instead the weary evangelist found shelter in a small hut owned by an elderly woman. When she learned he was traveling to the village across the river, she warned him to be careful.

"There's a terrible murderer living there," she said haltingly. "His name is Ramudu."

Instantly God impressed on Samuel's heart that Ramudu was the reason he had come on this assignment. He had no idea two other EHC workers had already witnessed to the murderer many months earlier, while he was in prison, but he knew he had been sent to "capture" Ramudu's soul for Jesus.

Samuel looked intently at the elderly woman. "Then Ramudu is the man I must go see."

The next day at dawn, Samuel thanked his hostess and crossed the river.

Reaching the first home on the far side of the village, which the woman had identified as Ramudu's, he called out boldly, "Ramudu!"

A man with a huge head popped out the door.

"Who's there?" he shouted. Then, seeing the bag of Gospel booklets over this stranger's shoulder and apparently recognizing that he was an evangelist, he lunged toward him.

Samuel flinched, then stood in amazement as the towering Indian fell at his feet in respect. This was the customary welcome to someone new, but hardly what Samuel had expected. All he could think about, this giant kneeling before him, was what the woman on the other side of the river had told him.

But something strange was transpiring. Ramudu stood to his feet and insisted Samuel step into his dwelling for tea.

By this time the entire village was gathering to see what was happening. Perhaps, as some suggested, Ramudu intended to murder the frail evangelist, and this was his way of mocking the man before the kill.

But Samuel stayed with Ramudu all day, listening to him and teaching him the truth of the Gospel. The seed first planted in Ramudu's heart months earlier in a prison cell was now taking root. By nightfall the apostle Paul's words would once again ring true: "If anyone is in Christ, he is a new creation" (2 Corinthians 5:17).

Frozen with Fear

Over the next 45 days Samuel continued his follow-up assignments in neighboring villages but came back repeatedly to see Ramudu.

"You must attend a church," the evangelist advised him on his fifth visit to Ramudu's home.

"But will they accept me?"

"I'll talk to the pastor of the church in the next village," the evangelist responded. "I am sure they will welcome you."

The elderly pastor expressed skepticism but agreed to look for Ramudu the following Sunday.

Meanwhile, Ramudu felt excited about going to church for the very first time. He got up early, washed and put on his best clothes. After a two-hour walk to the neighboring village, he stepped into the sanctuary.

Word had spread that Ramudu might be coming. Now the entire congregation, the men sitting on one side and the women on the other (a tradition in some Indian churches), turned to stare. The silence was deadly.

Ramudu, embarrassed, did not know what to do. Neither did the congregation. Then several fearful women stood in their section and slipped out the side door. In moments all the remaining women followed. Almost as quickly the men's section emptied. The only person remaining in the church was the elderly pastor standing behind the pulpit. Ramudu walked boldly up to him.

The pastor froze with fear.

"I trembled as Ramudu was coming," he testified later. "Everyone knew this man was a murderer. Even the authorities feared him. I didn't know what he was going to do."

Ramudu explained why he had come. He wanted to share his testimony, he said, and become a member of the church. Then the pastor realized Ramudu had indeed become a new creature in Christ.

Soon the congregation, watching and listening from outside the building, returned one by one to the sanctuary. That very morning Ramudu gave his testimony. And within a few months he had become a familiar face among the worshipers.

Not long afterward he asked to be baptized in water. He also asked that his name be changed. He had heard the New Testament story of Saul of Tarsus who became Paul the apostle following a dramatic conversion. He had learned that Paul had murdered Christians before he found Christ and had been in prison.

So as Ramudu came up from the waters of baptism in a stream near his village, his face lit up with a glorious smile.

"From today," he exclaimed, "I shall be Paul!"

Since his dramatic conversion, Ramudu (or Paul) has been a featured speaker in many of EHC's follow-up meetings called Seekers Conferences. He has been especially helpful in nurturing ex-offenders who have come to know Jesus Christ.

And it all began with a house call to a prison. Someone with "beautiful feet" had gone where an untouchable lived—someone who might never have been touched through conventional strategies of evangelism.

Touching the Untouched

In order to reach every person with the good news of Jesus, we must make special plans for those who fall outside the reach of normal methods of evangelism.

Ever since Jack McAlister's vision for reaching "all families of the earth" (Genesis 12:3, KJV), which we looked at in chapter 3, Every Home for Christ has worked to take a clear presentation of the Gospel of Jesus Christ to every home. But early on it became clear that not everyone lives in what might be considered a conventional home.

Some of the untouched, like Ramudu, occupy prison cells for a significant season of their lives. Others, like university and college students, live away from home for as long as four to six years while preparing for a career, and might miss a conventional house-to-house strategy. Others stay in hospital settings for prolonged periods, sometimes years—captive, in a sense, to a hospital bed. And there is an entire class of world citizens who travel the seas, living for months at a time on oceangoing vessels. The only time they see land is when the ship comes into port and they enjoy a few days of shore leave.

All these are untouchables when it comes to receiving a clear presentation of the Gospel. If a strategic plan of systematic (even "saturation") evangelism calls for reaching everyone, literally, with the Gospel by taking the Good News right where they live, a plan must be developed to take the message of salvation to each of these untouchable groups as well.

In the very first house-to-house Gospel initiative conducted by Every Home for Christ in Japan in 1953, an unusual conversion amplified this need. A Christian leader planning a citywide campaign suggested, almost as an afterthought, that every cell of the prison at Fukuoka, Japan, be visited and a printed Gospel message given to each inmate. Several pastors agreed, and the prison was included in the prayer-covered campaign.

Only one inmate out of hundreds of cells visited responded—a man named Uchida. But in the months after his conversion, Uchida led more than one hundred fellow inmates to Christ. Following his own water baptism within the walls of Fukuoka prison, he sought and obtained permission to baptize any converts who agreed. At least forty did, and they formed a small Christian fellowship.

The fruit that resulted from that one "seed" planted in a cell at Fukuoka prison made it crystal clear: The Every Home Crusade needed an Every Cell Crusade. True, radio or television might reach a small percentage of inmates in a few countries. But the means to receive such mass communication are still almost nonexistent in most prison cells in the world, especially in developing countries. And although some noteworthy prison ministries, like Prison Fellowship, have had significant global impact, many of the world's incarcerated will not be touched with the Gospel unless a massive effort is mounted to go to each inmate right where he or she lives—in his or her prison cell.

The Olmos Miracle

Just such a cell-to-cell campaign preceded a miraculous awakening at the infamous (but increasingly famous) Olmos Prison in La Plata, Argentina.[1]

For two decades a dark spiritual element within the prison (occupying the entire fourth floor) controlled inmate activity not only at Olmos but at prisons across Argentina. In the early 1980s Olmos was known as a center of occult worship. Inmates participated regularly in animal sacrifices and other satanic rituals.

But a crack in the door for spiritual breakthrough occurred in 1982. Every Home Crusade Argentina's prison ministry, Buenas Nuevas tras las Rejas (Good News Behind Bars), then headed by Ricardo Rocamora, targeted the prison for a systematic, cell-by-cell evangelistic campaign. By some standards it was not very successful. Out of more than two thousand inmates, only a handful accepted the Lord—about forty.

The next year an Assemblies of God minister named Juan Zuccarelli, not yet thirty years old, was walking the streets of La Plata when he sensed God calling him to prison ministry. It was difficult at the time for a Protestant to minister in a prison in an over-whelmingly Roman Catholic country. But a friend of Zuccarelli's who worked for the penitentiary service suggested he apply for a job as prison guard. Juan did so, and received word less than a week later (though his friend told him it would probably take six to eight months) that his application had been approved.

As a guard at Olmos Prison, Juan seized every possible opportunity to witness to both inmates and guards. And by the spring of 1984, the nucleus of believers numbered sixty. God would use this small handful of Christians, along with Juan Zuccarelli and another young evangelist from La Plata, José Tessi, to bring true revival to Olmos Prison.

In 1985 Juan Zuccarelli and José Tessi persuaded prison officials to permit an evangelistic crusade in the prison open to all the inmates. Other than the usual church services permitted for the small number of evangelical believers, nothing like this had ever happened at Olmos Prison. But reluctantly authorities agreed.

Now the challenge was to get inmates to attend. A gathering like this had to be voluntary, and getting inmates to attend an evangelistic meeting would be difficult, to say the least. But an idea came to these praying evangelists.

Normally when rock groups, movies or theatrical presentations came to the prison, the guards yelled, "*Acto*," to inmates, indicating some kind of special entertainment in the prison assembly hall. If a religious service was planned, they usually yelled, "*Culto*," as if to suggest that the meeting was organized by a cult in the prison.

Juan and Jose decided to yell, "*Acto-Culto*," which no doubt confused the inmates. Nearly three hundred attended, and an amazing one hundred gave their lives to Jesus. In a single meeting, the number of converted prisoners at Olmos had more than doubled. It was the beginning of the miracle.

By 1987 the seeds of revival had taken root. Entire cellblocks—averaging forty to sixty inmates each, but sometimes up to a hundred—were taken over by believers, with the prison authorities' blessing. By the end of 1987, new converts occupied at least one cellblock on all five floors of the prison. (Each floor consisted of twelve cellblocks.) By 1988 the prison officials decided to consolidate the evangelical cellblocks on a single floor. Amazingly, they took up six blocks on the fourth floor—the very floor that once controlled Olmos Prison and other institutions across the country.

The church, known by then as Christ the Only Hope, exploded with new conversions. By 1990 it had more than four hundred members. By 1993 that number approached nine hundred—almost thirty percent of the prison's population. By April 1995 at least twelve hundred inmates were members of the church, and another four to five hundred had received Christ who had not yet joined the church. And by mid-1995 eight cellblocks on the third floor, along with all twelve cellblocks on the fourth floor, were part of the church.

This conversion rate is even more remarkable when you realize that most of those incarcerated in Olmos Prison are awaiting their final sentencing, after which they are transferred to another prison in the province. So the prison sees a turnover of almost ten percent of believers a year, either because inmates complete their sentences or because they are transferred out. Inmates led to Jesus at Olmos are often instrumental in planting churches in other prisons. (This also explains how negative influences from the old fourth floor of Olmos had touched so many other prisons in the region before Christians took over the floor.)

Prayer has to be one of the primary reasons for the success of Christ the Only Hope Church at Olmos Prison. All active members are required to be part of the church's prayer focus. Corporate prayer meetings are held every night of the year, with all inmate church members expected to participate. Each member is also expected to spend one night per week (from midnight to 6 A.M., in three two-hour shifts) in personal prayer and worship, in Bible study and in intercession for other inmates, going from bed to bed to pray for their brothers who are sleeping. At least 120 men are involved in this strategy every night. Further, five complete cellblocks of sixty or more inmates each focus on nothing but continuous intercession 24 hours a day.

115

There is little doubt the miracle harvest at Olmos Prison is an act of God. But it is important we not forget that in 1982, a team of courageous warriors made house calls throughout this notorious institution, helping to establish the small nucleus of believers God would begin with to bring about this amazing prison awakening.[2]

Barley Paste and Pain

The ultimate goal of evangelistic house calls—whether to conventional homes, hospital sickrooms, university dormitories, berths on a ship or the cells of a prison like Olmos—is to bring people from darkness into light.

People like Kwonshik Lee of Korea. Kwonshik remembers when a guard at the infamous prison in Inchon, Korea, gave him his new name: No. 733. His head was shaved so guards and prison staff would know he was a prisoner, not one of them. As the barred cell door clanged shut behind him, Kwonshik, age 24, had plenty of time to reflect on his past.

He had been born into a destitute family that rarely had enough food for three meals a day. More often than not they ate simple barley paste. Many days young Kwonshik had to walk the streets begging for food.

He had only one vague memory of those who called themselves Christians. When he was very young, he was invited to a Christmas party sponsored by a nearby church in Uwidong. He could still recall the vast array of food, and how all the poor children of the village had been invited. It was his first time hearing names like *God, Christ* or *Son of God*. But the real reason he had gone was the food. It was the only time he could remember in all those years that his stomach actually felt full.

But his youthful soul remained empty.

Those were days of great political turmoil. Communism was sweeping throughout the north region of Korea, including his village of Uwidong. Eventually the country would be divided. Once the Korean War was in full swing, Kwonshik fled with his family from the North, ending up in an impoverished refugee camp not far from today's Demilitarized Zone. Even the children had to fend for themselves. Then his family split up. Kwonshik was barely a teenager, filled with bitterness, hatred and loneliness.

He began searching for a job to support himself and was finally hired as a janitor at a roadside restaurant. He worked hard and befriended many prostitutes who frequented the area. Eventually Kwonshik fell into sin. But something stirred his heart with remorse. One night he remembered a few of the ideas he had heard at the Christmas party years earlier, particularly that God loved him.

But could there possibly be a God? he wondered. *If so, why is He treating me so cruelly?*

The roadside restaurant went bankrupt and Kwonshik was fired. A few weeks later he was hired by a former patron of the restaurant who needed a cook in her own rice shop. The young man worked hard for several weeks but was fired again, ostensibly for being young and inexperienced. Rage filled his heart. And when he returned a few days later to receive his final week's salary, he was told he would not be paid, that his work had not been satisfactory.

"You should be grateful you even had something to eat while working here," the shop owner shouted.

Then it happened. Kwonshik lifted a broken beer bottle with one hand and grabbed a sharp kitchen knife with the other. In moments he was looking down at a lifeless body lying in a pool of blood. He had killed the shop owner, for which crime he was sentenced to death.

So as the door to Kwonshik's prison cell slammed behind him, he cursed God and his parents. He cursed his fellow human beings, his culture, even the country in which he had been born.

Sometime later he was transferred to the prison in Suwon, Korea, where his death sentence was to be carried out.

Meanwhile one day he spotted two young men about his age walking the corridors between the rows of prison cells, speaking to inmates and giving them booklets. Soon Kwonshik held one of the booklets in his hand. It was titled *Freedom Behind Prison Bars.*

It told him about a Person named Jesus Christ who could completely change his life, and it promised him something called eternal life. Anyone believing in Jesus, the booklet claimed, could experience total freedom—even if he or she had to live a lifetime behind prison bars.

The young man was fascinated with the message but uncertain about the concept of "receiving Christ as Savior." So he wrote the Korean Every Home Crusade office for more information. Then, in response to what they sent, he began working his way through the four-part Bible correspondence course. He studied the first lesson and sent in the answers, but still was unsure what it all meant. In Kwonshik's words:

> In the cold and lonesome prison cell I began to study about God, the Bible, sin and Jesus Christ. What a new world there was before me! After studying the second lesson, I accepted Jesus as my personal Savior. I couldn't believe that someone would die for a murderer like me. I was totally transformed.

By the time inmate No. 733 finished the Bible correspondence course, he had become a new person. The guards could tell. So could the warden. And some time later, without explanation, the government commuted Kwonshik's death sentence and pardoned him.

He never knew whether it had been a bureaucratic mistake or whether word of his behavior had touched key officials. In any case, shortly after his pardon, Kwonshik wrote this testimony:

> It has already been four years since I was put in prison. But these four years have been the most valuable and meaningful period in my life. When I first found myself behind the clanging prison bars, I was categorized as a Class-A suspected murderer. It was a terrible label to bear. It seems as if those fearful and rebellious days in Inchon prison were only yesterday—but it was four years ago. Then I was transferred to the Suwon prison to await execution. But today I am free because someone came to my cell to tell me about Jesus. Thank God they did not miss me!

118

Destined for the Gallows

Years ago Every Home for Christ founder Jack McAlister stood before 1,201 inmates of another notorious Korean prison, not far from where Kwonshik Lee had been incarcerated. Jack had flown more than six thousand miles from America to observe as well as participate in this amazing commencement ceremony.

As he prepared to give each inmate a graduation certificate acknowledging his completion of the simple, four-part Bible correspondence course, Jack could not hold back the tears. Hundreds of inmates sat crowded together on a cold cement floor, their faces filled with joy, and began to sing a song they had learned only recently, "There Is Power in the Blood."

Afterward the Buddhist warden of the prison, Commandant Lee, stood and declared, "Never in all my life have I seen so many men studying the Bible and learning about Jesus Christ."

These men had given their hearts to Jesus in response to a cell-by-cell campaign to provide every inmate a salvation message. Jack calculated that it had cost less than a penny each to present all 6,540 inmates at the prison with the Gospel, resulting in the 1,201 decisions for Christ.

Little could Jack have known that in the following several decades, more than six million inmates would be visited, cell by cell, and more than 120,000 of them would complete a similar Bible correspondence course and pray to receive Jesus as Savior.

Are these conversions genuine? An answer can be found in the testimony of one of the 1,201 inmates Jack met during the ceremony in Korea.

Indoh Park, a colonel from the North Korean army and a political prisoner condemned to death, was the first man to receive his diploma at the mass prison graduation. Earlier, after his conversion through a printed Gospel message given to him in his cell, Colonel Park had written the EHC office in Korea:

> All my life I have been afraid of what will happen after death. Even in the fiercest battle during the war in the North, this matter bewildered me.

But now, after accepting Christ as my personal Savior, my death sentence does not make me afraid. I can confess that I am truly happy. I will continue to study the Bible lessons until I lay down my life and go to be with Jesus.

When Jack McAlister left the prison, he embraced Colonel Park and encouraged him to be strong in the Lord. The condemned inmate smiled and responded, "Christ is nearer to me than ever before."

Colonel Park probably sensed what lay immediately ahead. His final appeal to the Supreme Court of South Korea was denied, and a few weeks later he was hanged. But those who knew him had little doubt Colonel Park was a new creation in Christ.

Perhaps of the 1,201 prisoners who found Christ at that Korean prison, there is special significance in the very last digit of that number. There was *one* named Colonel Indoh Park, and today he is with Jesus.

Anger of the Gods

The demons were angry. Sickness had spread across the deep valleys and towering hillsides of East Kwaio. Whole families lay sick or dying. Haribo heard their painful stories and offered the traditional means to appease the gods, whom he was certain vented their anger for no apparent reason. Perhaps someone had desecrated a Kwaio burial site unknowingly, angering an ancestral spirit, or maybe a warrior had failed to sacrifice a pig or chicken for breaking some tribal taboo.

Haribo, as the undisputed priestly leader of that region of at least ten small mountain villages, saw many pigs sacrificed—chickens, too; and received many as gifts in payment for his spiritual solutions to their painful plight. But deep in his heart, the eighty-year-old chief (or was he ninety?) sensed something missing in the beliefs of his people. The spirits were too angry and rarely forgiving. Sometimes he dreamed of a peaceful place with no pain or suffering, but he had no idea how to find that place.

Often at night as the old chief stared at the brilliant starry Pacific sky, he hoped that before he departed this life, someone would show him the way to eternal peace. But Haribo would have to wait at least ten more yam harvests before outsiders with the answers for which he searched found the courage to enter this remote area and bring with them those heavenly directions.

8

The "Must-Bring" Mandate

A stranger approaching the remote Sherpa village of Syabru in the foothills of the Nepalese Himalayas would be drawn immediately to the towering, thirty-foot-high flags blowing briskly in the breeze. They appear to be traditional Buddhist prayer flags with many glimmering streamers and larger, rectangular pieces of cloth at the top. Usually each family has its own personal flag, which bears the words of prayers to spirit gods in the names of departed loved ones.

But to anyone who knows the Sherpa or Tamang languages of the region, a careful look at the flags of Syabru reveals something astonishing. Almost a third of the homes scattered across this barren mountainside have flags that carry not prayers written for departed souls, but rather verses from the Bible.

The miracle of the good news of Jesus coming home by home to the families of this district of Nepal, including the village of Syabru, began in the 1980s with a ten-year-old boy named Gyal-sang, who was something of a child prodigy to the people of Syabru. Some were even convinced he was the incarnation of the primary spirit of their village.

Ten generations back, when the border of Tibet was moved as the result of a war, Gyalsang's ancestors had found themselves suddenly within the boundaries of the Hindu nation of Nepal, although they were strict Tibetan Buddhists. One of Gyalsang's forefathers, Kham Sung Wang Di, brought a gold-covered Buddha idol from Tibet for the temple that was eventually built near Syabru.

Generations later Gyalsang's father, Lharkyal, traveled a great distance as a boy of thirteen to the town of Sing Gompa, hoping to become a lama in the Tibetan Buddhist tradition. This did not happen, but he did become a devout Buddhist monk, studying under the great Khamba Lama for six years until he was nineteen. There was little Lharkyal did not know about the Tibetan Buddhist faith. Later, as an adult, he was guardian of the key to that temple near Syabru, and carried out his duties faithfully as the main caretaker.

But because Lharkyal was of the Tamang people and had married a Helambu Sherpa, his family showed their disdain by isolating the new couple in a small hut on a parcel of least desirable land, a steep hillside just outside the village. Though poor, they survived by breeding and selling jomos—female offspring of yaks and cows. Next to their modest dwelling stood a village idol where chickens were sacrificed regularly to the Buddha and villagers worshiped other evil spirits. Everyone was certain ghosts and demons lived at the site, and Gyalsang, one of Lharkyal's three sons, often saw his father hold out his huge, razor-sharp Gurkha knife in attempts to ward off evil spirits as he entered the house.

Gyalsang had his own destiny with the supernatural.

He attended school briefly in Syabru with twenty or so other village boys, but the teaching was in Nepalese, while the languages of his village were Sherpa and Tamang. Because he went to school only about once every two weeks, he learned little, never fully comprehending the Nepalese language. Instead, the boy helped his family tend their jomo herd in the Himalayan foothills, protecting the animals from wolves and snow leopards.

The Shadow Beings

In 1983, just after Gyalsang turned ten, he had his first encounter with the supernatural. He and his mother, Dolma, were watching their herd of jomos in the hills above Syabru on a cloudy spring day. At midday the boy lay down in the tall grass to rest and fell into a deep sleep.

Suddenly two "shadow beings" began surging back and forth before him, moving with lightning speed. Gyalsang began to cry out as if having a nightmare.

Dolma rushed to his side but could not awaken him. Splashing cold water on the child's face had no effect. She called for the help of other villagers tending nearby herds. No one was able to arouse the lad.

Finally Dolma carried her unconscious son back to their small hut. It was too late for her and Lharkyal to take Gyalsang to a witch doctor some distance away, so they decided to do so in the morning.

Meanwhile, Gyalsang was experiencing an astonishing vision. The shadow beings continued to surge back and forth until they finally spoke to the boy in the Sherpa language. They told him to instruct his parents not to see the witch doctor the next day, that he would be fine now. They also told the child to tell his parents to make a separate sleeping place for him, and that whenever he was asleep, they were not to awaken him.

By morning Gyalsang was conscious and told his parents all that had happened. Stricken with fear, the superstitious parents agreed to obey the boy's instructions to the letter.

The following night Gyalsang fell into another deep sleep. Again the strange beings appeared. This time they took the boy to a distant place far from Syabru, flying through a dark, unnatural place where no other living things existed. Suddenly Gyalsang saw a dimly lit image of the Buddha before him and heard a voice, either from the Buddha or from some other source, say, "From today I want to use you. I'll teach you about my way."

Then the shadow beings took the child back through the area of darkness to the special sleeping room that his father had made that day in their home on the outskirts of Syabru. But before they left, they told the boy, "From today you are not to mix with others. Stay alone with your parents."

Gyalsang's night encounters continued for more than two years. Often while he slept he was taken to the place of light, always through the dark region first, where he learned Buddhist teaching.

Gyalsang's father, Lharkyal, listened in amazement as his son told him what he had learned in the night. It corresponded precisely with what Lharkyal himself had learned from the Khamba Lama years before. In one encounter the shadow beings told the youth that his father was to obtain certain Buddhist religious attire, as well as drums and bells, which Gyalsang played perfectly though he had never been taught this difficult ritual.

A God Called *Yesu*

An even more remarkable encounter took place that almost defies explanation. One night the boy was taken back to the dimly lit image of the Buddha. This time he observed a plate or screen—similar to a computer screen, although no one in that remote Himalayan region had ever heard of a computer—attached to the Buddha's knees. Strange script was written on the screen, while a voice explained what each word meant.

When Gyalsang awakened, he was able to write in a notebook precisely what he had heard. He wrote in Nepalese (which at that time he had not fully learned) and in another language, which to this day no one has been able to identify. Yet Gyalsang could read every word.

The boy's parents realized something amazing was happening to their son. He could even tell them their thoughts and describe in detail the sins of their past simply by reading the script in what had soon expanded from one to several notebooks.

On a subsequent night journey, Gyalsang was given a list of 35 "gods" whom he and his family were to worship in ascending order, with number one the most important. Each Saturday he was to open his notebook and teach his parents and two brothers about the list. Insights simply came to his mind, and he communicated what he was feeling and hearing in his heart as he read from the strange script.

But one day the list included a new name listed in last position—Yesu, a name he had never heard before. It was the Sherpa word for Jesus, although no Bible was ever known to have been in the region of Syabru, nor was any Christian known to have entered this area.

This name, for reasons Gyalsang could not explain, kept moving up on the list from month to month as he taught from his notebook. With each change of position, Gyalsang gained more insight about the origin of the name. He learned, for example, that Yesu had descended directly from mankind's very first parents, Adam and Eve (whose strange and never-heard names, like the name Yesu, he recorded faithfully in his notebook). He also learned that Yesu was a special Person called "the Son of God."

Finally the name Yesu moved to second place on the list. Gyalsang was certain the name would soon move to number one.

That very night Gyalsang took another journey to the place of light, where he learned that Yesu was "crucified" on a "cross," and that after he was buried he "rose" from the dead. All these words were strange, and neither the youth nor his family knew what to do with this information.

125

Yesu Is Real

It was now the late fall of 1985. The family had moved with their jomo herd high into the Nepalese hills. But now, because winter was coming, they were returning closer to their permanent home near Syabru. On the way Gyalsang's father decided to visit some friends who owned a lodge catering to outsiders trekking into that part of the Himalayan foothills. There he saw a booklet in the Tibetan language that some outsider had left. He was immediately struck by the name *Yesu* that was noted prominently on the cover. Was it possible?

Lharkyal got permission from his friend to keep the booklet. It was the first outside confirmation that his son had written about a real Person.

When Lharkyal brought the tract home, he showed it to Gyalsang, who looked in one of his special notebooks and saw words he had written earlier that suddenly made sense. They said, "Keep the tract. It is good. Read it."

So Gyalsang's father read the message about Yesu to his son, confirming much of what Gyalsang had written about Jesus' death and resurrection. But because the family was bound by superstition, they thought the tract itself must be worshiped, so they bowed down to it repeatedly as just one more object of devotion.

A few days later one of Gyalsang's brothers, who had opened a tourist lodge near Syabru, hosted three men from a ministry called Gospel Recordings. Mingmar could not help but notice that the three men bowed their heads to pray before eating a meal.

Later two of the workers went out to explore the area while one stayed back. Mingmar entered into a conversation with him that soon turned to religion. In moments the worker was talking about a Person called Yesu and describing details about His life, death and resurrection.

Mingmar's face lit up.

"The things you have told me are exactly as my brother has told me," he exclaimed. "They do not differ in a single word."

"Where can I find your brother?" the worker asked excitedly.

"Well, Gyalsang seems to have gone crazy, but if you really want to meet him, I will gladly take you to him."

The members of the team had to return to Nepal's capital that day because one had to leave the next day for America. But the worker promised Mingmar he would return later with another Nepalese Christian.

Two weeks later he kept his promise, and the two men hiked to the village of Syabru, where the workers from Gospel Recordings were soon sharing details with Gyalsang's family about Yesu. They had brought with them an extraordinary resource—a tape-recorded message in the Tamang language to help them communicate the story of Jesus.

Thirteen-year-old Gyalsang listened intently to every word on the tape. Finally he jumped to his feet and rushed to get his notebooks. Flipping through the pages, the excited youth read aloud sections of his writings that corresponded to what he had just heard in the recording.

Christian workers who checked Gyalsang's writings later in detail determined that in only a single instance had he mixed up a fact while translating his visions. He had apparently confused the name of Pilate with that of Caesar in writing about Christ's trial. Everything else in his account was exactly as it unfolds in the New Testament—even though Gyalsang had never seen or even heard of such a Book.

A Final Vision

Late that same night Gyalsang experienced his final vision involving the shadow beings. He was taken back to the Buddha image, where the voice spoke for the last time: "Today you no longer need to serve me. One comes after me who is greater than I. You must do what the men say and follow Yesu."

The next morning Gyalsang described this vision to his father, brothers and the visitors from Gospel Recordings. (His mother was already out tending the jomo herd.) He declared boldly that from that day forward he would follow only Yesu. Christ was now his only Lord and Savior. He now realized, he added, that the family was never again to bow down to and worship a tract about Yesu, because Yesu dwells only in the heart. Then, in the presence of his father and brothers and these visitors, Gyalsang tore from his neck the charms and beads that had long been central to his Buddhist worship.

Both of Gyalsang's brothers, although not his father, quickly followed Gyalsang's example and declared their own faith in Christ. And later that day, when Dolma returned from tending the jomos, she listened to her son's testimony and promptly prayed a simple prayer to Yesu: "From now on You are my Lord. I don't know much, but You are my Lord." Soon even Gyalsang's staunchly devout Buddhist father received Christ. The entire family had been transformed.

Within days Gyalsang burned all the notebooks describing his encounters with the shadow beings, except the one containing specific messages about Yesu, including the details he had written about Christ's death and resurrection.

In 1993 Gyalsang's mother, Dolma, after a long battle with cancer, went to be with Jesus. Christian leaders of Nepal believe she is the first known Helambu Sherpa ever to stand before the throne of grace. Gyalsang's father, Lharkyal, today composes Sherpa and Tamang hymns and leads in Christian worship when believers of the Syabru area gather. Gyalsang and Mingmar have gone to Bible school to prepare for Christian ministry. Gyalsang, now in his twenties, has also recorded Gospel messages in the Sherpa language and has begun the translation of the New Testament into the same tribal language—the language of his heart.

So it is that numerous families in the remote mountain village of Syabru, who have come to know Jesus as Savior, have hoisted Christian prayer flags over the Sherpa countryside proclaiming promises from God's Word. Gyalsang's dream and goal is that someday every home in every village of Syabru and beyond will fly a similar flag indicating that their home has been transformed by the presence and power of Jesus Christ.[1]

Capturing Voices

Jesus described Himself as the only door through whom people can come to God. He spoke of "other sheep . . . which are not of this fold" (John 10:16, KJV), adding, "Them also I must bring."

Some of these "other sheep"—people beyond the bounds of conventional evangelism—I described in the last chapter, men and women like Ramudu of Tumella, India, who are living behind bars. Here we examine another group of the largely untouched: illiterate peoples scattered throughout the world.

How grateful I am that some Christian organizations are targeting those who cannot read! One of these organizations, with which Every Home for Christ has worked closely for years, is Gospel Recordings, the group that brought the Gospel to Gyalsang and his family in late 1985. This unique, behind-the-scenes ministry (which I am convinced will be pivotal in fulfilling the Great Commission in our generation) began more than a half-century ago as a result of the passionate burden of a young single missionary to Honduras who actually thought her ministry had ended.[2]

Joy Ridderhof had been in Central America only six years when she was forced to return home in 1937, her body ravaged by dysentery and malaria. Once back in her childhood home in Los Angeles, Joy could not escape the mental picture of individuals in the small Central American country of Honduras where she had intended to spend her life. She remembered in particular a poor, illiterate widow with a large family who lived in a village in the mountains.

The first time Joy visited the woman, not long before her return to the States, the widow listened eagerly to the message of salvation and prayed to receive Christ as Savior. Her daughter-in-law committed her life to Jesus, too. That night Joy walked the eight miles home through pouring rain, rejoicing at the opportunity of seeing two souls find Jesus.

Later Joy heard that the woman was being persecuted terribly for declaring her conversion publicly. By now Joy's health was declining rapidly. But she had a burden for this elderly woman living in the mountains who had not a single verse of God's Word to feed on. Nor would a Bible have helped, since the woman could not read a word.

If only I could teach her a verse of Scripture, thought Joy, *so she would really know it. It would be at least one weapon against sin and temptation.*

So Joy made the eight-mile journey into the mountains again and spent an entire day with the woman. For hours they sat together as the ailing missionary repeated a simple Bible verse over and over, phrase by phrase. The woman stumbled badly and grew confused every time she tried to commit a phrase to memory.

Joy left the mountain village hopelessly dejected. How she wished she could have stayed a few more days until the Word had taken root in the old woman's mind!

Months later, as Joy lay recovering in her parents' home in Los Angeles, she could not forget her feelings of anxiety and disappointment as she left that mountain village.

If only I could have left my voice behind, she thought, *to repeat that verse again and again, until by sheer force of repetition she had it committed to memory.*

"Just a voice," Joy muttered to herself as she fell asleep.

Joy spent most of the autumn and winter in bed. But God spoke often to her heart about His plan to get the Good News to those who might otherwise never receive it.

One day, as Joy lay recovering, her mind again wandered to experiences in Honduras. She remembered the shrill sounds of phonograph records being played in the saloons and shops of that impoverished nation. Then she recalled that she had been playing hymns on her own hand-cranked phonograph when a fellow missionary observed wistfully, "If only we had recordings of the Gospel like that in Spanish."

Creative insights began to flow.

Phonograph records, she thought. *Phonograph records that could be reproduced by the thousands.*

130

Was it even possible to do something like this on so massive a scale that it might actually affect an entire mission field?

A seemingly chance encounter several days later with a man who knew about producing records pointed Joy in the direction of still another man who understood the process even better. This man happened to be a former missionary to Central America, and the divine appointment led to the production one year later, in 1938, of the very first Gospel recording, which shared the message of salvation—including hymns and verses of Scripture—in Spanish.

The cost for that first recording was incredibly modest, just fifteen dollars (which included the studio time). By May 1940, eleven double-disk master recordings had been made for further duplication.

Joy determined from the start not to record the messages herself, because of her accent, but to use only native speakers of the language. (This policy would prove critical to the overall plan as God accelerated the recording of messages into many hundreds of languages.) She also sent out modest prayer letters to friends who had expressed special enthusiasm for the evangelization of the illiterate. They wanted to pray—and help!

From the very first arrival of these unique recorded messages on the mission field of Honduras, they were received enthusiastically. Little did Joy realize, working out of her attic in Los Angeles (which was her office as well as "distribution center"), how dramatically the ministry was to expand. People of other tongues and dialects would soon find out what was happening in the Spanish language and appeal for help in their own languages.

In 1943 a special request came to Joy from Wycliffe Bible Translators. They wanted a Gospel recording for the Mazahua Indian tribe living in northern Mexico. But when Joy and her co-workers were ready to receive several members of the Mazahua tribe in Los Angeles to record the Gospel messages in their own language, the visa applications for these tribal representatives were denied, since the U.S. was currently entrenched in World War II.

Then it occurred to Joy: To capture the voices of the Mazahua, so they could hear the good news of Jesus in their own language, did not necessitate their coming to the Americans; the Americans could go to them.

On a practical level the idea involved considerable challenge. The tiny portable tape recorders so familiar today were unknown at the time. Recordings still had to be made directly onto disks, and the machinery was unusually cumbersome.

Still, the first team to the Mazahuas left Southern California in March 1944 and did not return until early 1945. A succession of miracles helped the team capture not only the voice of the Mazahuas, but an amazing 32 additional languages as well, 25 of which were Indian tribal languages. Each recording was brought back to the U.S., transferred onto acetate, reproduced in quantity and taken back into many regions of Mexico.[3]

"A Tree Tied Crosswise"

Capturing the voices of remote tribes, obviously, was difficult. The Gospel had never gone to most of those tribes and many had no written language. So it was necessary to find someone from the tribe who could understand at least one other language and through whom a recording team might be able to communicate. Then a worker had to provide that unique person with a script he could translate into his mother tongue. But because that person probably could not read, the message had to be communicated verbally through an interpreter in the second language, and this had to be done sentence by sentence.

In November 1948 Joy Ridderhof and a team from Gospel Recordings made their first trip to the Philippines to begin capturing voices from numerous remote tribes using this unique multi-translation method. If they could use this means to capture the language of a group of aboriginal Pygmies, a language never even reduced to writing and which not a single missionary could speak, it would be possible to replicate the method elsewhere.

How did it work? Let's sit in on the actual recording session, as described by Phyllis Thompson in her book *Faith by Hearing*.

132

Joy and several co-workers, including her partner, Ann Sherwood, and a Filipino interpreter named Mrs. Maggay, sat with an eighteen-year-old member of the Negrito tribe and an elderly tribesman, a toothless, half-naked man barely five feet tall who spoke the Ibanag language (another language of the region) as well as Palanan Negrito, the language they intended to record. He even spoke a limited amount of English.

The message prepared for recording described how "the Son of the Chief of Sky" came to earth "to die on a tree tied crosswise, to bear the punishment of the sins of all people everywhere, to save them from the wicked village down below, a place called fire." It went on to explain that "whoever believes in 'Jesu,' Son of Chief of Sky, will become himself a child of Chief of Sky, and when death comes will enter immediately into the good village above, where everything is pretty and happy."

The message concluded that the Holy Spirit, "the Spirit shadow, good, who belongs to Chief of Sky, will come to dwell in the heart of the one who believes in Jesu."

Now, sitting with her fellow team members and the two Negrito tribesmen, Joy took the microphone and said clearly in English, "God, the Creator of earth and sky and everything in them, has sent a message to all men that dwell upon the earth. . . ."

Then she handed the microphone to Mrs. Maggay, who repeated the sentence in the Ibanag language to the alert little man. Then Joy passed the microphone to him. The toothless tribesman took it excitedly and spoke the same sentence in jerky Palanan Negrito.

Next to him sat the slight, eighteen-year-old Negrito whose task it was to record the Gospel message that day. He was to speak clearly into the microphone exactly what he heard from the old man, so he listened intently as the elderly tribesman interpreted the first sentence of the Gospel message in their native language. As the young man listened, his lips quivered and his small, brown body tensed. Then he took the strange little object that the others had been talking into and repeated the sentence he had just heard loudly in his own language.

133

Afterward Joy asked Ann Sherwood excitedly to play back the message that had been recorded in three languages. First came Joy's voice talking about God, the Creator of the earth and sky. The young Negrito man sat rigid as Joy's voice resonated from the box.

Then came the calm, matter-of-fact voice of the Filipino woman, Mrs. Maggay. The young Negrito showed no emotion.

Then came the jerky, excited voice of the old, toothless tribesman. Still the Negrito displayed no emotion.

Finally the voice changed again, and this time the Negrito heard himself proclaiming loudly, "Chief of Sky, He who made sky and earth and all in it, He sent already message to all people of the world. . . ."

The young man was overwhelmed with emotion. Never in his eighteen summers had he heard or seen anything like this! His own voice was speaking to him out of that tiny box! He threw himself back and laughed until every part of his body shook with joy.

It took several minutes before he was able to control himself so that the missionaries could continue recording. Each segment had to travel from Joy to the Filipino woman to the old tribesman and then to the young Negrito. And each segment had to be replayed to make sure it had recorded properly, causing the young Negrito to burst into laughter. Needless to say, it took many hours to record the whole message.

Later Ann Sherwood edited the recording, preserving only the young Negrito's segments for a finished Gospel message. She had to make 150 separate splices to get it correct. But when she finished, those who spoke Palanan Negrito had the good news of salvation in their own language. This acetate disk concluded,

> Words of Chief of Sky say: "Whoever receive Jesu, He give power to become child of Chief of Sky, whoever believe name His."

It was the Gospel in the Palanan Negrito language, and many would receive Christ because of what happened that day in the rugged, remote hills of the Philippines.

A year later, when Joy Ridderhof and Ann Sherwood finally left the Philippines, they had obtained recordings of 92 indigenous tribes and dialects using the same method. And although missionaries from throughout the region had provided invaluable assistance, the team had ventured into many areas so remote that not a single missionary had ever been there.

Obeying the "Must-Bring" Mandate

In the months following, the work of Gospel Recordings accelerated amazingly. By the end of 1949, Gospel presentations in 230 languages and dialects had been recorded on tape. By the end of 1950 that number had skyrocketed to 350. By 1955 one million records had been produced and sent into 1,401 language groups. By 1963 Gospel Recordings had passed the 4.5 million mark in total records produced, capturing 2,900 languages.

In that same year, the ministry developed an amazing "talking booklet" that earned the award of the year from International Paper for the most unusual use of cardboard. It represented a breakthrough in making the Gospel available to the illiterate or those with no written language.[4]

For years Joy Ridderhof had said, "All that's needed to play a record is something for the record to turn on and a needle to go into the grooves." Such a simplified device was required, she knew, for the most remote areas of the world in which no record or cassette player would be available. Even if one could be made small enough (which eventually happened), the cost of distributing it in vast quantities to tens of thousands of illiterate villages still without the Gospel would be prohibitive.

Much experimentation thus went into the development of the talking booklet called "cardtalk." Plastic proved unsuitable. And only by accident did those involved in the project say they discovered that corrugated cardboard was the best choice of material because of the way it reverberated the sound. Even the placement of the corrugated grooves made for better sound reproduction.

135

Later, when the cardboard was coated to make it waterproof, the sound improved even more.

One small cardboard player, consisting of three pieces of cardboard about eight inches square on little hinges, cost less than a dollar to produce and reverberated the sound of a recorded message throughout a large room or hut in which as many as thirty or forty people were gathered.

To date 936,698 cardtalk players have been distributed among illiterate peoples throughout the world. Every Home for Christ has distributed more than five hundred thousand of these to more than one hundred thousand illiterate villages scattered across India. The total of almost one million cardtalks distributed is in addition to the millions of regular records distributed in the earlier years of Gospel Recordings, as well as the impossible-to-count number of cassette recordings in hundreds of languages that have since gone to indigenous tribes.

Later came Gospel Recordings' development of a hand-cranked cassette player, a marvel in itself, that functioned without motor or batteries. All that was necessary to operate the player was turning a small hand crank to generate power. These unique cassette players, which could be operated by anyone and had no mechanical features to break down, were manufactured by the thousands very economically in China.

In many parts of the world, entire villages were touched by the message of Christ as the result of a hand-operated cassette player left in each village—with not only a cassette containing the Gospel message but recorded Christian songs as well, all in a people group's own language.

Today at least 4,679 different languages and dialects have been captured on recordings, and plans are underway to mobilize the necessary teams of "recordists" to go into a decreasing number of tribes that still await any written or spoken presentation of the Gospel.

The fruit continues to prove it is possible to reach previously unreached people using this simple means of communicating the Gospel. In Nepal, not far from the village of Syabru where Gyalsang and his family came to Christ, three unreached tribes were targeted by Gospel Recordings and Every Home Concern (EHC) of Nepal: the Sonha tribe, consisting of some ten thousand gold-panners and farmers; the Hayu people, one of Nepal's smallest tribes, with only 1,500 tribesmen; and the Thami tribe, consisting of twenty thousand stone-cutters and hunters. Each group, nearly illiterate, was given recorded Gospel messages and, for the very few who could read, printed messages in their languages.

According to a report from the evangelism team penetrating the Sonha:

> We were a total of eight Christian workers fulfilling the Great Commission. With great confidence and faith we began our work. Now we see how marvelously the Lord heard our prayers. He brought 23 people to understand there is a God who loves and forgives. These 23 accepted the Lord as personal Savior and made vows to live for Him alone. We distributed forty cassettes in the Sonha language, two hand-wind cassette players and some EHC tracts in the Nepalese language for those who might be able to read. Isn't that wonderful? They had never heard the Gospel before. They were astonished that the cassettes spoke in their language. Now most of the Sonha villages have been covered with the Good News.

These "other sheep" Jesus spoke of in His must-bring mandate of John 10:16 are clearly having a chance to hear the Good News in their own languages.

But what of those who live in closed or restricted nations in which the Gospel cannot freely be shared? As you will soon see, they possibly represent the greatest miracle of all that is emerging on the horizon of world evangelization.

Another Child of Destiny

Most East Kwaio villagers thought Chief Haribo had lived almost ninety yam harvests. Even Haribo was not sure how many he had seen. But the people loved his stories as he recounted the Kwaio traditions he knew so well.

The villagers would sit around the fire late at night in the chill of the rugged Kwaio mountains and sing and dance and tell their island tales, interrupted occasionally by brilliant shooting stars streaking across the ink-black Pacific sky. Haribo was always quick to explain that these strange occurrences were reminders that ancestral spirits were near, somehow acknowledging their presence. But deep inside he wondered what the stars really were and how they had come to be.

In spite of his own inner questions, Haribo always had answers for those he served as high chief. The people, in turn, loved and respected Haribo. In fact, when a new Kwaio child was born and ceremonially dedicated to their ancestors, villagers wondered if that little one might someday become their future priestly chief when the old patriarch was gone. Others wondered if Haribo could ever be replaced.

One night, as naked Kwaio warriors warmed themselves by a crackling midnight fire, another child with a destiny like Haribo's was born on the other side of the world, deep in the rain forest of central Africa. It was early afternoon on that continent as Pygmy parents, surrounded by their clan (more than forty members in all), offered their baby, a future Pygmy chief, to the spirit of the trees. Lendongo would, like Haribo, be used by God as an entry point for the Gospel to penetrate his people.

Warriors of the Night

Night seems darker in China, and this night was no exception. Perhaps it was the absence of street lights, I thought. Or perhaps it was the spiritual darkness that seemed to hover over this section of high-rise apartments on the outskirts of one of China's large northern cities.

It was past midnight, and the team of night warriors I was working with had already distributed almost a thousand

Gospel messages. Our small team of four had split up into two groups. Another group of four had gone to a different area of the city. For several hours we had been darting in and out of shadowy entrances to apartment buildings, keeping our eyes open for the authorities or anyone who might detect what we were doing. Cars, although common these days in China, were scarce at that time of night, and anytime we caught the glare of headlights, we knew they were from either a taxi or a police car. Discovery by either could lead to serious consequences.

Suddenly we heard someone coming through the entryway of one of the apartments where we had just distributed scores of Gospel messages. We darted once again into the shadows. My heart pounded as we stood in absolute silence. But it was a false alarm. No doubt the person thought he had heard something, and then walked back quietly into his apartment.

I took a deep breath and thought to myself again, *I can't believe I'm here in the middle of northern China breaking the law! What on earth ever came over me to agree to do this?*

For years I had had a special burden for China and had prayed for that nation every day that I could remember for more than nineteen years.

Every Home for Christ also took the call to prayer very seriously. Two decades earlier the ministry had printed thirty separate pamphlets for prayer, each focusing on a different province of China.[1] We were also involved with various Christian organizations and indigenous church groups to get Bibles and other Christian literature into China. As far back as the early 1960s, we had filled balloons with Gospel booklets and released them with favorable winds from Taiwan into the coastal areas of southern China. It was the best we could do at the time, and a modest but encouraging number of mailed responses indicated fruit. Still, the doors seemed to be closed tightly to any kind of systematic activity to take the Gospel home to home in China.

Now here I was, in June 1995, with a small team of Western Christians in the middle of the night, going from apartment to apartment, sharing the good news of Jesus Christ and hoping we would not get caught.

We were part of an emerging strategy that fascinated me—one that I had heard about only recently, and which had been implemented for little more than sixteen months throughout China. It had all been started (as I was to discover) by a passionate 21-year-old British lad with only a ninth-grade education and a call from God to forsake everything and go to China.

Meeting Brother Mac

My unusual experience with these "warriors of the night" began five months earlier, when ten EHC national directors from East and Southeast Asia gathered in January 1995 to strategize for the remaining years of this decade. China was high on our list of priorities. But the big question concerned the feasibility of conducting systematic, home-by-home evangelism there. We had heard many remarkable reports coming out of that vast land, some indicating as many as 35,000 conversions a day. But all forms of open evangelism were outlawed, even though we knew that if a systematic plan ever were permitted, the numbers would be far higher. Most of us at the meeting agreed that a systematic plan to evangelize China simply could not be implemented, at least for now.

Then I met a young British brother whom I will call, for security reasons, Brother Mac.[2]

I might not have met Brother Mac had it not been for an unexpected encounter with a respected missionary who works in China. I talked with him only moments after my arrival in East Asia for the EHC leaders' conference. Exhausted from more than 24 hours of nonstop travel, I was ready to fall into bed when the phone rang.

The missionary, with whom I had hoped to meet while I was in the area, was calling to inform me he was leaving for the U.S. early the next morning. If I wanted to touch base with him, it had to be that night.

141

Something within me—I know now it was God's Spirit—urged me to see him in spite of my exhaustion. So moments later we were seated in the hotel lobby as he related to me incredible stories of what was happening in China.

Suddenly, almost mid-sentence, he looked me in the eyes and asked, "So, Dick, what are your plans for China?"

I explained the vision of Every Home for Christ and how our ultimate goal was to work with believers in China, as we have done in more than 170 other countries, to take a printed message of salvation to literally every family.

I was startled when the missionary interrupted me.

"I think that's already begun," he said. "There's a British chap here, only in his twenties, who's doing an amazing work just as you're describing. You really need to see him."

"Is that possible?" I asked excitedly.

"Yes. He just arrived today from Beijing and will be here through the weekend. It's great you came this week," he added. "This brother shows up here only a few days every other month. The rest of the time he's running all over China."

As I tumbled into bed an hour or two later, I knew in my heart that God had been setting up circumstances for a strategic encounter that would change my thinking about the evangelization of China.

Less than 36 hours later I met Brother Mac. His wrinkled blue sport coat fit tightly on his thin frame, and his narrow, old-fashioned tie clashed with his shirt. But style, I soon realized, mattered little to Brother Mac. He cared only about souls. And he had left his home in Great Britain because Chinese people by the millions needed to hear about Jesus.

Only a few days after first meeting Brother Mac, and after a night of prayer, God impressed a thought on my heart: *You can never know the joy of giving people the Gospel in a restricted nation until you've experienced it for yourself.*

So it was that I found myself, five months later, joined to a team of Western warriors of the night, distributing Gospel literature in one of the closed nations of the world.

142

A New Home

In some ways, Mac is about as ordinary as you get. Some might even say he is less than ordinary. As a seventeen-year-old he left school after the ninth grade and volunteered to work free on a pig farm near his home while the owners went on vacation. He worked so hard they kept him on after they returned. Later Mac's parents, pleased with his determination to make a way for himself, gave him a hundred acres of farmland to help him get started in life with his own small farm.

Mac was destined to be a farmer, it seemed, reaping a harvest of sorghum and beans. But God had another kind of harvest for him. Someone shared the good news of Jesus with him and his life was transformed. He knew, though he was still in his teens, that God had a plan for his life. If that meant sorghum and beans for Jesus, then sorghum and beans for Jesus it would be.

But Mac was stirred in his heart about the possibility of full-time Christian ministry. He knew he lacked a good education, but he also knew God could help him make up for it.

Then in 1987 a small team of Christians came to Mac's little church in central England to recount their experiences taking Bibles into China. When they said they planned another trip into China just four months later, Mac was instantly convinced this was what he should do. He just knew.

"I honestly didn't even pray about it," he told me as we talked. "I just told everybody, 'I'm going to China.' To be honest, it sounded like fun."

Four months later he accompanied that team to one of East Asia's key cities, where they were briefed on how to take Bibles inconspicuously into China. They would not deliver their Bibles immediately to Chinese contacts, but wait several days while they saw the sights like all tourists. Then they would meet some local believers—they were given specific instructions as to where and how—and give their precious "bread" to them.

As Mac cleared customs with a backpack and other luggage filled with Bibles, he heard a still, small voice speaking to his heart: *You've arrived at your new home.*

This message, which had flooded his heart in an instant, would change his life.

"I just knew I was home," Mac told me. "From then on there was no question about where I was to live."

The more he saw of the Chinese people, the more his heart was broken. There were so many in China who had no understanding of salvation through Christ. He would lie awake at night wondering, *How can we get the Word to them? How can we give them the Good News?*

While traveling to Beijing on that first trip, something happened to Brother Mac that would influence the direction of his mission for China.

Having given the bulk of his Chinese Bibles to his contact, Mac wondered how he might best use his remaining Bibles. They were just a few compared to the vast multitudes in Beijing. Trusting the Holy Spirit to guide him, he walked casually to a busy street corner. When it appeared that no one was watching, he placed a Bible on a ledge near a lamppost, then darted quickly into the shadows. The very first person who spotted the Bible snatched it up as though he were seizing priceless treasure.

So Mac sauntered back to the spot and, after a few moments, dropped another Bible. It, too, was grabbed up.

After repeating the process several times in several locations, the young Brit realized that even if he could continue this pace of distributing God's Word in China indefinitely, it would take centuries to make a dent in the vast spiritual need of the Chinese people. On the one hand, he felt encouraged that a few seeds had been planted. But he was troubled at the seeming impossibility of the task of getting the Gospel to the millions of Chinese.

When Mac's short visa expired, he had no choice but to return to his homeland—in spite of the impression from God that his new home was really China. But within three months he had sold all his possessions and, in January 1988, returned once again to China.

In Beijing, through a Chinese Christian he had met earlier, he approached several universities and offered them his services as an English teacher, although he realized he lacked the educational qualifications for a teaching job. Sure enough, the moment they heard he had only a ninth-grade education, they declined. Mac became increasingly discouraged and soon began questioning the Lord. Had God really told him China would be his new home?

Then in prayer he became convinced he had been operating in his own strength, rather than in God's strength, and decided to turn the matter over to the Lord. Only God could get a twenty-year-old with a ninth-grade education a job as an English teacher in China!

The following Sunday Mac was invited to visit a small gathering of Christian students in Beijing. Following a Bible study, several of the students were chatting about spiritual things. Then one of the female students addressed Mac.

"I understand you are looking for a job teaching English?"

Mac was stunned. How had she known?

"Yes, I am," he replied.

"Well, I'm teaching English in a hotel, and they're looking for other teachers."

She named the number-one hotel in all of China for foreigners at the time, and agreed to set up an interview.

Within days Mac was teaching English to excited Chinese students who wanted desperately to learn the language. They had no idea their instructor was staying up late into the night trying to figure out the difference between verbs and adverbs!

The job lasted a full year—just enough time for Mac to establish a base and to learn the Chinese language for himself. Also during that time, God began to show the young man His plan for communicating the Gospel systematically, through the printed page, to every family across China. Fittingly, it all began in Beijing, China's capital city.

Brother Mac noticed quickly that Beijing's city center, the original part of the city, consisted of lanes—very narrow streets with small individual dwellings along either side. This was a holdover from the British influence more than a half-century earlier. Most of the newer, outer parts of the city consisted of huge, multifamily high-rises (typical in Communist-ruled countries). All those high-rises, as Brother Mac was quick to note, had mailboxes (or, as the British would say, *letterboxes*), which would make it easier to reach every family.

A plan was emerging in Brother Mac's mind. He recalled how readily people snatched up the few Bibles he had put onto ledges near street corners just a few months earlier. Because he had done this discreetly and no one had seen him, he knew he had not been reported to authorities. What if he dressed up as a Chinese and went out at night on his bicycle distributing Gospel messages? Wouldn't it be possible to reach hundreds of families a night and no one be any the wiser?

Trouble in Tiananmen Square

During those days, as the vision grew in Mac's heart, a devastating event occurred in China that affected him deeply. In fact, he found himself strangely caught up in the middle of it.

Mac had just turned 21 and had been in China only a year and a half. For reasons no one fully understood, huge throngs of university students were flocking to Beijing's famous Tiananmen Square. They brought with them a unified call for democratic reforms. Everyone was filled with excitement. No one seemed to sense the turmoil that lay ahead.

On June 3, 1989, Mac went to see an eighty-year-old Chinese woman we will call Mildred who often served as a stopping-off point for Gospel literature that had come into China from outside sources. Mildred told Mac she had just received a shipment of more Gospel messages. Did he want them? Mac had exhausted nearly all of his supply and was delighted to accept a large tote bag half-full of unfolded Gospel messages. It easily contained three thousand tracts. Mac could not wait to distribute them.

Shortly before midnight, as he was riding his bicycle back to his hotel, he passed Tiananmen Square. Thousands of young people were still gathering, and hundreds of tents had been erected. Then he thought of his tote bag, and a strange burden flooded his heart, accompanied by a sense of urgency.

He was dressed in his usual Chinese garb—a dark blue Mao jacket with dark pants and a typical Chinese hat with its long bill. He knew he would be inconspicuous. So he pulled the bill of his cap down over his forehead and pedaled toward the center of the square.

Then Mac did something unusual. He stopped his bicycle and stood quietly, lifting his face toward heaven. In Jesus' name he claimed authority over the forces of darkness, binding them as Jesus instructed His disciples in Matthew 16:19: "Whatever you bind on earth will be bound in heaven, and whatever you loose on earth will be loosed in heaven." Then Mac claimed souls that night for Jesus. It was exactly midnight.

Clutching his tote bag tightly, Mac began to walk among the hundreds of tents set up in the square. When no one was looking, he threw a handful of messages into a tent. If he could hear students in the tent talking, he lay a small stack of messages by the entrance and walked hastily on.

Scores of tents were served with the Gospel in those late-night hours. Mac nearly emptied his bag. Then he prayed, *Let them read the message tonight, Lord. Open their eyes to Your plan of salvation.*

Less than 24 hours later, hundreds of these very students would lie lifeless in pools of blood, their bodies scattered across the massive square.

Late that night, back at his hotel, Mac heard gunfire. And the following morning, when he rode his bicycle back to Tiananmen Square, he discovered carnage in all directions, and buses everywhere turned upside-down and burning. The crackdown on the pro-democracy movement had started.

Suddenly one of the soldiers fired tear gas and everyone scattered. Mac pedaled to the other side of the square, opposite the famed Hall of the People. When the soldiers were not looking, he took out his camera and began taking pictures. Instantly and without warning, a row of soldiers began opening fire in different directions. People were screaming and running, and Mac took off like a rocket. He knew he was in a war zone.

At the hotel, Mac was told that all foreigners had to report to the airport immediately. And soon he found himself on his way once again back to his homeland. His China call would be interrupted for several months. But as soon as he was able, Mac returned to China—this time, Lord willing, for good.

Bicycle Baskets and Doorsteps

Mac's experience at Tiananmen Square convinced him he had to do all he could to get the Gospel to every Chinese person possible. Soon he was riding his bicycle late at night, every few nights, up and down the lanes of central Beijing. He tossed Gospel messages, when no one was looking, into bicycle baskets and onto doorsteps. Dropping a tract into a bicycle basket, Mac knew, was the same as leaving it in their home, since everyone in China, it seemed, had a bicycle.

During his first year Mac visited some ten thousand homes, always trying to keep a record of where he had been so he would not cover an area twice, especially when so many parts of the city had not been reached once. At first Mac still taught English during the day, while at night he put on his Chinese garb and went out with the Gospel.

"My greatest hindrance," Mac told me, "wasn't the lack of sleep, but the lack of literature. Sometimes I had to wait many weeks before another team came from the outside with a fresh supply of Gospel messages."

After the Tiananmen Square massacre, the work accelerated dramatically. Until then Mac told no one about his activities, not even missionary friends. He felt it was too risky.

Then one day a fresh team of couriers, led by his friend John, came from the West with Bibles. He met them at the border and agreed to help them make contact with Chinese believers. But first they had to wait three days. Mac suggested to John that perhaps there were some tourist sites they might see.

"Look," said John, "I didn't come to see sights but to save souls. Isn't there something we can do to help get people the Gospel?"

Mac decided to tell his friend what he had been doing, and invite him to try it a night or two. John accepted with joy, and they decided to invite the others on the team to join them.

So successful was the outreach that they planned several more night campaigns. John and his team would return to their country and invite other courageous believers to join them. Soon a plan was underway to help the teams move out into many additional Chinese communities.

As Mac began to research the towns and cities of China, he discovered there are at least 574 large cities with a population of between three and four thousand. (Other much larger cities, like Beijing and Shanghai, have populations in the millions.) Within the next 24 months, Mac would visit two hundred of these cities personally, planting Gospel seeds in each one but also gathering maps of the various locales to prepare for systematic tract-planting outreaches. Then the young strategist compiled this information in small, printed "tourist guides" for each province to be targeted (information that proved an invaluable aid to the team of night warriors I joined in June 1995).

Mac also realized that many of the larger cities, at least five hundred of them, could serve as bases from which teams could travel to smaller towns at night and share the Good News. They could come into a city during the day, and late that night share printed Gospel messages throughout an assigned area of the city. By the next morning, usually before dawn, they could catch one of the typical Chinese minibuses and leave town, even as the residents of that city were waking up to discover life-giving salvation messages in their bicycle baskets or mailboxes or even on their doorsteps.

There was yet another dimension to Mac's literature distribution ministry that fascinated me, facilitated by those Chinese minibuses, which carry fifteen to 25 passengers each to towns throughout China. He calls it "tract-bombing."

In one of his early trips to a distant town, a trip that took at least five hours, Mac decided to sit in the rear of the bus by a window. Beside him was his bag loaded with Gospel booklets for distribution in the town where he was heading. As the bus rumbled through small villages, rarely slowing down even for pedestrians, an idea came to him. Mac decided, when no one was looking, to toss a handful of booklets out the window.

The result was amazing. The wind hit the booklets and scattered them across the road like a white carpet of paper, while people came running from all directions to retrieve one of them. Some even stood in the middle of the road as they read the Gospel message.

Other teams eventually came to participate, and tract-bombing became an exciting part of the evangelistic experience.

I experienced it firsthand—including the delight of tossing more than two thousand Gospel booklets in small "cluster bombs" out a minibus window into the Chinese countryside. One cluster scattered near a group of schoolchildren, who came running from everywhere. As the bus rumbled on, I turned and watched as one girl, probably not more than ten years old, stood in the middle of the road reading the message intently.

By the time my team's two-week mission was completed, more than two hundred thousand Gospel messages had been planted within hand's reach of waiting Chinese.

Conflicting Commandments

One of the great challenges in attempting to evangelize a nation considered closed to the Gospel is how to reconcile the Scripture passages that on the one hand command believers *everywhere* to take the Good News to *everybody,* and on the other hand admonish followers of Jesus to obey those in authority.

The disciples in Acts 5:17–29 were told by the ruling authorities to cease all teaching about Jesus. Up to that point they had been going about freely throughout Jerusalem and seeing significant results as multitudes turned to the Lord. But, we read, "The high priest and all his associates, who were members of the party of Sadducees, were filled with jealousy" (verse 17). They had the apostles arrested and jailed.

It was another opportunity for a miracle, as an angel appeared to them at night and released them. He told them, "Go, stand in the temple courts . . . and tell the people the full message of this new life" (verse 20).

The disciples obeyed, and on the very day of their release were again spotted in the Temple teaching people about Jesus. Again they were arrested and brought before the high priest for questioning.

> "We gave you strict orders not to teach in this name," he said. "Yet you have filled Jerusalem with your teaching. . . ."
>
> Acts 5:28

Quite simply, the apostles had been breaking the law. But Peter and the others replied, "We must obey God rather than men!" (verse 29).

Through the intervention of Gamaliel, a respected teacher of the law, they were released, but not before being beaten and ordered once again not to speak about Jesus.

But we read only two verses later not only that they continued to testify about Jesus, but that they did it "day after day, in the temple courts and from house to house" (verse 42). That verse adds, in fact: "They never stopped teaching and proclaiming the good news that Jesus is the Christ."

In contrast to the disciples' clear violation of the law, what do we make of Paul's equally inspired directive in Romans?

> Everyone must submit himself to the governing authorities, for there is no authority except that which God has established. The authorities that exist have been established by God. . . . Therefore, it is necessary to submit to the authorities, not only because of possible punishment but also because of conscience.
>
> Romans 13:1, 5

Certainly it is in direct opposition to the governing authorities of a nation to engage in evangelism when it is strictly prohibited. We must recognize, however, that we have a mandate from the Lord to take the Good News to literally every person (see again Matthew 28:19 and Mark 16:15). The conduct of the apostles shows us that whenever manmade laws contradict the clear teaching of God's Word, the believer is duty-bound to submit to God first.

Numerous examples in Scripture (in addition to the Acts 5 examples above) illustrate this principle. Here are three:

1. *The midwives who refused to obey Pharaoh's order to kill all male babies born to the Hebrew women in Egypt* (see Exodus 1:15–21). God rewarded those midwives for what they did.
2. *Shadrach, Meshach and Abednego,* who refused to worship the idol the Babylonian king had set up and found themselves thrown into the fiery furnace (see Daniel 3). God delivered them and even caused them to be promoted by the king.
3. *Daniel,* who continued to pray to his God in defiance of King Darius' decree forbidding prayer to any god except the king himself (see Daniel 6). God "sent his angel, and he shut the mouths of the lions" (verse 22) after Daniel was punished for breaking the law. God not only kept Daniel from certain death, but actually prospered him during the reigns of Darius and Cyrus.

So I felt comfortable, biblically speaking, darting up and down those darkened alleyways (even though it did not lessen my anxieties of the moment!). We were breaking Chinese law, but I also knew we were obeying the Commission Christ gave the Church to go into all the world and preach the Good News to everybody. Further, I had the distinct sense that if we were caught, we could trust God to deliver us in His own way, just as He did Daniel and the early disciples.

A Minibus Miracle

Best of all, we saw firsthand evidence that God was honoring the planting of these seeds. One testimony came to our attention the very last day of our June 1995 evangelism adventure.

As we gathered for a final debriefing, two of the brothers on the team, who had journeyed the farthest into the province, shared a most incredible encounter.

While they rode their minibus to a remote town, they told us, they began releasing clusters of booklets out the back window whenever the passengers seemed distracted. They were helped inadvertently in the process by a Chinese woman in her early twenties who was sitting near the front of the bus, reading to other Chinese riders from a booklet in her hand and explaining its contents.

Suddenly one of the Christian workers, a foreign brother who had learned a few expressions in Chinese, turned to his partner.

"She's talking about Jesus!" he exclaimed with a stunned look on his face. "I'm sure of it!"

He listened more carefully, picking up words and phrases like *repentance* and *personal Savior*. To his amazement, he realized she was now giving an invitation to receive Christ—and several on the bus were responding!

When she had finished, one of the young workers approached the student evangelist and asked if she spoke any English. She understood enough to communicate, and told the workers she had found Christ four years earlier. When they asked her how she had come to Christ, she pulled a sixteen-page booklet from her purse that she had used in her preaching.

"This booklet told me about Jesus," she explained, clutching it happily. "I found it by my door one morning four years ago."

"Is this the original booklet?" asked one of the workers.

"Oh, no," she answered quickly. "This is a copy. I've made many copies of the booklet since then, and I've given them away to people who want to meet Jesus."

"Do you have an extra copy I might keep?"

"Oh, yes, I have many extra copies."

Now, as our evangelism team sat together in our final debriefing, one of the brothers from the team produced the booklet for the entire group to see.

In that instant I happened to be looking at Brother Mac, whose eyes filled with tears. Quickly he spoke up.

"This is one of the very booklets I planted in that same town late at night four years ago," he said, "when I first came to map the cities of this province." Then he smiled like a child who had just won a prize. "I must have left that booklet by her doorway."

I smiled, too, as I felt Brother Mac's joy. And I thought of God's promise to Isaiah: "[My word] will not return to me empty, but will accomplish what I desire and achieve the purpose for which I sent it" (Isaiah 55:11).

10

Naked in the Forest

Lendongo Botshemba was born into the family of Bokimba of the Bosuka Pygmy people in central Africa. The infant was assured of his future position as chief of his people because that was Bokimba's role, which he would inherit.

The traditions of the Pygmies are similar to those of the Kwaio, although they live in an equatorial rain forest continents away. Lendongo's people worship nature—trees and animals—as well as ancestral spirits, just as the Kwaio have done for centuries in the western Pacific Ocean. Pygmies especially reverence the forest itself, affectionately calling it *Father*.

Like the Kwaio, the Pygmies of the central African rain forest (consisting of many tribes, clans and languages) are deeply superstitious. Witchcraft and black magic permeate all aspects of life. These "people of the trees" believe their high death rate from malaria and other diseases is actually caused by black magic or evil spirits. So they take special pains to appease the spirits of their ancestors, whom they believe come back in anger to afflict them with these diseases.

Short in stature and nearly naked, some Pygmies tend to identify more with the animals of the forest, particularly the chimps and monkeys, than with the taller African Bantu people of the region. Indeed, the Bantu so ravaged the Pygmies in earlier generations that the people of the trees fled even deeper into the forest for protection—further from an opportunity to hear the one message that could change their destiny.

But for these Pygmies, soon to be led by their young chief, Lendongo—as well as for the Kwaio and their old priest, Haribo—a plan was underway that would transform them forever.

A Weakening Giant

The global Church has entered a season of falling giants. In fact, missions strategist George Otis, Jr., in his timely book *The Last of the Giants* (Chosen Books, 1991) speaks of the penetration of various long-closed cultures and belief systems with the good news of Jesus. When his book was first published, the Soviet Union was just beginning to crumble, and signs on the spiritual horizon suggested that other giants were starting to weaken. Otis and others wondered: Might Islam be next?

A Christian brother we will call Erik Duran thinks this giant is already beginning to fall.

Several years ago Erik and his wife, Beth, sensed a divine directive to give their lives to help plant churches in the Middle East. Not surprisingly, friends and mission leaders told them it was an impossible task. Still, they pursued their calling and found themselves in the heart of the Middle East, in a nation not far from the Persian Gulf states.

Like other Islamic nations in the area, the country they had chosen had a modest number of resident expatriate Christians from various non-Islamic countries who had formed cluster groups of believers. Such expatriates usually hold down jobs the nationals tend to avoid. The nation Erik and Beth chose for ministry, although predominantly Muslim, is one of several in the area that tolerate a limited amount of Christian activity, although converting Muslims is strictly forbidden. But because their goal was church planting, Erik and Beth knew they had their work cut out for them.

From the outset, in order to overcome any suspicion that they were trying to change the Muslim way of life, the Durans were careful not to refer to their work as "church planting." Instead they simply sought to start small Bible study groups. They also avoided any Sunday meetings. Instead, their Bible study groups met on Tuesdays, Fridays or Saturday nights.

Because this Islamic nation served as a central business location for many other Middle Eastern countries, it was possible to gather numerous Arab believers from places like Egypt, Lebanon, Sudan, Jordan, Syria and other nations in the region for training conferences. Soon this led to gatherings that lasted up to fourteen days, and Erik and Beth found themselves part of a team of some thirty full-time staff workers involved in year-round activities. Their annual meetings gathered as many as 150 Christian leaders from throughout the region.

God clearly was beginning to bless the work significantly. Could it be that the legs of the giant of Islam were beginning to weaken?

Leaders from outside the region, meanwhile, were sensing a special concern for the Middle East. One such brother, a Swede we will call Gustuf Janic, had served in a diplomatic capacity in the Middle East for some time. About thirty, married and the father of several children, Gustuf was a devout Christian with a passionate burden for the lost. Gustuf spoke no Arabic and very little English. After finishing his tour of duty, he decided to stay in the region.

The Janic family moved to a very poor area in their Muslim city, where he rented a small home for just forty dollars a month. Since only one church back in Sweden sent him any support, Gustuf had to work odd jobs to provide for his family. But he used as much of his income as possible to buy Christian literature in Arabic from various sources and use it for personal evangelism.

A Brilliant Idea

In September 1994 Gustuf approached Erik Duran, the church planter, with what he considered a brilliant idea. He proposed to go to Scandinavia and get a big tent for evangelistic meetings that had been offered him by someone in the church back home.

How, Erik asked, could Gustuf possibly use a tent for evangelistic meetings in a nation that prohibited proselytizing, especially among Muslims?

Gustuf did not know, but reminded Erik the tent was free.

In any case, the idea seemed moot a few weeks later. First Gustuf was interrogated by Muslim militants, who threatened to kill him and his family if they stayed in the country. Gustuf would not budge. But this made local authorities aware of Gustuf's witnessing activities among Muslims, and they ordered him and his family to leave the country and return to Scandinavia.

When Erik and Beth said good-bye to the Janics, they were sure they would never see them again. So you can imagine Erik and Beth's surprise three months later when Gustuf drove up in a beat-up British Land Rover with something huge tied to its top.

Gustuf bounded from the vehicle shouting in his awkward English, "My brother, we have tent! Let's go Muslims. Let's preach Jesus!"

Amazingly, Gustuf and his family had received new visas and driven their aging Land Rover, with the tent tied to its top, all the way from Scandinavia. It had taken them several weeks. Equally astounding, they had actually moved back into the same house where they had lived before the government ordered them to leave, and from which Gustuf had been taken and interrogated by Muslim militants.

Gustuf Janic's ministry picked up right where it had left off. During his earlier evangelistic activities, Gustuf had befriended a Christian man in the southern part of the nation who owned a small chicken restaurant. Now his friend, whom he told about his tent, promptly encouraged him to come to his city and "tell all my friends" about Jesus.

Gustuf asked Erik if he thought it was possible to set up the tent for evangelistic meetings. Erik, convinced it was impossible but not wanting to show a lack of enthusiasm, responded, "Sounds great to me. If you can get the permission, I'll come down and help you."

To Erik's amazement, two days later Gustuf showed up at his doorstep.

"Come down, Brother Erik," he shouted happily. "We set up tent. We have permission. We preach in two days!"

Gustuf had obtained permission from the head of the Islamic party in the town. But Erik was troubled. The more he quizzed Gustuf, the more convinced he became that the old Islamic leader, who apparently knew some English, must have given permission because he did not understand what Gustuf, in his limited English, had really been asking. Still, Erik agreed to go with Gustuf to the town of the planned campaign in hopes of meeting the leader who had granted the "permission."

When he met the Muslim leader, Erik explained exactly what they were going to do. He fully expected the leader to say, "Get out of here now. That's impossible. We follow Islam." To his amazement, the leader answered simply, "That would be great."

Now Erik wondered if *he* had been properly understood. So he explained exactly what it meant to preach Jesus.

"We want to come and teach Muslims about who Jesus Christ is," he said, "and teach the holy Bible."

"Are you coming to build church buildings and make us Christians?"

"What do you mean by 'make us Christians'?"

"I mean, do you want us to change our identity cards, which now say we are Muslims, so they say we are Christians?"

Erik explained carefully that they did not plan to build church buildings or "make Christians" in the way the man was thinking.

"We don't care about religion at all," Erik added. "We just want to teach about Jesus."

Somehow Erik's response put the leader at ease. He agreed to give his permission for public evangelistic services. He suggested, to Erik's amazement, that if their tent was not big enough for the crowds, he could get them bigger tents normally used for large gatherings of Scout troops. He even offered the use of a piece of land right in the middle of town.

Erik and Gustuf went to look at the land. It was a field at a fork in the road where the main road split to become two branches, both leading directly into the city. The tent would be erected at a point at which only a hundred yards separated the two roads, a field where children from the city normally played soccer. They could not have found a better place for their campaign.

The People of the Tent

Two days later, as Gustuf had arranged, the first of four nights of evangelistic meetings, attended by several hundred adults and nearly as many children, was conducted in which Christ was shared freely. During the day workers went from home to home sharing Gospel literature and inviting people to the meetings. One night they were even permitted to show the *Jesus* film in its entirety. No one could believe they were doing something like this in the heart of a Muslim community!

On the morning of the final night, Erik was visited by a group representing influential Muslims in the town concerned about the growing impact of the Christian witness. They had heard that Erik had instigated the gatherings and questioned him repeatedly regarding his motive for being in the area. Unless he came to meet and debate their sheik, they said, perhaps even a live debate on television, he and Gustuf could not conduct their last meeting and would have to go home.

Convinced they were trying to intimidate him, Erik answered quickly, "No! Go back and tell your sheik that if God wants us to come and debate, we'll come. And if God says, 'Go home,' we'll go home. But no man can tell us what we must do."

These words surprised even Erik, and he felt certain the Lord had put them in his mouth.

The response also brought raised eyebrows among the members of the group.

"You mean you want *us* to tell our sheik *that?*" asked the spokesman.

"Yes, I do."

Two hours later, the small delegation returned, smiling. Each Muslim shook hands with Erik and Gustuf.

Then the spokesman announced, "Our sheik said your answer was a very good one, and he would like to meet you. He also says you may conduct your final meeting."

Which they did that night in the tent. And two days later the sheik representing those influential Muslims actually came to where Erik and Gustuf were staying. After they talked, he granted them permission to hold four more evangelistic meetings in the same place a month later, using the same tent.

Those meetings, too, were filled to capacity. But another *imam* (religious leader) in the town felt the sheik had gone too far in granting permission for the meetings. He began railing against them, using a loudspeaker from his own mosque to declare that Muslims should boycott the meetings.

But the ranting and raving became the best advertisement. People came from everywhere to see what was happening outside of town each night, and by the final night the tent was packed. Word had spread even beyond the town. Delegations from neighboring villages actually began arguing during the meetings over which village would get the tent ministry next, and the evangelism team became known as "the people of the tent."

Several of the meetings were concluded with a "reverse altar call." Before giving an invitation to receive Christ, Erik explained the plan of salvation, then graciously asked all who did not wish to hear any more to leave.

"But if you want to know more about Jesus," he said, "stay and join in small groups, where we'll explain more about what it means to be a follower of Jesus."

Each night dozens of people stayed in their seats as the rest departed. Many found Christ.

How were Erik and Gustuf able to hold open evangelistic meetings in a closed nation, and go door to door systematically with the Gospel and watch the fruit multiply? The legs of the giant of Islam were indeed weakening.

A Sea of Mud

By now Erik and the rest of the evangelistic team realized the best way to influence a Muslim community spiritually was to go to every home, share the Gospel with every family and invite them to the tent meetings. Door-to-door witnessing soon became even more fruitful than the evangelistic meetings. Behind closed doors Muslims seemed far more likely to express their needs and receive the Gospel. Many professed their faith in Christ after inviting workers in for coffee or tea. And evangelistic literature was always given so people would have something to reflect on long after the personal contact.

Soon the evangelistic team had gone to five towns in the area, canvassing every home in those communities. Nearly one thousand families were given the Gospel. Then a miracle opened new doors for evangelism in the region—the doors of fellowship halls of Muslim mosques.

In December 1994, the team arrived in the small town of Saran (not its real name) where permission had been granted to conduct a three-night tent crusade directly across the road from a large mosque. The first night the tent was filled. It was a powerful meeting, and many responded to the "reverse invitation" to hear more about Jesus. On the following day, however, it rained so hard that the field turned into a sea of mud. It was virtually impossible to get to the tent. Even though some people would be traveling great distances from other villages, the team faced the unhappy prospect of canceling the meeting.

As they pondered the dilemma, Erik eyed the large mosque across the road with its attached *hosseineye*, fellowship hall. While the mosque is used for Muslim worship, the *hosseineye*—a huge room, usually including a podium, pictures of sheiks or imams and large posters featuring verses from the Koran—is used for occasions like weddings and funerals. What would it take to get permission to use the *hosseineye* of this mosque?

It would not hurt to ask. So Erik and a colleague we'll call Len, who led the door-to-door phase of the outreach, set out with an interpreter to find the imam in charge of the mosque. (Although Erik and Len both spoke Arabic well enough to carry on a conversation, they brought the interpreter along to make sure nothing was miscommunicated.) When they finally found someone they thought was in charge, he explained that there was another, more important imam who would have to give permission.

The team finally located the other imam, an older man. Again Erik felt God guiding his words as he explained what they wanted to use the room for that night.

"The other imam said if it was O.K. with you, it was O.K. with him," he said. "I'm not sure which of you really has the authority to make such a decision. If you don't, perhaps we can go back to the other imam."

The older imam promptly granted permission and handed Erik the key. Then he authorized the generator to be turned on to provide electricity for the evangelistic meeting that night.

So when the people arrived at the muddy field that rainy night, they were directed to the mosque. Nearly 150 people gathered in the *hosseineye* as the team sang Gospel songs and Erik taught about Jesus under a huge portrait of the long-deceased Ayatollah Khomeini (still greatly revered by Muslims throughout the Middle East).

The next day the rains increased and the field of mud became more like a bog. So again the next afternoon Erik, Len and the interpreter approached the older imam for permission. This time he said no, that continuing the meetings would be too dangerous. If, on the other hand, he added, Erik and his team could get written permission from the head imam for the entire region, the meetings could go on. He seemed to snicker as he spoke of getting this permission, as if to say, "Don't hold your breath."

That head imam, the chief spiritual leader of the Shiite Muslims throughout the region, lived in a neighboring town about thirty minutes away. The tent meeting was scheduled for just two hours away. The three evangelists were off like a shot.

A Handshake and a Sermon

Thankfully, they found the imam's house quickly and soon stood at his door, anxious for an audience with him. The Muslim cleric, an aide told them, was taking a nap. They would have to wait. They waited only half an hour outside the door when the aide appeared again. The imam would see them now.

Erik and Len and their interpreter suddenly found themselves staring into the cold, gray eyes of an elderly imam. Easily ninety years of age, he was leaning weakly on a well-worn cane. His long white beard and carefully wrapped turban reminded Len and Erik of pictures they had seen of the late Ayatollah Khomeini. Erik glanced at his watch. They had barely an hour before the meeting in Saran. Could they possibly make it?

They all shook hands with the aging cleric, who had his own interpreter present. Suddenly the old man, who was hard of hearing, launched into a tirade. Erik and his co-workers were stunned. They understood enough Arabic to know, without translation, that he was berating them for being Christians and warning them that unless they became Muslims, they would rot in hell. He alone could give them permission to use the mosque in Saran, but it had to happen within the next thirty minutes, and they were off to a bad start.

Then the imam calmed down.

"Why did you want a meeting with me?" he asked.

Erik began to explain about the tent and the permission granted by the two imams to conduct meetings in their towns. Then he described the heavy rains in Saran the day before and how they had been given gracious access to the *hosseineye* for their meeting.

As he was describing how much he appreciated the use of the *hosseineye*, the elderly cleric interrupted again, rebuking them vigorously in Arabic and ranting that unless they all became Muslims, their destiny would surely be hell. Finally he calmed down once again and waited for Erik to continue.

The missionary spoke only one sentence, a question: "Could we have your permission to use the *hosseineye* in Saran?"

The old imam began a third tirade against Christianity, this time almost shouting. Then, just as suddenly, he stopped and declared calmly, "Why, of course you can."

So startling was the cleric's response that Erik asked, "Excuse me, sir, what did you just say?"

"I said, of course you can have my permission to use the *hosseineye*."

Erik was almost shaking. "Would it be possible for you to put your permission in writing?"

"Of course." And the old imam pulled out a pad and pen from his desk drawer and began to write slowly.

Len leaned quietly toward Erik.

"This is going really well," he whispered. "Why don't you ask permission to use all the *hosseineyes* in the area, not just the one in Saran?"

"You're crazy," Erik whispered back. "Why don't *you* ask him?"

"You're the leader of the team. You ask him."

Suddenly a holy boldness came over Erik.

"Excuse me, sir," he said loudly to the hard-of-hearing imam.

The imam looked up. "What do you want?"

"Would it be possible," he asked hesitantly, "for you to give us written permission to use *all* the halls connected to mosques throughout the entire region?"

The imam did not quite understand the question. He turned with a quizzical look to his interpreter, who translated it again. They both stared at each other for what seemed an eternity. Suddenly he rose to his feet and blasted forth with the loudest burst of sermonizing yet.

Then, as before, the old man sat down calmly and said, "O.K., why not?"

He continued writing on the same page, apparently expanding his permission, while Erik, Len and the interpreter glanced at one another, stunned. And minutes later, after expressing their gratitude, they rushed from the cleric's residence for the drive back to Saran, unable to believe what had just happened.

They arrived just in time to show a shocked local sheik the written permission they had received to use the *hosseineye* in Saran, as well as all such halls in the region. And the meeting was held that final night with three hundred people present.

Nearly nine hundred people in all heard the Gospel at the mosque in Saran over three nights. Erik stood behind the podium in front of a huge picture of Ayatollah Khomeini and talked about the life, death and resurrection of Jesus Christ. He realized as he preached that the ayatollah portrayed behind him was clearly dead, while, as he declared, "Jesus is alive!"

The Face of Jesus

One worker conducted home-by-home evangelism among Muslims in this very country for two years in the early 1990s and prayed with not a single person to receive Jesus. But in the past 24 months, he says, he has seen more than two thousand Muslims surrender their lives to Christ during home-to-home ministry.

Why this amazing breakthrough in so rigid a Muslim region? Erik and Len are quick to explain that prayer is the key.

When they launched their mission, the entire team often gathered for a half-day every week, and sometimes several days a month, just to pray. Len especially is convinced that prayer is essential for the success of the house-to-house ministry he supervises. After one evangelism outreach, he recalls, a group of believers informed their team that they had been praying for the villages of that area by name every evening for seven years.

Prayer is also the reason, Len and Erik believe, for the increase of signs and wonders in some areas of the Middle East, particularly in the nation in which they minister. In one recent seven-day outreach, for example, according to one of Erik's colleagues, several Muslims spoke of having dreams about people coming to their homes with printed booklets. Two actually said they "saw" the very persons who ultimately came! Three other Muslims told of specific dreams about a person called Jesus. One of these was a young Sunni Muslim I will call Kabul Ali, who was about nineteen years old when he first heard the Gospel.

Kabul Ali was standing on a street corner in one of the poorer areas of his nation's capital city when a European worker approached and handed him a Gospel booklet in Arabic.

The youth's eyes opened wide when he saw the pamphlet. It was about a Person named Jesus.

"I can't believe it!" he exclaimed. "This tells about Jesus. I can't believe it!"

And he went on to tell the evangelist about an unusual dream he had had just two nights earlier. It was so real he thought it was actually happening, and he trembled as he described it.

"I dreamed I was standing on the edge of a great black pit," he said, "and then I fell into it. I was falling and falling, when all of a sudden I was caught in something like a big net. I couldn't get out."

The European evangelist was listening, transfixed. Kabul cleared his throat. "Then, in an instant, a rope was lowered over the edge directly toward me. I remember thinking, *All I have to do is take this rope and I'm saved*, so I grabbed the rope tightly. As I did, it began to pull me up from the pit. I could look up and see the end of the rope and two beautiful hands at the top reaching over the edge and pulling me up. I watched as those hands pulled on the rope and I rose from the pit. When I reached the very crest of the pit, I knew I was going to be rescued."

Kabul paused for a moment and then said, "I couldn't wait to see who it was who had rescued me. As I passed the crest of the opening, I looked into the most beautiful face I had ever seen. Something within me said, *This is the face of Jesus,* even though I had never seen any picture of Him; I had only heard His name through the Koran. I had no idea who He was or what He looked like."

"Then how did you know it was Jesus?" asked the European evangelist.

"I don't know how I knew. But His eyes were so filled with love, I just knew."

As Kabul Ali stood with the Gospel booklet clutched tightly in his hand, his eyes filled with tears.

"I can't believe it," he said again. "I had this dream about Jesus just two nights ago. Then you come to tell me about Him."

Indeed, the giant of Islam truly is beginning to weaken. And surely the young Sunni Muslim who gave his heart to Jesus that day is, along with many of his fellow Muslims all over the world, one of the "other sheep" the Lord spoke of in His must-bring mandate of John 10:16—sheep who are also being called into the fold of the Good Shepherd.

11

A Beginning for the End

Lendongo began early to learn the ways of the Pygmies. As a three-year-old he made his first primitive bow and, with the help of his father, several arrows with the tips whittled sharp. By the age of eight he was an expert marksman.

Lendongo also learned how to acquire small pieces of metal acquired from bartering honey and monkey meat with Bantu peoples, the taller natives. Then, with the aid of a portable foundry and billows made from woven palm leaves, he learned to build a fire hot enough to melt the metal, which could then be fashioned into sharp metal tips for arrows or spears. Deadly poisons squeezed from roots and a special tree bark made the weapons even more effective when piercing their targets.

Lendongo was five years old when his father, Chief Bokimba, helped him kill his first wild pig in the rain forest near Bosuka.

Bosuka, in the language of their people, means "the end," for not much lies beyond Bosuka but dense forest. In that forest the Pygmies of Bosuka, like those in other parts of the equatorial and Ituri rain forests of central Africa, live without permanent dwellings. Some call them "the people of the trees," since they live literally in the trees—sometimes on the thick leaves, sometimes under them.

A nomadic people, the Pygmies of central Africa move quietly about the dense forest in clans and cluster groups, living along some stream or tributary like the Momboyo River, gathering fruit and hunting and fishing until all the resources are depleted. Then they move on, seeking out some other region of the forest rich with game and in which the streams are filled with fish.

Bosuka, the place called "The End" was, for the first time in this tribe's history, soon to see a new beginning, as were a people called the Kwaio living in the distant Solomon Islands.

A Child Shall Lead Them

Sagiono's first reaction was rage. His young son, Punijan, had rushed into their modest dirt-floor dwelling and begun to talk excitedly about Jesus Christ. The ten-year-old had learned about Jesus from a booklet at school where Every Home Contact workers had visited that day. But Sagiono's family was staunchly Muslim, and their region in Indonesia was steeped in spiritual darkness.

Years earlier the distribution of such Christian "propaganda" would have been against the law in Indonesia, but now the government permitted the sharing of religion. It was an outflow of the official ideology called *Pancasila,* or "Five Principles," affirming belief in one God, humanitarianism, national unity, democracy and social justice. So Indonesia enjoyed religious freedom, even though officially ninety percent of the population was Muslim.

Such was the case in the tiny village of Sawahan, where Punijan's family lived. Sawahan can be reached only by a sometimes treacherous journey of several hours into the hilly regions near Yogyakarta, a metropolis considered by some to be Indonesia's seat of culture. Located 270 miles southeast of the capital city of Jakarta, Yogyakarta is the cradle of many demonic traditions.

A few miles from Yogyakarta, for example, is Prambanan, a soaring cluster of tenth-century Hindu temples. And just outside of Yogyakarta, on the way to the village of Sawahan, stand the towering ruins of Borobudur, once one of the world's largest and most magnificent Buddhist temples. In Yogyakarta itself is the Kraton, the sprawling palace of Java's last sultan, who died at the age of 76 little more than a decade ago. The sultan was so respected that, according to scholars, strips of his clothing and even pieces of his hair and fingernails were offered up annually to the Lawun Meripa volcanoes and cast into the waters as a sacrifice to the goddess of the southern seas.[1]

Thus has the geographical area surrounding the village of Sawahan been bound by forces of darkness for countless generations.

But now Punijan, whose family was caught up in the spirit of Islam, had discovered something he had never heard of before. Although only ten years old, he understood that he held something significant in his hand. He promptly told his father, Sagiono, that he believed what the booklet said.

Sagiono realized what would happen to anyone in his family who embraced another religion. Sagiono's father, Rejoprawiro, was, after all, the chief of the village and one of the most respected Islamic leaders of the district.

But as Sagiono began reading the booklet about Jesus that his son gave him, he had the strangest sensation that the message was true. So he did exactly as the booklet suggested: He asked Christ to enter his heart. Instantly Sagiono was filled with a sense of peace.

He knew something significant had happened. So, guided by the Holy Spirit, Punijan's father followed his son's example and took the same Gospel message to his own father, Rejoprawiro, the village chief. To his amazement, the old chief read the simple message with the same intensity and declared that he, too, wanted to ask Jesus Christ to be his Savior.

In a matter of a few hours, three generations of a Muslim family had prayed to receive Christ as personal Savior.

Word of the conversions spread quickly throughout Sawahan and the surrounding area. One after another of the villagers read the message brought home from school by the ten-year-old Punijan. Soon an amazing 88 people in the village had prayed to receive Christ, including the village's highly revered witch doctor, Coba Niat, who owned much property in the area. Not long after his conversion, Coba gave a parcel of land in the village for a church to be built.

Today in Sawahan, more than two decades after the conversion of Punijan, more than twenty children and 150 adults have received Christ and been baptized. One of the converts, a woman named Rudh Sudini, pastors the Bread of Life Christian Church. Coba Niat died several years ago at the age of 87, but his wife, Ibu Juminem, still attends the church. So does their daughter, Tugina.

I had the joy of traveling up the bumpy road from Yogyakarta to Sawahan in June 1995 to see firsthand the impact of a single Gospel booklet on a Muslim village. Although Punijan moved long ago to the capital city of Jakarta (typical of young people, who tend to leave smaller villages for big cities), his parents, Sagiono and Sarjiyem, still worshiped at the church regularly. So did Punijan's elderly grandfather, Rejoprawiro, along with his frail wife of almost seventy years.

I was also especially encouraged to learn how seeds of the Gospel planted among a handful of children at the school near Sawahan have produced fruit in other regions of Indonesia. One of Punijan's classmates, for example, a lad named Pujito, received one of the same Gospel booklets distributed years ago and was swept up in the mass Christian conversions of the region. Recently Pujito finished several years of theological training at a Baptist seminary in Jakarta, and today is pastoring a growing church in Central Java.

Reaching the Children

Surely children—who, once reached, reach out in turn to others—are some of the "other sheep" Jesus is bringing into His sheep fold for that final praise gathering for all eternity. So any systematic plan to provide everyone on earth with reasonable access to the Gospel must reach the youngsters, too.

For one thing, many countries have more children than adults. For another thing (as was the case with Punijan), giving the Good News to a child has the potential to influence other generations. And in some homes, especially in illiterate areas, only the children can read a Gospel tract or booklet.

Such was the case with Rae Barchi, the ten-year-old son of a merchant in North India. Affectionately named "the Little Doctor" because of his unique desire to help people who were hurting, Rae Barchi was excited when two young Christian workers showed up at his home. The evangelists said they were traveling from house to house as part of a plan to reach every family in North India with the Gospel. They handed the young boy two Gospel messages, one titled *Are You Happy?* and the other, *He Wants to be Your Friend* (specifically designed for children).

By the time Rae's father got home from work, the Little Doctor, an excellent reader, had read both messages three times.

"What's that?" the tired father asked Rae, who was still engrossed in one of the booklets.

"Visitors came to our house today," Rae explained, "and they gave me these."

That night after supper, the father, who could not read, asked his son to read both of the messages aloud. As Rae concluded, he mumbled, "Religious talk—that's all it is. Just religious talk."

But for the next several days, the young boy kept mentioning the messages. Finally his father asked him to read them again. This time he advised him, "Tell those people to send us more reading materials."

So the Little Doctor wasted no time writing to the Every Home Crusade office in Lucknow, the capital of India's northern state of Uttar Pradesh. A few days later the boy was thrilled as the first lesson of *The Way to a Happy Life*, a four-part Bible correspondence course, arrived.

"It arrived today!" Rae told his father excitedly.

"What arrived, son?"

"The written lesson you told me to write and ask for."

The Little Doctor completed that lesson and the next three as they came. And in the process, he opened his heart to Jesus and became the first Christian in his family.

The transformation was obvious to everyone, and Rae's father was keenly interested. He asked Rae to read him each Bible correspondence lesson. Soon casual interest turned into serious inquiry, and the older Barchi used his son as a secretary, asking him often to write to the Every Home Crusade office in Lucknow. Finally he, too, welcomed Christ into his heart as personal Savior.

Then he began inviting illiterate townspeople to his house and asking his son to read from the two messages, as well as from the Bible lessons. The villagers asked many questions, which Rae answered to the best of his ability.

And within a year, four townspeople had accepted Christ—all because a child has the potential to influence other generations for Jesus.

A Tract on a Tractor

Several time zones to the east, not long after the Little Doctor's conversion in Northern India, another Gospel seed fell on the soil

173

of a young heart, this one in the northern Japanese prefecture (or district) of Iwate. The seed would lie seemingly dormant for almost a decade and a half before yielding its life-giving fruit.

Iwate, by any measurement of missionary advance, would have been classified as unreached. The people of that mountainous region were primarily Buddhist or Shinto, or else they believed in one of a variety of folk religions or modern cults. The diverse mixture of generational religious influence had long established the spiritual climate of Iwate.

But fifteen small evangelical churches in the early 1980s longed to see this climate changed. They formed an interdenominational alliance to conduct a house-to-house evangelistic initiative for Jesus Christ throughout Iwate. They divided the prefecture into three regions and committed themselves to visiting every family in at least one of the regions every summer, providing literature for adults and children supplied by Japan Every Home Crusade. The goal: to take the Gospel to literally every family throughout the prefecture.

In the middle of that first summer of outreach in Iwate, the temperature was unusually warm. One brilliant day the mercury reached a hundred degrees Fahrenheit—extremely hot for such a mountainous area. Setsuko Motoi, a twelve-year-old Japanese girl who had just lost her mother, was on her long trek home from school with a Shinto friend. Setsuko lived almost two hours beyond her friend's house, on the edge of the Buddhist mountain village of Tamayama.

As the young girl waved good-bye to her classmate, she noticed a brightly colored piece of literature reflecting the sunlight from the seat of a tractor parked in her friend's front yard. It was resting conspicuously on top of a stack of paper trash and old magazines. Obviously the pile was about to be burned. Setsuko stepped into the yard, picked up the pamphlet and began to read.

The message fascinated her, so she asked her friend's mother if she could keep the booklet. The answer was an emphatic no. Her friend's mother did not want her to have this shameful "religious propaganda." They were, after all, strict worshipers of Shinto, the oldest surviving religion of Japan.

174

So Setsuko walked home disappointed. Two hours later, as she picked up the local newspaper at the door of her house as usual, two booklets, including the one she had wanted so desperately from her friend's yard, dropped from the newspaper.

Setsuko sat down immediately and read the two booklets—one titled *Invitation for Happiness* (for adults) and *Who Created the Universe?* (for children).

Over the next few months, she read the booklets many times. Then she decided to enroll in the Bible correspondence course.

Setsuko completed the course several weeks later, and the EHC office in Tokyo sent her a beautiful graduation diploma. They also introduced her to the Tsukiga-oka Lutheran Church in Morioka City, pastored by the Reverend Olson, which had participated in the evangelistic campaign. To get to the church, however, twelve-year-old Setsuko would have to walk for an hour and then take two consecutive thirty-minute bus rides.

Setsuko attempted the journey once, but could not find the church and came home with a broken heart. The following day she mustered her courage, called the Reverend Olson and told him what had happened. After that she received numerous kind letters from the church encouraging her in her newfound faith.

But because of the distance, Setsuko decided it was impossible to attend. She also feared what the people of her village, mostly Buddhists, might say. In a small village like Tamayama, anyone who did anything different became the subject of gossip. Also, since her mother had died the year before, Setsuko was now under the authority of her aunts, who no more approved of Christianity than her friend's mother had.

The girl felt deep pain in her heart that she could not confess her Lord publicly. But through the years she never lost her faith.

Ten years later, Setsuko was a gifted tailor in her early twenties. One day as she was driving through Morioka City, she caught a glimpse of a sign in front of a church that included the name *Reverend Olson*. Setsuko had never forgotten that name. She stopped at once and went inside to find out whether it was the same Mr. Olson she had spoken with more than a decade earlier.

It was his son, she learned. The other Reverend Olson had gone to be with Jesus. And the house of worship she had stopped at was none other than the Tsukiga-oka Lutheran Church—the very church recommended to her ten years earlier by the EHC office in Tokyo. Setsuko decided to attend there regularly and is an active member today.

Later she learned there was a man in the church named Osumi who first brought the Gospel messages to her village of Tamayama a decade earlier. (He, too, had gone to be with Jesus.)

Little could Osumi have realized on the day of his visit to Tamayama that one of the seeds he was planting would touch the heart of a child and sustain her for more than a decade until she grew into fellowship with other believers at his very church.

The Mouths of Babes

In some countries of the world, teams of children trained and supervised by adults are themselves beginning to evangelize boldly house to house. In some cases signs and wonders accompany their efforts, as happened to a team of boys and girls visiting every home in a small Fijian village.

Villagers pitied and feared the old woman who lived at the edge of town. For years she had had a variety of serious medical problems that affected her mind. Christians in the area believed she was also possessed by demons, captive in both body and spirit, bound by an enemy she failed to recognize and could not fight.

Then the unexpected happened. The group of children from a larger, adult-supervised Every Home Fiji evangelism team knocked on her door.

How could one resist the enthusiasm of children? She invited them in.

Although several of the children in the group were older, a five-year-old boy was asked to pray. With a child's innocent faith, he prayed for the old woman to be completely healed. Then, because he had seen it done in his church, he ordered the demons to come out of her in the name of Jesus.

Regardless of whether the boy fully understood what he was doing, the demons understood perfectly. The old woman was suddenly and totally delivered. She surrendered her life to Christ and became a believer.

God had used the faith and simplicity of a child to free a woman long bound by Satan, and bring her into the Kingdom of God.

The apparent fresh release of faith for the miraculous among children may be an indicator that the Church is headed for an even greater season of the miraculous globally. Indeed, in Part 3 of this book, we will look at the increasing role signs and wonders appear to be playing in the evangelization of the world, and explore some of the surprising ways God has intervened to let the good news of Jesus be known. As you will discover, sometimes the Holy Spirit has even distributed Gospel literature Himself!

Harvest Wonders

*The Supernatural Factor
in Reaching Our World for Jesus*

Theological disputes aside regarding the miraculous (including any discussion of the purpose or even validity of modern accounts), reports of highly unusual happenings are clearly on the rise as the Gospel spreads globally.

Muslims who know nothing of a New Testament Jesus are seeing dreams and visions of our Lord, and thousands are seeking out Christians to inquire about what these encounters mean.

The Holy Spirit takes printed messages of salvation and literally blows them into the paths of unbelievers steeped in false religions who soon are converted (sometimes instantly) and later become powerful evangelists for Christ, winning multitudes to Him.

Dramatic accounts of angelic intervention increase sharply, and isolated reports are received of the most questioned miracles—the dead coming back to life, if even for a short time—but always in the context of bringing people to a knowledge of Jesus.

Join me in the pages that follow for a look at just such reports and how they are becoming a factor in Christ's great, end-time harvest.

12

Accompanied by Angels

The children sat in awe as the old chief, Haribo, told stories of the spirits of those who had gone before them, and how the spirits must be angry since the yam harvest was not very good during this season of the rains. But in his heart Haribo still looked to the heavens and wondered if his people had not missed the real reason there was so much suffering on earth, the real reason for the lives of human beings on earth.

By now Haribo had lived at least 85 yam harvests. Some believed it was surely more—perhaps 95. But in any case, this would be the last yam harvest during which an outsider was slain near Kwaio territory.

By another standard of measurement, it was 1975. The incident involved a medical missionary and his son, both of whom were murdered by indigenous people over a land dispute. Neither Haribo nor any of his clan deep in the interior of East Kwaio was involved in the dispute; in fact, it happened closer to the coast than to the interior. But the incident brought fear to the hearts of Christians living in the coastal areas of the islands.

Many of them were actually of Kwaio descent. Their forefathers had come to the coast decades or even generations back. But these Christians avoided the interior and often talked about the fierceness of the mountain people. So Haribo and his people would wait another fifteen yam harvests before anyone had the courage to visit them.

But when they did, they would not come alone. They would be accompanied by angels.

Winds of the Spirit

Sabir Ali Khan was proud to be a Pathan—a member of a high-caste orthodox Muslim family in India. Many generations earlier his ancestors had come from Kabul, Afghanistan, settling in a town that became known as Tilhar, 260 miles east of India's capital, New Delhi. Although they were originally cloth merchants, Sabir's ancestors soon became farmers, scratching out a difficult existence in the ever-changing climate of the region. But Sabir, a well-educated Pathan, was proud to have risen above all this.

181

Tilhar, Sabir's hometown, had a population of thirty thousand people, of whom forty percent were Muslims, forty percent were Hindus and the remaining twenty percent represented a variety of cults and castes prevalent throughout India.

Sabir often declared he would die for Islam. And what he had heard about Christians caused him to look down on anyone who professed to be one. Years earlier he had heard that two Muslim men from his caste had converted to Christianity and established a Methodist church in Tilhar. But long ago the forty Christian families resulting from those early conversions had moved to bigger cities, and now the church building lay in ruins, so Sabir had never really met a Christian. Still, he despised them.

His Muslim indoctrination had begun when he was enrolled in an Islamic preschool at three years of age. By the time Sabir was eight, he knew many passages of the Koran by heart and had already begun to study other Islamic writings. During all those years, he could not remember missing a single day of saying his prayers or fasting on the required occasions, such as the annual month of Ramadan. Friends and family thought Sabir would surely become a great Islamic spiritual leader someday.

But Sabir became troubled as he moved into his teenage years. Once he read in the *Hadees Tirmizi,* a holy book written by Muslim priests, that during the creation of humankind, Allah had waved his right hand over Adam's back, declaring, "These have I created for heaven," and then waved his left hand, saying, "These have I created for hell." Sabir wondered, meditating on this passage, which hand he had been created from. If it was with Allah's right hand, then no matter how sinful a life he lived, he would still go to heaven. But if he had been created with Allah's left hand, then no matter how good and pure a life he lived, his final destination would still be hell.

For weeks anxiety filled Sabir's heart. And over the next few years, he hungered for true peace and happiness.

A Paper-Wrapped Power Encounter

In 1971, like other 21-year-olds in India who had just finished school, Sabir faced poor prospects for finding a job, so he decided to visit his sister for several weeks. She lived near Lucknow, the capital of Uttar Pradesh, India's northern state. Her husband worked in management for the Indian railways and owned four racehorses.

One day Sabir sat dejectedly in a park near the outskirts of Lucknow, munching on a small package of peanuts he had bought from a street vendor and contemplating his dissatisfaction with life. As he crunched the last peanut, Sabir noticed that part of the wrapper, which must have been recycled, had printing on it. These words leaped from the paper:

> "Peace I leave with you, my peace I give unto you: not as the world giveth, give I unto you. Let not your heart be troubled, neither let it be afraid."
>
> John 14:27

Sabir did not understand what the word *John*, followed by a strange set of numbers—14:27—meant. But he read more words on the wrapper:

> "Come unto me, all ye that labor and are heavy laden, and I will give you rest."
>
> Matthew 11:28

Rest, true peace, was what he had been seeking!
The paper included still another sentence:

> "Him that cometh to me I will in no wise cast out."
>
> John 6:37

The rest of the message was missing, but an address in Lucknow appeared at the bottom of the wrapper to which an interested

183

inquirer could write for additional information. So Sabir wrote, asking what the words on the wrapper meant. In less than two weeks he received two booklets on what it meant to be a follower of Jesus, plus the first lesson of a four-part Bible course.

Sabir Ali Khan was so stirred by the literature that he traveled to Lucknow and located the address on the wrapper, the Every Home Crusade office, where he showed up on the front steps. He spent more than four hours talking to the director, M. M. Maxton, about Jesus and what it meant to follow Him as Lord and Savior. On subsequent visits Mr. Maxton and another EHC leader, Suresh Mathews, provided food and shelter for Sabir when he was in Lucknow, pursuing his intense spiritual hunger.

In 1974, three years after his "power encounter" with the peanut wrapper, Sabir was baptized in water and declared himself publicly a follower of Jesus Christ. Afterward he went straight to his sister and her husband, with whom he was still living, to witness to them for the first time and explain what had happened to him.

Devout Muslims, they became furious, demanding that he recant and even refusing to feed him. During the next few days, Sabir was given nothing to eat but tamarind—a sour fruit used much in India for cooking. His sister and brother-in-law also insisted he find a job.

Sabir found a job pulling a rickshaw for just a few rupees a day, equivalent to less than five cents in today's currency. It was enough to provide him with food. But when Sabir's brother-in-law found out he had taken such a menial job, he beat him with a horsewhip for not trying harder to find a better job, and ordered him angrily to leave their house.

A few days later, God led the young Christian to a good job in a shoe company, where he worked for two years while continuing to study Scripture in his spare moments. His passion to serve Christ grew.

In 1977 Sabir showed up again at the EHC office in Lucknow, inquiring about serving Jesus in a ministry to Muslims. Before long he was working full-time even as he continued his education. In his first few months as a field worker, Sabir led thirty Muslims to Christ.

He also met and married a beautiful young woman who, like himself, had been saved out of a strict orthodox Muslim family.

In 1992 Sabir was invited to join Trans World Radio as program producer and evangelist for an Urdu-language program called "Noor-e-Ilahi" (Divine Light) for Muslims. The program, which is still broadcast from the Moscow Center of Trans World Radio every Monday through Friday, touches Muslims and other Urdu speakers across Asia. More than three hundred letters a month come from listeners, most of them Muslims, saying they have received Jesus as Savior.

And it all began with a small portion of a printed message about Jesus wrapped around a handful of peanuts. It was a message the wind of God's Spirit carried to a Lucknow street vendor for its appointment with a youth named Sabir Ali Khan.

A Seed on a Staircase

It is amazing what happens when the Holy Spirit blows a Gospel message—literally!—on a breeze of divine destiny at the most timely moment.

So it was with Necitas Nicodemus of the Philippines. In 1984 Necitas could no longer endure the pain of her troubled marriage to Marcelino, a chronic womanizer. More than a year earlier, Necitas had tried to take her life by swallowing a bottle of pills, but her husband found her just in time to save her. The couple tried to work out their differences, and Marcelino made many promises. But now the situation was much worse.

One evening when Marcelino was out, the distraught housewife again took an overdose of sleeping pills. But they only gave her a terrific headache and made her feel groggy. Then a thought came to her: the train tracks. They were just a short walking distance from their apartment. This time she would not fail. She would lie down on the tracks and let a speeding train end her misery.

Necitas went tearfully down the stairs of their apartment building. Then, at the bottom of the stairwell, she glimpsed some-

185

thing on the floor that looked like a postcard. She bent over to pick it up.

It was obviously part of some other message. The brief statement on the card encouraged the reader to check one of two boxes, then mail the card to the address on the other side. The first box said simply, "I believe this message and have received Christ as my Savior. Please send me more information about my new life in Christ." The second box advised, "I do not understand the message but I would like to know more. Please send me additional information on what it means to receive Christ as my Savior."

Perhaps her husband had picked up whatever had accompanied this card and thrown it away, not noticing that the card had fallen out. Or perhaps the message had been dropped inside the doorway and the wind had carried the rest of it out into the street, leaving just the card at the foot of the stairs.

Whatever the case, Necitas had never heard language like this before. She stood for a moment wondering what the accompanying message might have said. As she hesitated, holding the card in her hand, she felt a strange inward impression, almost like a voice. It said simply, *This is the answer to what you are searching for.*

Necitas had no idea what was happening within her, but realized her depression, strangely, had abated. So instead of continuing with her plan, she turned and headed back up the stairs. The desire to take her life was suddenly gone, and she felt the first small measure of hope.

Back in her apartment, she took a pencil and filled out the form. Because she did not have the accompanying message explaining what it meant to receive Christ as Savior, she checked the second box. Then she hid the card and went to bed, not knowing when Marcelino might arrive home.

The following day Necitas mailed the card to the address on the back, the Every Home Crusade office in Manila.

Several days later she received the first lesson of a four-part Bible correspondence course. Studying it, she learned what it means to receive Christ as her Lord and Savior. Convinced of the truth of the message, she committed her life to Jesus Christ.

As Necitas contemplated filling out the answer sheet at the end of the lesson, which she planned to return to the EHC office, she wondered how she might get Marcelino to study the same material. This message would change his life, she felt, and perhaps their marriage as well, but she knew he would refuse if she told him the Bible study would do him good.

Suddenly an idea came. Necitas penciled in several answers to the study questions, answering them incorrectly. When Marcelino arrived home later that evening, Necitas told him she had written for a free study course about Jesus Christ, and that if she finished it properly, she would receive a diploma. But she wanted to be sure she did not get any of the questions wrong. Would he help her?

Marcelino agreed happily.

One question read, "Are all people sinners or only those who do bad things?" Necitas had answered, "Only those who do bad things." Marcelino was not sure himself, so he read the text of the lesson and discovered that the Bible plainly says, "All have sinned."

So Marcelino corrected her, "No, no, Necitas. Look at what the lesson says."

Necitas looked with him at the text, erased the incorrect answer and penciled in the correction.

She said nothing further as she worked with Marcelino that night to finish the questions. Then she thanked him for helping her answer the questions correctly.

About two weeks later the second lesson arrived. Again Necitas asked for Marcelino's help. He read through every word carefully, making sure his wife answered each question properly.

During the third lesson, as Marcelino helped Necitas answer a question about Jesus, he turned to his wife and said, "Necitas, I believe all this is true. I believe salvation *does* come through trusting in Jesus Christ alone."

Necitas invited Marcelino to pray with her and invite Christ into his heart. And in an instant, an unfaithful husband's life was transformed. Marcelino became a new creation in Christ.

Marcelino quickly proved an able Bible teacher. Soon as many as one hundred people were studying the Bible with him, using

EHC's correspondence course as a text. A strong nucleus of believers formed in Marcelino's village, and he and Necitas visited the EHC office in Manila and asked for help. EHC sent a staff member, the Reverend Rudy Delez, who began guiding the group into the deeper truths of God's Word. Later the new believers were baptized in a river at a neighboring municipality, burning the fetishes they had once used in worship as Rudy and the entire EHC staff looked on with joy.

Today Necitas and Marcelino Nicodemus, who went on to receive intensive Bible training, have planted four churches in the Philippines. The last has grown to more than two hundred worshipers and has a new chapel erected on land donated by one of their converts. And it all began with only a decision card blown by the Spirit of God into the stairwell of their apartment on the very day Necitas intended to take her life.

A Booklet in the Breeze

In all our strategic planning to reach the world for Jesus, we must never forget that the Lord alone is in charge of His harvest (see Matthew 9:37–38). We are merely His witnesses, His seed sowers. We must plan methodically, of course, and pray mightily. And if we do not want to miss anyone, we must go systematically to where people live. But even then, only God can produce the fruit.

Recall Paul's words to the Corinthian believers—when he was dealing with factions in that church—about seed planting and harvest:

> I planted the seed, Apollos watered it, but God made it grow. So neither he who plants nor he who waters is anything, but only God, who makes things grow.
>
> 1 Corinthians 3:6–7

If we plant the seeds of the Gospel prayerfully and carefully, God will cause these seeds to produce fruit at the right time:

"As the rain and the snow come down from heaven, and do not return to it without watering the earth and making it bud and flourish, so that it yields seeds for the sower and bread for the eater, so is my word that goes out from my mouth: It will not return to me empty, but will accomplish what I desire and achieve the purpose for which I sent it."

Isaiah 55:10–11

Some of the seeds may represent a harvest in and of themselves. As someone wisely said, "Any fool can count the seeds in an apple, but only God can count the apples in a seed."

So it was with an eight-page Gospel booklet blown by a humid monsoon breeze toward its divinely appointed destination in Bangalore in southern India. The target: Vasudeva Rao, the eldest son of an orthodox Brahmin family.

Vasudeva had grown up according to strong Hindu tradition. Twice a day he offered his *poojas* (Hindu prayers) to the many deities adorning their home. Some were pictures and some were statues, but all were worshiped. Vasu, following in the footsteps of his father, an ardent Hindu worshiper, sought to attain the special divine enlightenment that Hindus call *Moksha*.

But Vasu was confused as to which god out of the many hundreds, even thousands, he should seek after and worship in order to receive this divine enlightenment. He read many Hindu scriptures and discovered repeatedly that his gods had committed many sinful actions.

Something within Vasu's conscience would not allow him to accept these beings as real gods. His search for the true God continued. He even prayed a prayer (to whom he was praying, he was not certain): "If there really is a true God, let Him reveal Himself to me." But nothing seemed to happen.

Finally Vasu joined a gang of young criminals, harassing people in Bangalore and indulging in petty crimes. But even this did not last long. Vasu entered into a season of depression and considered ending his life.

Then one day Vasu was walking along a busy Bangalore boulevard. The monsoon breezes, which were beginning to blow briskly, caught a pocket-sized pamphlet and were tossing it playfully in different directions. Suddenly it flew directly toward Vasu and rested quietly at his feet. Vasu retrieved the booklet and stood on the side of the busy road, reading it carefully. The message was simple. It explained how a person could receive Someone called Jesus Christ, the Son of God, as his or her Lord and Savior.

Vasu responded to the message instantly. Even as cars and cattle carts jostled about along the busy boulevard, the young man opened his heart to Jesus.

Vasu's faith in Christ met severe opposition from both family and friends, but he continued to grow in Jesus. He received follow-up materials from the EHC office in Bangalore, including a New Testament, which he soon was devouring every day.

Less than a year later, Vasu applied to work at the EHC Bangalore office, and after careful training became a valued member of the follow-up staff. Hundreds of Hindus who responded to Gospel booklets given home by home received carefully prepared follow-up letters from Vasu. Each was filled with appropriate Scriptures, answering even the most complicated questions. Vasu soon became a popular counselor at seekers conferences (the meetings for new converts) and Christ Groups (the small groups of new believers I described in chapter 6).

In the months after joining the EHC ministry and completing the necessary training, Vasu led a remarkable three hundred people to Jesus, most of them Hindus. Of this number he personally baptized 231. To Vasu's special joy, this initial harvest included all his own family members, including his staunch Brahmin parents.

And it all began with a simple eight-page Gospel message that had been blown his way by a brisk south Indian breeze—and the wind of God's Spirit.

13

The Spirit of the Trees

Lendongo Botshemba, who stood a full head taller than most of the Pygmies, climbed with the agility of a chimp from a towering Malapa tree deep in the rain forest near the Momboyo River. Carefully he tied several short branches with long, oval leaves to a strip of leather attached to his waist. This, he believed, captured the spirit of the trees and protected Pygmy warriors like himself from harmful evil spirits.

The young Pygmy, destined for a role similar to that of Chief Haribo in the Solomon Islands, was about to assume leadership of the Pygmy clans of the Bosuka region in central Africa. He was twenty years old.

Stories had circulated among these Pygmies about a white man who had visited their forest long ago. He had brought a strange message about the Creator of all things who had a Son. But most did not understand this new religion, even fewer believed it, and any impact from the white visitor's message had long since died away. Most of those in the deep forest beyond Bosuka could not remember ever seeing the face of a white man, never mind anything of his strange religion.

Lendongo's tribe, numbering at least six thousand, had no idea they lived on a continent called Africa, or that their rain forest fell within the boundaries of a nation now called Zaire. The Pygmies, like the Kwaio of the Solomon Islands, knew little of the outside world. They had no concept of a modern calendar or that they were living in the last decade of the twentieth century.

But in a matter of months all this was to change dramatically. And most of the peoples of Bosuka, like the Kwaio of the Solomon Islands, would see their lives transformed by that Creator who has a Son.

The Sleeves of God

Sanji Adonga clutched his bag of Gospel messages tightly and proceeded to the next apartment in the central district of Yan (not its real name), a sprawling Muslim city in North Africa. Few Christian workers labored in this city of more than a million Muslims, but Sanji had an assignment from God. He was part of a tiny army of believers committed to visiting every dwelling in this North African Muslim enclave.

It had not been the best of days; most people who appeared at their doors had refused the message. But when they closed their doors, Sanji usually put a booklet on the front step anyway, so these individuals would not be missed in the house-to-house evangelism campaign. And if no one answered his knock, the young evangelist slipped the good news about Jesus under the door. Sanji wanted every Muslim to meet Jesus. After all, he himself was a Muslim who had found Jesus.

Now Sanji was approaching the next Muslim apartment. Knocking tentatively on the door, the worker was greeted by a man in his mid-twenties. Sanji smiled and handed him the message.

"I give you the truth," he declared boldly, handing the young man a Gospel booklet.

The man took the booklet, glanced at it briefly and opened it. Then, apparently seeing a reference to Jesus Christ, he began cursing and ripped the booklet into pieces.

"This is not truth!" he shouted. "This is a lie!" With that he threw the torn booklet into the face of the evangelist. "Leave now—and don't ever return, or I'll kill you!"

Shaken, Sanji headed hastily for the next apartment just up the street, where he continued his work until early evening.

A Voice in the Night

The man at the door was 25-year-old Abdulai Masa, the son of a wealthy local merchant. He helped direct one of his father's businesses.

That night Abdulai fell into a deep sleep. He had forgotten the experience with the evangelist earlier that day. But during the night the young Muslim felt two powerful hands grab his shoulders in the darkness and begin to shake him violently. Was it a dreadful dream or was it real? At first he was not sure. The hands gripped tighter and Abdulai, convinced that a thief had broken into his apartment, swung his arms wildly to fend off the unseen intruder.

But in the darkness he could feel no body to go with the hands grabbing his shoulders.

Abdulai's heart was beating like a loud African log drum, and he sat up shaking.

"Who are you?" he shouted. "What do you want?"

He reached up and turned on the lamp hanging over his bed. The room was empty. Still shaking, he lit a cigarette, hoping it would calm his nerves.

"Who are you?" Abdulai asked again, thinking perhaps this had been just a dream after all.

A voice filled the room.

"You have torn up the truth," the voice said with authority.

Abdulai's eyes darted in every direction. Obviously another person was in the room with him.

"Where are you?" he shouted again. "What do you want?"

"You have torn up the truth," the voice repeated. "The message you were given by the visitor at your door was God's truth that points to eternal life. It tells of the only way to lasting peace and happiness, and you have torn it up."

Abdulai was still shaking. "But what can I do now? Surely the pieces of paper have been blown away by the wind."

"I will tell you where you may find another booklet. Take paper and pencil and write this address."

Abdulai could not believe he was hearing a voice with no visible body. But he grabbed a paper and pencil and wrote down the name and address of Sanji Adonga.

"If you want another booklet," repeated the voice, "you must go to this address when the sun rises. You will find the same man who stood at your door today."

Abdulai Masa slept little the remainder of the night. At the crack of dawn he dressed and headed for the address on the paper.

Sanji had just risen when he heard a knock at his door. Wiping sleep from his eyes, he opened the door and stood in disbelief as he looked into the face of the young man who the day before had threatened his life. How had this man found his address in a city of more than a million? He was certain no one had followed him the previous evening, and the only address on the booklet was a postal box in a distant city. Besides, this man had torn up his booklet.

"What are you doing here?" Sanji asked, swallowing hard.

"I've come for another booklet," Abdulai answered. "I must have a new copy of what you gave me yesterday."

"But you threw it in my face. And how did you find my address?"

"The voice in the night," the Muslim explained, describing how the hands had shaken him awake and the voice had said he had torn up the truth.

"The voice gave me your address," Abdulai concluded. "It also told me you would give me another booklet."

An amazed Sanji retreated to his bedroom and returned with a booklet. Then, for more than an hour, he used the pamphlet to explain in depth what it means to receive Christ as Lord. By the end of the explanation, Abdulai was convinced the message was true. He repeated the sinner's prayer and gave his life to Jesus.

When he announced his conversion to his family, Abdulai, who had already changed his name to Abraham, was fired from his father's business and banned from all family contact. His father even organized a plan to have him kidnapped and killed, but one of his sisters told him details of the plan. So Abraham fled to the only Christian he knew, Sanji Adonga, who helped him escape three hundred miles to the south, where the national office of Every Home for Christ is located.

Abraham was grateful Sanji had helped him escape, because only a few weeks later, another Muslim, the teenage son of an emir (a top Muslim leader) who had found Christ in the same door-to-door outreach, was bludgeoned to death by the emir himself on the grounds of his palace. The youth's entire family, as well as palace personnel, looked on as he refused to deny that Jesus was the only Son of God, and was slain brutally by his own father.

But Abraham arrived safely at the EHC office to be nurtured and discipled by the director himself, even living for a time in his home. Soon he was doing odd jobs around the office and, in a few months, going out and witnessing house to house, telling others what Jesus had done in his life.

Now Abraham has finished an intensive Bible course and has become involved in house-to-house evangelism in regions of his nation that are heavily Muslim.

An Age of Wonders

These kinds of experiences—being instructed by a voice in a dream, as just one example—are, as remarkable as it sounds, increasing dramatically on a global scale. God clearly has something up His sleeves, and we do well to remember—putting aside any theology of how God might dress (see Psalm 104:1–2)—that *God has really big sleeves!* And one thing appears certain: The exploding global prayer movement is clearly related to what God is releasing from those "big sleeves." As J. Edwin Orr often preached, "Whenever God is about to do something new with His people, He always sets them to praying."

If this is true (and I find myself in full agreement), then we should not be surprised by the dramatic increase in signs and wonders being reported by missiologists and Christian leaders worldwide, or by the rapidly expanding global harvest of lost souls. These are signs offering us hope that the fulfillment of the Great Commission may be closer than we think.

Some Christian leaders believe there is ample biblical reason to anticipate even more occasions of the miraculous as we move toward the end of this present age and the "closure" of the Great Commission. The supernatural, they suggest, may become the norm rather than a seldom-seen phenomenon.

The word *supernatural* comes from the two words—"super" and "natural." *Super* means "above" or "greater than." *Natural* means "what is normal or common." Thus, an event or occurrence might be considered supernatural if it is above or greater than what is normal or common. *Miracle,* an overused word in today's culture, refers to "an event or action that apparently contradicts known scientific laws." A miracle might also be defined simply as "a remarkable thing" or "a marvel."

Events like a young Muslim hearing a voice in the night, giving him the address of a believer in a city of a million, is a remarkable occurrence that appears to contradict known scientific laws. But should we classify it as a biblical miracle?

Biblical Reasons for Signs and Wonders

Miraculous occurrences can be controversial theologically. But I am sure all believers agree that, when it comes to the miraculous, God can do whatever He wants.

Still, it is a matter of biblical record that signs and wonders accompanied many of the evangelistic advances of the early Church. The writer of the epistle to the Hebrews explained, for example, that signs and wonders confirmed the truth of our salvation:

> This salvation, which was first announced by the Lord, was confirmed to us by those who heard him. God also testified to it by signs, wonders and various miracles, and gifts of the Holy Spirit distributed according to his will.
>
> Hebrews 2:3–4

The apostle Paul emphasized the role of miracles in his own missionary work, confirming the reality of the Gospel:

> Therefore I glory in Christ Jesus in my service to God. I will not venture to speak of anything except what Christ has accomplished through me in leading the Gentiles to obey God by what I have said and done— by the power of signs and miracles, through the power of the Spirit.
>
> Romans 15:17–19

Let's note what the Scriptures themselves reveal about miracles and why God performs them. It will help us measure the validity of signs and wonders today, especially as they relate to the acceleration of the worldwide harvest of people coming to Christ.

Miracles Reveal God

First, it is clear from a careful study of Scripture that God performs miracles to reveal His glory, and that "the earth will be filled with the knowledge of the glory of the LORD" (Habakkuk 2:14).

An example of a miracle revealing God's glory is found early in the book of Joshua when the two Israelites were sent to spy out the city of Jericho. They lodged in the house of a prostitute, Rahab, but the king of Jericho, who heard about the intruders, demanded that she produce them. Instead Rahab hid them in stalks of flax on the roof and told the king's messengers that the spies had fled. Then she told the Israelites,

> "I know that the LORD has given this land to you and that a great fear of you has fallen on us, so that all who live in this country are melting in fear because of you."

> Joshua 2:9

Further, she said,

> "We have heard how the LORD dried up the water of the Red Sea for you when you came out of Egypt, and what you did to Sihon and Og, the two kings of the Amorites east of the Jordan, whom you completely destroyed."

> verse 10

Rahab's conclusion contains a key insight into the reason God performs miracles:

> "When we heard of it, our hearts melted and everyone's courage failed because of you, for the LORD your God is God in heaven above and on the earth below."

> verse 11

Clearly God used these miracles to reveal His power and glory to those who might stand in the way of His ultimate plan.

Biblically speaking, then, we might consider putting all supposed signs and wonders to this test: *Do they reveal something of the nature and character of God and His ways? And in the end, is God glorified through them by revealing Himself to those who do not know Him?*

Miracles Reveal Christ

A second reason for the miraculous is to reveal and glorify Jesus Christ. The apostle John, like the other Gospel writers, described many miracles that Jesus performed. Then, after recounting the resurrection and how Jesus confronted the doubts of Thomas, John concluded:

> Jesus did many other miraculous signs in the presence of his disciples, which are not recorded in this book. But these are written that you may believe that Jesus is the Christ, the Son of God, and that by believing you may have life in his name.

> John 20:30–31

The miracles Jesus performed, then, attested to the truth of who He was (and is!). And since we know that "Jesus Christ is the same yesterday and today and forever" (Hebrews 13:8), we should not be surprised to see miracles continue in ways that reveal and glorify Jesus, especially in convincing the lost of His reality.

Thus, we can put signs and wonders to this second test: *Do they reveal the Person and work of our Lord Jesus Christ as the only way to salvation? Do they truly bring glory to Jesus?*

Miracles Reveal God's Mercy

A third biblical purpose for miracles is to reveal the mercy of God and His unfathomable forgiveness and compassion, especially for those lost in sin. For reasons beyond our ability to explain or understand, God sometimes performs miracles simply out of His mercy. Feeding the five thousand (see John 6), feeding the four thousand (see Mark 8) and raising the widow's son from the dead in Elisha's day (see 2 Kings 4) are examples.

James, the brother of our Lord, refers to those who endured pain and suffering until victory came:

> Brothers, as an example of patience in the face of suffering, take the prophets who spoke in the name of the Lord. As you know, we consider blessed those who have persevered. You have heard of Job's perseverance and have seen what the Lord finally brought about. The Lord is full of compassion and mercy.
>
> James 5:10–11

Job was blessed after he suffered simply because God chose to manifest His mercy and compassion on him. We cannot discount that God, in His sovereignty, may choose to perform the supernatural in certain situations purely because He wants to.

And wasn't the redemption of lost people often key to these manifestations of the miraculous in Scripture? Consider Saul of Tarsus. He did not deserve the supernatural Damascus road encounter that resulted in his conversion (compare Acts 7:60 and 8:1 with Acts 9:1–9), any more than Abdulai Masa in North Africa deserved to hear a voice in the night. God simply chose to save Paul in that way to reveal His mercy and compassion, prompting a final biblical test we might use to measure the validity of ostensible signs and wonders: *Is there a strong basis to believe that God has acted sovereignly in this situation to manifest His mercy? Does the miracle measure up to a biblical understanding of God's way of showing His compassion so that people might know Him?*

Theological disputes aside—specifically regarding the issue of whether miracles ceased with the apostles or continue to the present day—we must ask if there is any reason the miraculous would *not* have the same effect today as in early Church times. That is, wouldn't miracles today have the same impact in confirming the reality of the Gospel and drawing more people to a saving knowledge of Jesus Christ?

Dreams and Visions

Dr. Bill Bright of Campus Crusade for Christ, a respected states-man in the Church and one of my personal mentors, reported in a letter to Campus Crusade partners dated August 1995 the "astounding phenomenon" of dreams and visions confirming the reality of Christ, particularly among Muslims.

Thousands of letters from Muslims in North Africa and the Middle East, responding to a radio program aired throughout the region, describe dreams in which Jesus appeared to them, saying, "I am the way." When these Muslims heard the radio broadcast, they understood what they had experienced in their dreams and requested more information about this Person called Jesus.

Dr. Bright also reported numerous Muslims in Algeria who had dreamed about Jesus. Later they discovered that their friends had had the very same dream, right down to the words Jesus had spoken. Several of these Muslims obtained Bibles and formed a small Bible study group, which is growing rapidly.

One fanatical Muslim woman nearing the conclusion of a four-year prison term for political activities had a vision of Jesus in her cell. Jesus explained to her personally the meaning of redemption, she testified, so she surrendered her life to Him. Today she is ministering to Muslims as a staff worker with Campus Crusade for Christ.

These wonders are by no means confined to North Africa, nor was the voice in the night that confronted Abdulai Masa the only such encounter reported by Every Home for Christ workers. Thousands of miles away, in Kashmir in northeast India, a devout Muslim named Jalaluddin had a visitation just as remarkable.

Jalaluddin had studied the Koran faithfully for years. But as time passed, he felt increasingly dissatisfied with the Islamic message. No Christian worker had ever visited Jala, nor had he ever heard the Gospel, but Jala knew something was missing. Every attempt to find true peace eluded him.

One night in a deep sleep, Jala had a dream. A man wearing a white robe appeared before him asking, "Do you want real peace?"

"Yes," Jala replied. "I am seeking peace but I've been unable to find it."

"Read the holy Scripture."

"What is the holy Scripture and where can I get it?"

"The holy Scripture is the holy Bible, and you can get it from the India Every Home Crusade, 3 Bishop Rockey Street, Faizabad Road, in Lucknow."

So vivid was the message that Jala sat straight up in bed. The address was etched in his mind. He grabbed a piece of paper and wrote it down.

A few days later the EHC office in Lucknow received Jala's letter, which said, in part:

> I don't know who you people are or whether this address is correct, but I am writing exactly as I was told in a dream. If you receive this, would you please immediately send me something that is called a "holy Bible"?

About ten days later Jala received the first lesson of a Bible correspondence course, along with the Bible he had requested. Soon he had completed all four lessons and read through the entire New Testament. Jala wrote once again to the EHC office, affirming two truths that Muslims often have great difficulty accepting: "The course has enlightened me about the reality of the Trinity, as well as the truth of the Sonship of Jesus Christ."

Within weeks Jala was attending a Christian church and witnessing freely to other Muslims about his newfound faith in Christ.

Kashinath's Confirmation

Hindus, too, are being touched by the supernatural—like Kashinath Hayak of the remote village of Pandiapathar in India. Located in the state of Orissa, in a dense forest about 140 miles from Orissa's capital city of Bhubaneswar, Pandiapathar is a Hindu village filled with anti-Christian sentiment.

Kashinath grew up in a hut made from thatched leaves and mud. His ancestors were strict Hindus, worshiping many deities, idols and demon spirits. He could not recall a true sense of peace or meaning from his early years. The people of his village had always quarreled. As far as Kashinath was concerned, no one knew true happiness.

And always they had to honor their gods. Religious festivals were all-consuming, and there were so many of them. Orissa Hindus liked to say, "There are thirteen festivals in twelve months," and a good Hindu was expected to take part in each of them.

One sweltering, humid morning, an EHC worker from Bhubaneswar came to Kashinath's village—one of many in the district that Saral Singh had been assigned to reach with the Gospel. Soon he stood at the entry of Kashinath's modest thatched hut. Saral explained that only through Jesus Christ could one find eternal salvation. And it was really very simple, he added. No painful rituals were involved. There was a simple gift called "grace" that made it all possible. Forgiveness was free, final and forever. All Kashinath had to do was believe.

But believing seemed impossible for the well-trained Hindu. All his life Kashinath had been taught that it was necessary to honor many rituals and customs in order to satisfy his deity. Hinduism as a religion just made more sense. Surely, he reasoned, salvation had to be earned by worshiping many gods, and required far more than the simple faith this evangelist described.

So Kashinath rejected the message of Saral Singh.

But early the next morning, just before waking, Kashinath had a dream in which he saw a Man standing before him dressed in beautiful white clothing.

"Kashinath," asked the Man, "how many parents do you have?"

"One father and one mother."

"Why, then, do you worship so many gods and goddesses? I am Jesus, the true way to God the Father."

With that Kashinath awoke from his deep sleep. It was early morning, and he set out immediately to find the evangelist.

Brother Saral Singh had not yet left the village, and he listened intently as Kashinath described his unusual dream. Then the evangelist explained again the message of the Good News.

This time, when he spoke about Jesus, Kashinath knew exactly whom Saral was referring to. He had seen Him in his dream. And before mid-morning Kashinath had placed his trust in Christ.

Why? Because his life-changing dream had confirmed to him the reality of the Gospel.

Bewildered but Believing

God also uses signs and wonders sometimes to break strong resistance to the Gospel.

An EHC field evangelist named Zechariah was making his weekly visit to a district hospital in one of Fiji's 106 islands, ministering to the patients. An elderly man we will call Raja Kali, from Fiji's Vanua Levu island, had been admitted, suffering from an illness that had left him paralyzed. As Zechariah approached the old man to tell him about Jesus, a strange sense of spiritual authority filled his heart. It was impossible to explain, but Zechariah sensed that God wanted to restore Raja to health.

Zechariah was a man of faith but had never done anything so audacious. Only later did he recognize that he was exercising the gifts of faith and healing given him by the Holy Spirit (see 1 Corinthians 12:9).

Without any explanation, he commanded Raja boldly, "In the name of Jesus, rise up!"

Raja Kali felt a twitching sensation in his legs. Something was happening in his body. Bewildered but believing, he rose slowly to his feet.

Then Zechariah placed his hands on the old man's back.

"In the name of Jesus," he declared, "walk!"

The thrust of the evangelist's hands seemed to propel Raja for the first step or two. Then, as a nurse and several patients looked on in amazement, Raja took some tentative steps and began walking freely down the narrow corridor.

Before the end of the day, the old man had also heard the plan of salvation and asked Jesus to be his Lord and Savior. Zechariah gave him a printed Gospel message, encouraged him to read it often and write the EHC office then located in Labasa, Fiji, requesting the four-lesson Bible correspondence course.

The miracle had only begun. About a week after Raja's return to his remote village, one of his relatives from the interior of Vanua Levu island appeared at the EHC center in Labasa. The entire village, he reported, wanted to hear about Jesus. Could they send someone that very day?

Two workers were dispatched promptly for the lengthy journey into the interior, first by bus and then for many hours on foot. It was clearly a Holy Spirit-ordained opportunity.

The two evangelists were greeted warmly by Raja's entire family, then asked to tell the story about Jesus. Within a few hours, the family had prayed to receive Jesus as Lord and Savior. Then the workers were asked to bring back a larger evangelistic team as soon as possible to reach the whole area with the Gospel.

Four workers returned, and many in that remote area of Vanua Levu received Christ. After a third outreach took place, half of Raja's village responded to the Gospel. Soon it had a thriving church.

As word of the miracle spread, the Every Home Fiji staff realized that Raja's healing was even more significant than they had first realized. Eight months earlier, as it turned out, another two-man team of evangelists had gone into that same area to proclaim the Gospel, village by village and house by house. But a townsperson in Raja's village had led in public opposition, until the chief of the village (whose word is final) refused the workers permission to distribute literature, visit homes or conduct any public meetings. The workers had to leave without witnessing to a single family.

And the identity of the man who had led the initial opposition? It was Raja Kali himself—the man who had been touched by God in the hospital!

Now he had been healed and become God's instrument for touching two entire villages, including the chiefs and their families, for Christ.

Technological Wonders

Some harvest wonders are miracles that combine the technology of our day with God's power in order to reveal Christ.

In a remote part of the Arctic in Russia is an Eskimo village nicknamed "The End of the Earth," since nothing lies beyond the area but huge ice floes and the Arctic itself. One of the few modern conveniences: an earth station and satellite dish to pick up television signals for the isolated village.

In the town lived a young Eskimo woman who was depressed about her circumstances and about living in so remote a place. Attractive, in her mid-twenties, Misa reached such a point of despondency that she finally decided to take her life. At the time, the generator that supplied much-needed electricity to the village had failed, cutting off power for days.

As Misa sat contemplating how to die, power to the generator was suddenly restored, sending electricity surging into the homes throughout the small outpost. Misa was surprised as her television set came to life. Apparently it had been on days before when the power had been cut.

Now, as the picture sharpened, she saw a man looking straight into the television camera and declaring, "The Lord has just impressed on me that you are contemplating taking your life because you think nobody cares about you."

It was Pat Robertson and "The 700 Club." The earth station had apparently been focused on a cable system that carried the program the moment the generator began to function.

The television evangelist pointed directly at the camera—and seemingly at Misa.

"But God cares about you," he said, "and He loves you."

The beautiful Eskimo girl heard it in her own language. And as the American evangelist prayed for whomever that person might be, Misa could not hold back her tears. She gave her heart to Jesus and was born again.

So profound was the change in Misa's life that she began telling her neighbors about the miracle she had experienced. Soon her testimony touched the entire village, resulting in more than six hundred conversions. Today Misa serves as pastor of a thriving village congregation at "the end of the earth."[1]

The technological wonder she experienced is just one of the miraculous happenings occurring today that reveal

> the nature and character of God and His ways to those who do not know Him;
>
> the Person and work of our Lord Jesus Christ as the only way of salvation;
>
> the sovereign compassion of God, demonstrated so that people might understand Him.

So we should not be surprised if the spread of the Gospel continues to accelerate amid ever-increasing signs and wonders. After all, God has really big sleeves.

And from those big sleeves, as we will discover next, comes another extraordinary phenomenon taking place as the Church advances toward the completion of the Great Commission.

Mysterious Mountains

14

Their assignment was the Solomon Islands—the chain of volcanic islands east of New Guinea in the western Pacific Ocean. The two dedicated missionaries from Fiji, a thousand miles southeast in that vast ocean, had participated in an in-depth training program to prepare them to take the good news of Jesus to remote places on the estimated 23,000 inhabited islands throughout the Pacific.

The missionaries had agreed to go by faith to the Solomons to help train a small army of evangelists who would visit all one hundred islands in the chain, village by village and home by home. Christian workers had labored there for several generations but never undertaken a systematic effort to tell every family in every village on every island about Jesus. This is what the two missionaries had been trained to do.

Both had seen the awesome results of such a strategy in Fiji, where all 106 inhabited islands, over a period of just a few years, had been visited systematically, village by village and home by home. They had seen the birth of more than five hundred small groups of new believers, baby churches, often in remote and rugged areas. Many of these groups had grown into full-fledged fellowships, some numbering many hundreds of believers. The same miracle, Matthew and Suva believed, would occur throughout the Solomons, especially in areas where the Gospel had never penetrated.

But little did these two pioneers realize the means God would use to bring this miracle about. It would involve an old chief named Haribo, living—though dying—in the mysterious mountains of Malaita, one of the Solomons' largest islands. What would happen to Haribo would prove to Matthew and Suva, and the workers who would first encounter Haribo, that Jesus Christ is indeed "the same yesterday and today and forever" (Hebrews 13:8).

Agents of the Invisible

Mental weariness was taking its toll. I decided I could not go on.

I'll just resign, I said to myself as I boarded the plane for yet another tiring assignment.

The West Coast organization I served was large, with numerous vice presidents (of which I was one) and hundreds of full-time staff. I was barely thirty when I began. But now the frailties of some of the senior staff, mine included, were beginning to show. Leadership was in transition, and some in the organization were jockeying for position.

For months I had carried an unusually heavy burden that often kept me awake all night. On one occasion at work, long before dawn, I had found myself prostrate, all alone, just inside the office entryway of our ministry, weeping and crying out to God for personal and corporate cleansing. But for weeks nothing seemed to happen. My emotions were drained.

I fastened my seatbelt as the plane taxied down the runway for the three-hour flight to Chicago's O'Hare Airport. There I would catch a connection for the East Coast to appear on a nationally televised Christian program discussing the very work that now seemed to be robbing me of my joy. I felt even more depressed. How could I share testimonies of spiritual victories with integrity when I felt such defeat?

I'll just resign, I said to myself again as the plane began its final approach into Chicago. *I'll quit, that's what I'll do.*

I stared at the huge Sears Tower that loomed over the skyline. Suddenly an unexpected spirit of determination flooded my mind. I knew God had called me to this ministry, and I knew He had not "uncalled" me. Indignation filled my heart against Satan, who must be trying to rob me of my joy. It was not God trying to *call* me out of the work, but the enemy trying to *force* me out.

I began to pray fervently in my spirit as the plane descended toward O'Hare. I grabbed both armrests firmly. So intense was my prayer against what I perceived to be Satan's harassing demons that I know my body was shaking noticeably, even though my prayers were silent.

Inwardly I shouted, *I will not quit. You can't make me quit! I will stay in the battle, no matter what its outcome.*

Instantly my anxiety and depression lifted. It seemed that fresh oil began to pour over me. As I exited the plane, I felt almost lighthearted, renewed.

O'Hare was packed with people as I stood at the gate waiting for my connecting flight to board. A man with a dark pinstriped suit and attaché case came and stood beside me.

Perhaps he's on the same flight, I thought.

The man never spoke. He just stood, staring straight ahead. Then another man came, wearing an identical suit and carrying a similar attaché case.

Strange.

He stood directly beside the other man and, like him, stared straight ahead.

For a moment it was just another O'Hare oddity—the kind of strange sight you see in busy public places when you are watching people. But suddenly I sensed this was different.

"Hey," said one man to the other, still staring straight ahead. "Whatever happened to that Eastman fellow? I heard he was going to quit the company."

I caught my breath and looked out of the corner of my eye to see if either one of them would acknowledge my existence. Could they possibly know my name was Eastman, and that only a short time earlier I had thought of quitting my company?

The other man kept looking straight ahead.

"Oh, I have some good news," he said. "I just talked to headquarters. The chief told me Eastman changed his mind. He was hanging by a thread, you know. We thought we were going to lose him."

Then, with a slight smile, he concluded, "Yeah, the chief says Eastman's going to stay in the battle."

"I'm really glad to hear that. There's a great future for him in the company."

I am not sure what kept me from turning to either of those men and saying, "Hey, who are you guys, anyway?" But the next instant they walked away and went around a corner perhaps thirty feet away. I looked for them later but did not see them.

Whether they simply blended into the crowd or literally disappeared, I do not know. And whether this was merely a very odd coincidence or a divine encounter, the incident became a great source of encouragement for me in an otherwise deeply difficult time.

Over the years I have often wondered if those men were "agents of the invisible" come to deliver an encouraging confirmation for me to stay in the battle long enough to see victory. Of one thing I am certain: There *are* angels out there, and they are clearly at work.

Dispensers of the Divine

Centuries ago John Calvin, writing in the *Institutes of the Christian Religion,* advised:

> Angels are the ministers and the dispensers of the divine bounty towards us. Accordingly, we are told how they watch for our safety, how they undertake our defense, direct our path, and take heed that no evil befall us.[1]

Billy Graham adds thoughtfully:

> I am convinced that these heavenly beings exist and that they provide unseen aid on our behalf. I do not believe in angels because someone has told me about a dramatic visitation from an angel, impressive as such rare testimonies may be. . . . I do not believe in angels because I have ever seen one—because I haven't. I believe in angels because the Bible says there are angels; and I believe the Bible to be the true Word of God.[2]

There is little doubt biblically and experientially (my strange O'Hare encounter aside) that God does send angels on specific assignments to accomplish His will, especially regarding world evangelization.

Biblically speaking we see angels involved in the work of evangelism from the very birth of Christ, when one of them announced the Good News to frightened shepherds:

> "Do not be afraid. I bring you good news of great joy that will be for all the people. Today in the town of David a Savior has been born to you; he is Christ the Lord."

> Luke 2:10–11

210

If we accept the definition of evangelism as "sharing the Good News," then this angel was involved in evangelism. In fact, he was specifically dispatched to deliver the very first declaration in history that Jesus Christ, the Savior of the world, had been born.

The Bible says much about the ministry of angels, referring to them (in differing angelic categories) some three hundred times. Their functions are defined as twofold: service and worship (see Isaiah 6:1–4; Hebrews 1:13–14; Revelation 4:8–11). We may even infer from the rhetorical question of Hebrews 1:14—"Are not all angels ministering spirits sent to serve those who will inherit salvation?"—that "all" angels are involved somehow in the harvest of souls.

Angels Are Everywhere

Isaiah's vision of the throne room (see Isaiah 6:1–4) involved unique angelic beings called seraphs, each with six wings, praising God for His holiness. Isaiah did not tell how many seraphs he saw, but simply referred to them in the plural. The apostle John referred to four living creatures, each with six wings, likewise worshiping God for His holiness (see Revelation 4:8–11). Perhaps Isaiah and John were describing the same angelic worship leaders orchestrating praise around the throne.

But no matter how we define angels—or differentiate between cherubim (see Ezekiel 10:8–15) and seraphs (see Isaiah 6:2), or between seraphs and archangels (see 1 Thessalonians 4:16; Jude 9), or between all of the above from the living creatures of Revelation (see Revelation 4:8; 7:11)—one thing is certain: Angels are real and seem to be everywhere.

In the Old Testament

Elisha and his servant saw the hills full of beings described as "chariots of fire" (2 Kings 6:17). As Jacob slept on his journey to

Haran, he saw a stairway leading into the heavenlies on which "the angels of God were ascending and descending" (Genesis 28:12).

When Jesus Was on Earth

Angels were vitally involved in events surrounding Jesus' birth (see Matthew 1:20–21; Luke 1:26–38; 2:13–15) and temptation in the wilderness (see Matthew 4:11; Luke 4:10). They were also present during His ministry to His disciples (see John 1:51) and as He confronted the powers of darkness in Gethsemane (see Luke 22:43). They were with Him in His resurrection (see Matthew 28:2–7), at His ascension (see Acts 1:10–11), and will be actively involved in His second coming (see Matthew 16:27; 24:36; 2 Thessalonians 1:7–9).

Note that it was the angel Gabriel who proclaimed to Zechariah the impending birth of the Messiah's forerunner, John the Baptist (see Luke 1:11–20). The same heavenly agent informed Mary that she would give birth to the Messiah and that she was to call His name Jesus (see Luke 1:26–38). And during Joseph's engagement to Mary, he was told by an angel that his wife would soon give birth to the Christ child (see Matthew 1:20–23).

Angels were involved in the entire process of the incarnation.

In the Early Church

God's agents of the invisible, who sometimes showed up clothed in human bodies, were also significant in the emerging early Church.

An angel opened prison doors, allowing the apostles to go free and continue evangelizing throughout Jerusalem (see Acts 5:19–20), and an angel gave Philip his Gaza Strip assignment, which led him into the desert to encounter and convert the Ethiopian eunuch (see Acts 8:26).

God sent an angelic representative to Cornelius to commend the centurion for his faithfulness in praying and giving (see Acts 10:3–4) and instruct him to send for Peter (verses 5–6), who would bring the message of salvation to Cornelius' family. Once again the preaching of the Gospel to lost people is linked with angelic intervention.

An angel was sent to deliver Peter from prison while the disciples prayed for him "without ceasing" (see Acts 12:5, KJV). And in the same chapter we read that Herod's death came at the hands of an angel (see Acts 12:23).

Paul was also touched by these agents of the invisible. As he sailed to Rome, for example, he was told by an angel that he and those aboard ship with him would be saved from drowning, and that he would stand trial before Caesar (see Acts 27:23–24).

A study of Revelation reveals a dramatic increase in angelic activity as this present age concludes. The seven angels sound seven trumpets of judgment that announce the establishment of Christ's Kingdom on earth (see Revelation 8–9, 11).

Ed Silvoso reminds us:

> The reality of angels cannot be denied. The book of Acts contains 20 references to angels. On almost every occasion, when the Church was in danger or in confusion, angels were dispatched to the battlefield to help. This is not something that ceased with the completion of the biblical canon. All over the Third World, where the Church is on fire, we find ever-expanding numbers of testimonies of dramatic angelic intervention on behalf of the Church.[3]

The idea of angelic ministry is indeed biblical, and angels *are* out there. And because they are "ministering spirits sent to serve those who will inherit salvation" (Hebrews 1:14), we should not be surprised to see an increased level of their activity as the Church advances toward "closure" and the conclusion of this present age.

A Failed Execution

Hawa Ahmed was the daughter of an emir, a revered Muslim leader. Beautiful and talented, she was pursuing a nursing degree at a university near her home in North Africa, when she received a simple evangelistic booklet in her dormitory room one day.

She had never read a message like it. She had heard of the "prophet" Jesus from the Koran, but this message pictured a different Jesus. This Jesus was more than a prophet; He was the very Son of God who actually forgave people their sins—something Mohammed could never do.

Hawa discussed this amazing message with her friends, some of whom also were interested. One of her friends knew the young worker who had distributed the messages, and arranged a meeting so Hawa could hear more about this Jesus.

Hawa Ahmed listened intently as the worker explained the plan of salvation. Then, convinced of its truth, she received Christ as her Savior.

Because she was the daughter of an emir, Hawa knew her family would be devastated when they learned she had become a Christian. Certainly they would disown her. Many Muslim converts to Christianity in North Africa had been severely persecuted. So Hawa (who changed her name to Faith) decided not to tell her parents about her conversion until the end of the school term.

That day finally arrived. Faith sat before her father and mother one evening and told them about her encounter with Jesus Christ. A strange spirit of boldness came on her as she realized she was preaching the message of the cross and telling her parents about Jesus' resurrection—themes clearly absent from Islam.

But Faith never imagined how angry her father would get. He stood by the only door into the room and called her brothers to come immediately. Then he told the family that Hawa had disgraced them as well as Allah and his prophet Mohammed. She was a heretic, and unless she recanted he had the authority as an emir to sentence her to death.

Faith refused several opportunities he gave her to renounce her newfound faith. So he announced that he would execute his "wayward" daughter by electrocution that very night.

The emir and his sons attached a large metal plate to a chair, to which they wired a cord connected to a 240-volt source of electricity. He had no idea how long this crude electric chair would take to kill her, but he himself would watch until the task was done.

Faith had anticipated rejection by her family, but never anything like this. She waited, terrified, as her brothers stripped her naked and tied her to the chair.

"Put my Bible in my lap," she begged them. "Please."

Amazingly the emir allowed it.

"If you wish to die with your false teaching," he said, "then so be it."

Her older brother added, "This will prove your Christian teachings have no power."

Faith was able to touch the Bible with one of her hands, although she was tied to the chair. As she did so, she felt a strange peace, as if someone was standing beside her. Was Jesus there? Or was it an angel? She just knew she was not alone.

Then one of her brothers plugged the cord into the socket. Nothing happened. They fiddled with the cord and tried again. Still nothing happened. Then they tried another socket. They made four attempts. Each one failed.

Suddenly the emir untied the cords that had bound her, rebuking her loudly.

"You are no longer my daughter," he screamed.

He beat her severely, then pushed her out the door, still unclothed, into the humid African evening.

Stunned by the unbelievable events of the last few hours, Faith found herself outside her own front door without a stitch of clothing. Humiliated, the young student ran naked through the streets of the city, passing people along the way as she raced to the apartment of one of her Christian friends at school. She could think of no place else to go.

Faith soon stood knocking breathlessly at her girlfriend's front door. In moments Sarah answered, then stared in shock to see Faith standing naked on her doorstep. She rushed her inside and wrapped something around the tearful, trembling girl, who explained the entire episode—the rejection by her family, her near-electrocution, the humiliation of running so many blocks unclothed.

Sarah took Faith in, and she and other Christian friends helped to meet her physical needs as Faith considered her future.

The following day, meanwhile, Sarah was talking to several neighbors, who told her they had seen Faith running down the street the night before.

"How sad it is," Sarah commented, "that my friend was thrown out of her home and forced to run through the streets unclothed."

"What are you talking about?" asked one of the neighbors.

"I'm talking about that young woman who ran naked to my door last night. She ran right past you."

"You must be mistaken. The girl who ran past us last night was wearing a beautiful white gown."

The others agreed.

"Yes," added another, "we wondered why someone was running down the street dressed so nicely."

Sarah caught her breath as she realized the extent of God's provision for her friend.

Can angels clothe a naked woman running through the streets, when she herself is unaware of being clothed? Was it an angel who spared Faith's life? One thing is certain: Faith, who is now a full-time evangelist for Every Home for Christ in her predominantly Muslim nation, is an heir of salvation whom angels (as we recall from Hebrews 1:14) are assigned to serve.

The Crocodile River

There is no biblical basis for praying to angels, but we can pray to God, asking Him to send His angels to work on our behalf. As the psalmist asked, "Let those be put to shame and brought to dishonor who seek after my life. . . . And let the angel of the Lord chase them" (Psalm 35:4–5, NKJV).

Two Every Home for Christ field workers found themselves in 1994 claiming the release of angels to "chase" a very strange enemy! Jack and Andrew were doing systematic, home-to-home evangelism in villages throughout the western province of Guadalcanal, the main island in the Solomon Island chain. One settlement was located on a wide river that cut through the region. Jack and Andrew visited every home in that village, sharing the Good News with all who would listen.

In the afternoon, after visiting with the last family, they looked across the river and noticed another village almost hidden in the trees. That village, too, had to be reached, but they had no means of crossing the river. They inquired about the availability of a boat, but everyone who had a boat was fishing on the river. The workers waited for a boat to return but none came.

It was now well into the afternoon, and Jack and Andrew realized that if they were to do any more evangelism that day, they would have to cross now. So they decided to find some logs and hold them together as a flotation device to help them swim across the river.

As they tossed several logs into the river and prepared to wade in, a village elder rushed over. "What are you doing?"

They explained their intention to swim across the river using the logs.

"Oh, no," cried the old man. "You'll be eaten!"

"What do you mean?" Andrew inquired.

"The river is filled with crocodiles. In all my years in this village, I have never known anyone to swim across this river successfully."

Still, Andrew and Jack knew they had to cross, and there was no boat available.

"We'll just have to ask God to send His angels," Jack told the elder, "as He did for Daniel in the lions' den."

The old man had no idea what the evangelist meant, and stood bewildered as the Christian workers entered the water. Pushing several logs together, they placed their bags of Gospel literature carefully into the center of the logs. Then, their bodies half submerged and their feet kicking furiously, they headed out toward the center of the river.

The swimming evangelists could soon see crocodiles lunging into the water and moving toward them. The reptiles formed a small line of observers, loglike above the surface of the water, following their moves but appearing strangely uncertain about coming any closer. Andrew and Jack could also see a lone man watching from the other side of the river.

As they approached the shore and began to gather up their Gospel literature, the man exclaimed, "You are the first people ever to swim across that river without being attacked by crocodiles! Even dogs who swim in this river never make it across. They're swallowed up."

Andrew and Jack thanked God for keeping the crocodiles at bay, and set about to visit every home in the village, leaving Gospel messages for those who could read, and taking time to tell those who could not the story of the Savior. By evening word had spread about how the young men had crossed the crocodile-infested waters untouched, and how "unseen beings" must have protected them.

That night Jack and Andrew began singing Gospel songs in the village center to a gathering crowd. Andrew was soon preaching, telling the story of Daniel in the lions' den. Many in the village received Christ.

When the young men headed back across the river, they took a boat. Daniel had been in the lions' den only once, they reasoned, and they did not want to be presumptuous! But they never doubted that invisible agents had crossed the river with them and kept the mouths of the crocodiles shut.

The Scent of an Angel

Agents of the invisible working on behalf of those carrying the Gospel to unreached peoples may manifest their presence in peculiar ways. But is it possible for an angel, though invisible, to give off a scent as humans do, if there were some purpose for it?

As unlikely as it seems to find a biblical answer to this question, four brave field evangelists in Nepal wonder if this scenario is not only possible, but exactly what happened to them in 1993.

These EHC workers—Sanjeev, Ruben, Naveen and Yubal—were assigned to visit villages in the early autumn of 1993 in the Taplejung district in a remote area of Nepal, and they were stopping at every home in every village. They especially wanted to give the Gospel to the unreached Limbus people prominent in the region.

For two days the young men were unable to find food, and they spent several chilly nights out in the open. They wished, as they wandered through the hilly countryside, that either the crude maps available or the directions from villagers were a little more accurate. But one evening they were thankful to find the village of Lingtheb, where they could get food. An old man agreed to let the four stay in his home, since they did not relish spending another chilly night in the hills. But the man's only son, in his mid-twenties, protested his father's invitation so fiercely that the workers were forced to leave.

It was late at night. As they were leaving the old man's residence, Sanjeev spotted the son slipping out the back door carrying a huge, Nepalese Gurkha knife. He whispered to the others what he had seen, and soon the workers were walking briskly. Within moments they were running for their lives. Instead of following the main path by which they had arrived, they took a shortcut they had seen.

As they sprinted into the hills, they saw nearly a dozen strong-looking men from the village less than a quarter-mile behind them, led by the old man's son. The villagers' flashlight beams glinted like lightning as they reflected off the blades of their Gurkha knives. A few paces ahead of the villagers was a Tibetan dog. He had apparently caught the scent of the workers and was leading the men on in the darkness.

The EHC workers hurried on, stumbling uphill in unfamiliar country with neither flashlights nor weapons. Crossing what seemed to be a main road, they turned up another, less traveled path. They were convinced they would soon be overtaken.

Then Yubal spotted a dark, low nook off the side of the path and motioned to the others. Desperate, they climbed in and huddled there, waiting tensely as the voices of the villagers grew closer. Were it not for the dog, it would be the perfect place to hide. But they knew he could easily follow their scent.

Sure enough, the dog, fierce-looking as he approached in the darkness, led the armed band of men across the main road and up the small path directly toward the evangelists. But just a few feet away from their hiding place, the dog stopped abruptly, looking agitated. Something had caught his attention. Lifting his nose, he sniffed in all directions. Only a few feet further and he would have sniffed out the young workers.

Suddenly, as though he had picked up a stronger scent in the opposite direction, he turned and bolted back down the path. The villagers rushed frantically after him.

Sanjeev, convinced the villagers would discover their mistake at any moment and return to kill them, burst into hysterical laughter. His friends tried to quiet him, but to no avail. His mind was so flooded with the thought that they would soon be with Jesus that all he could do was laugh. And so great was his joy that he simply could not stop.

That triggered the second miracle of the night. The gang of villagers was so consumed with chasing their dog, who was now tearing down the hill away from the evangelists, that they were apparently oblivious to Sanjeev's laughter. Something must have kept the sound from their ears.

The young men, meanwhile, emerged from their hiding place and hurried on up the path into the hills, farther from Lingtheb. More than an hour passed before Sanjeev was able to control his laughter. And by one in the morning they came to a beautiful grove of chestnut trees, where they lay down peacefully to sleep the remainder of the night.

Later they learned that the son of the old man of Lingtheb, who had led the chase, was a notorious criminal in the region. Perhaps he thought the evangelists had been carrying valuables in their literature bags.

In any case, less than a month later, two other EHC workers, Nirrai and Tikaram, went to Lingtheb and finished reaching every home in that village with the Gospel. And they never saw the dog.

15

The Threshold of Eternity

The evangelistic training camp on the coast of Malaita was filled with anxiety as the thirty young Christian workers looked toward the rugged mountains inland. Maps of the interior of the Solomon Islands were nonexistent, and that mountainous area—the next target for systematic, village-to-village evangelism—held great mystery.

Fear gripped many of the workers as they talked about the rugged terrain and the rumors that abounded about the fierceness of the Kwaio peoples living there, some still in caves. This fear had been effective for generations in keeping the Gospel from being planted in the area. The workers had no idea that an old chief named Haribo had waited more than 110 yam harvests to hear about Jesus. He could not wait much longer. The old Kwaio chief was dying.

Amid the uncertainty of which workers would be the first to go into the interior, they agreed on a special season of prayer and fasting to confront the spiritual strongholds there. Afterward several teams were formed and departed for the mountains.

It would take less than a day for one of the teams to stumble upon the Kwaio village where the old chief stood on the threshold of eternity. A miracle was about to happen. These mountains of mystery would soon mirror the majestic prophecy of Isaiah 55:12 (KJV): "The mountains and the hills shall break forth before you into singing, and all the trees of the field shall clap their hands."

Mountains of Mystery

Rain fell in sheets for more than two hours as five chiefs of several nearby Kwaio villages sat on the dirt floor of the primitive thatched hut. In the adjacent hut, their beloved chief was dying. Because Haribo was so revered, and because there was no official system for appointing a successor to someone who had become a legend, they were meeting to determine what to do if he passed away.

Meanwhile, the old chief in the next hut lay in an "earth bed" carved out of the ground, where a few family members and friends attended him as he struggled for each breath.

Chief Haribo was the personification of a people to whom missiologists refer as the unreached. The Gospel of Jesus Christ had reached the coastal areas of the island of Malaita in the 1880s, about the time Haribo was born. But the Good News had touched neither his village nor his area, though it was little more than ten miles as the crow flies from the coastal settlements that were home to several thriving churches. It was as if a veil had been held over the interior of Malaita.

It was not that no one had cared for the Kwaio people in this rugged mountain area. Attempts had been made early in the century to take the Gospel to the mountain Kwaios. But they were intensely fearful of outsiders and became known as a fierce people who rejected every attempt to reach them.

Some traced this fear back to 1927, not long after the first missionaries from Australia and New Zealand brought the Gospel to the people living along Malaita's coast. In that year William Bell, a district officer of Great Britain, which controlled the southern Solomon Islands at the time, came with a band of thirteen officials to survey the land for the purpose of taxing the people. But the mountain Kwaios, afraid the stranger and his small army had offended the gods of their territory, massacred the entire party at a settlement called Kwaiawbe. The British government in Australia responded by sending a warship to shell that part of Malaita in an attempt to let these "heathens" know who was boss. Before it was over, two hundred Kwaio people had been killed, creating an even greater animosity among them toward outsiders.

Over the years several missionaries attempting to Christianize the Kwaios in the interior met with a similar fate. Several Roman Catholic priests were martyred by the Kwaios as they tried to establish a base for the Catholic Church in the mountain region of the island. In 1965 a missionary from New Zealand was killed trying to evangelize the Kwaios. Most recently, in 1975, the Kwaios killed a Seventh-day Adventist medical missionary and his son. Some say it involved a dispute over land rather than the preaching of the Gospel. But it gave the impression once again to outsiders, Christian workers in particular, that the Kwaios were bent on resisting any incursion into their territory. Anyone who had attempted to preach to them—few in number and for the most part long before the second World War—gave up quickly because there was no fruit.

All this is why Haribo had lived through more than one hundred yam harvests without ever hearing anything of the Gospel.

The Decision to Advance

In the spring of 1990, a team of Christian workers mobilized by Every Home for Christ underwent weeks of training for a systematic campaign to share the Gospel with the Kwaios right where they lived. Leading the team were two workers from Fiji who had been part of an earlier campaign to reach that island chain in the southwest Pacific. All 106 of Fiji's inhabited islands had been visited by Christian workers, village by village and home by home, resulting in more than 35,000 new converts and seven hundred small groups of new believers.

Afterward, these two Fijian evangelists had responded to the challenge to branch out to other remote places throughout the estimated 23,000 inhabited islands in the Pacific, so that all unreached peoples could hear about Jesus. Specifically, Matthew and Sova had traveled a thousand miles northwest to the Solomon Islands, where many young workers were being trained to take the good news of Jesus to all one hundred inhabited islands, dwelling by dwelling, hut by hut. Several thousand people so far had given their hearts to Jesus. And now the work had reached Malaita, the second-largest of the Solomon Islands after Guadalcanal.

The trained team of about thirty workers started where it was easiest to work, in the coastal area, where they visited every village and home. Now their work along the coast was concluding.

Sitting around the fire of their base camp in early May 1990, the evangelistic team—the older Fijian workers and the younger

223

trainees—were discussing what to do next. One of the Fijians pointed to the rugged, hilly terrain of the interior of Kwaio.

"Are there people living there who have yet to hear about Jesus?" he asked.

"Yes," responded one of his younger colleagues. "It's one of the most difficult areas in all of the islands to evangelize because of the rugged terrain and the hostile people."

"Good," responded one of the Fijian workers, adding a faith-filled declaration: "Tomorrow we advance into the interior."

Someone raised a fervent objection, emphasizing the fierceness of the mountain Kwaios and their many taboos that would endanger outsiders. Another worker explained that anyone who had ever tried to penetrate the mountainous interior had been attacked by the Kwaios and either driven out or killed (probably an exaggeration). Another mentioned the Catholic priests and the Seventh-day Adventist doctor and his son who had been murdered. Someone mentioned the story of the shelling of the Kwaios by the navy ship from Australia early in the century. It almost seemed as if a case were being built to suggest that the mountain Kwaios should be evangelized by some other group, if at all.

"Besides," as one worker stated, "someone tried to reach these people earlier this century and they wouldn't listen."

The discussion continued for some time. Then one of the Fijian brothers reminded the group that Christ's Great Commission included "all the world" and "every creature" (Mark 16:15, KJV), and that they had not come all the way from Fiji to leave the task unfinished.

Soon the influence of the older Fijians on the young trainees gained a foothold, and everyone agreed it was time to step out by faith and penetrate all the regions of East Kwaio. Still, concern was voiced all around the campfire. Many dangers existed in the interior. The people there lived much as they did centuries ago. Cannibalism had been practiced in the region as recently as the end of the last century. Who could know for sure if it had ceased? Also, the area was known to be controlled by demonic powers.

The workers finally agreed that before a team went into the East Kwaio mountains, they would spend at least seven days in fasting and prayer.

Prayer Preparation

The season of prayer began the following day. The evangelistic team used insights from the Lord, as well as information from coastal Kwaios who had once lived in the interior, to list the demonic powers that controlled the region. Some of these Kwaios had become Christians and knew much about the powerful spiritual forces at work in the interior. Several were former witch doctors who could actually name the spirits worshiped by the Kwaios.

Soon the team had a list of at least 87 different known evil spirits. Then, point by point, they confronted each spiritual force boldly in prayer. Each of the strongholds, for seven days, was assaulted by intensive, focused warfare prayer. (More about warfare praying in chapter 20.)

On the eighth day, twelve members of the team of thirty were selected to make the first trip into the mountains. This group was further divided into two-man teams, each of which would head in different directions into East Kwaio.

Kwaio Christians from the coast, especially the former witch doctors, taught the teams about taboos in the region. They explained, for example, that the people of the interior were intensely superstitious and fearful of the "gods" of other people. They did not want any "outside spirits" offending their gods. They also taught the young workers that, once inside a village of mountain Kwaios, they must not pray in any noticeable way inside their huts, because the Kwaios believed this would offend their gods.

Two of the young workers, Jack Alfred and Japta Labo, both relatively young Christians, were about to face this taboo firsthand. Thankfully, they (like the other members of the team) were operating under unusual divine protection and spiritual authority resulting from the seven days of fasting and prayer. (Some of the team would continue their fast for thirty days.) Unknown to the believers, Kwaio priests in the interior would be able to sense this protection and authority.

On the eighth day, Jack and Japta joined ten other Christian workers, including Matthew and Sova, on the day-long trek into the remote hill country. The journey took them over some of the most jagged rocks imaginable. Once they reached the outer edges of the interior, the twelve workers split into two-man teams, so each could move through the region visiting every village they could find, keeping a record as they went of where the villages were located. No maps were available for the area, so teams would move as they sensed God leading them. Sometimes villages would seem to pop up out of nowhere, usually consisting of six to ten dwellings each. And often the way to determine where the next village lay hidden was to ask someone in the last village if another village was located nearby.

Jack and Japta headed off into the hills without an inkling they had a divine appointment. They were about to experience a miracle that would advance Christ's Kingdom dramatically among the Kwaios and prove to the evangelists that miracles still happen today.

A Divine Appointment

About five o'clock that afternoon, having picked their way all day over razor-sharp rocks, the two young Solomon Island workers stumbled onto a village. A warm mountain mist covered the hillside like a foggy shroud. A large gathering of people had assembled for some reason—considerably more people than the small population of the village. What was going on?

Jack and Japta were surrounded immediately by several large warriors, larger than most of the small-framed Kwaios. They wanted to know who these visitors were and why they had come. Jack explained as quickly as he could in the Kwaio language that they were bringing the Kwaio people good news. But the burly guardians led them away to be questioned by five village priests or elders of the area. These were the elders who had gathered in anticipation of the impending death of their chief. The strangers had arrived at a sacred moment and might be infringing on the customs of the Kwaios—a taboo of taboos that could meet with dire consequences.

As the area elders began to question the two EHC workers, many of the Kwaios standing about them, only partially attired, held 24-inch machetes. Others gripped bows with poison-tipped arrows. Jack and Japta could not help recalling the rumors about the fierceness of the Kwaios. The ensuing conversation was tense.

The elders asked the workers why they were there.

"We have come to share good news," the workers explained again, describing the one true God who had created everything—the hills, the trees, the animals, even the Kwaio people themselves.

"Our eternal God," they said, "sent His only Son to be like us, a Man, and to sacrifice His own life willingly on our behalf."

The visiting elders had never heard a message like this and discussed among themselves whether it could possibly be true. Some thought it might be. The others thought it was impossible.

Then a spokesman told the evangelists, "We cannot believe anything you say unless our chief believes."

The workers had been trained to adapt to other cultures when sharing the Gospel. They knew it was customary to get permission from the chief of a village or area before doing anything, and that, once they had such permission, they could go everywhere freely since their presence had been blessed by the chief. So Jack and Japta requested permission to see the chief.

The elders refused. Their respected chief was very old and dying, they said, and seeing him was out of the question.

Then one of the workers had an idea.

"When Jesus Christ came as the Son of God," he explained to the elders, "He came not only to deliver men from their sins, but to heal sick people, too. God is quite capable of healing your chief."

Two of the five attending elders felt the workers should be given a chance to talk with the chief. Two others disagreed. One was uncertain. So about seven in the evening, two hours after they had arrived at the village, the young workers were placed in seclusion in a nearby hut while the elders engaged in a prolonged discussion.

The two elders who agreed with the young men suggested they be given a chance to pray to their God for the chief's healing. The two in opposition were certain this would offend their gods and cause them to seek retribution. Finally the elder who had not made up his mind became convinced these young men might represent a God who had great power and just possibly might restore Chief Haribo—no matter how many yam harvests he had lived—to see yet another.

Jack and Japta waited the entire night locked in the hut. Careful not to appear to be praying, they could see and hear through the thatched walls as the elders argued incessantly around a fire. The elders appeared to be chewing a special nut from a particular tree in East Kwaio that Jack and Japta had heard about. It had a druglike effect, keeping them awake and making them unusually talkative.

At seven in the morning the elders finally returned. The two workers would be permitted to pray for the chief.

A Being in White

Jack and Japta could see, as soon as they entered the hut of Haribo, how very sick the old chief was as he lay in his earth bed, struggling for breath. If they had understood his condition, would they have been more careful in explaining their theology of healing to the elders? In any case, rather than speak to him about physical healing or even pray for his healing, Jack shared with him quickly God's plan of salvation, explaining that Jesus was the only way to eternal life.

Haribo was fascinated with the message.

"I have waited my entire lifetime to hear this story," he said. "I have always felt there was some sacred message like this. But no one ever came to bring us such words. How can I receive this Jesus into my life?"

Jack and Japta led Chief Haribo in a simple sinner's prayer. And a few moments later, God's peace seemed to fill Haribo's eyes. It was clear, even to the village elders, that something remarkable had occurred. So they permitted the two young workers to leave.

About two hours later the old chief died. The attending elders sent a villager running after the workers to bring them back. Perhaps they blamed them for offending their gods and killing their chief with their prayers. Possibly they wanted the workers to pray once again that their chief would be restored. But the villager did not find the workers and returned alone.

Chief Haribo lay in his earth bed the entire day, lifeless now, as his body was prepared for the traditional Kwaio burial. The elders waited just outside his hut. Then, about five in the afternoon, Haribo sat up quietly and began to speak.

"Let the elders gather," he said, to the utter amazement of those standing nearby. "And let someone go and find the boys who came earlier to tell me about Jesus."

No one had seen anything like it. Their beloved chief, who had lain in state all day, had come back from the dead. Now Haribo, who had captivated villagers for many yam harvests with his stories, told a remarkable account.

A being dressed in glorious white (apparently the Kwaios have no word in their language for *angel*) had taken him a great distance to the most beautiful place he had ever seen. There a Person called Jesus Christ, the Son of God the young men had told him about, was being worshiped by a huge crowd of people. The glorious being explained to him that this beautiful place was where people who believed in Jesus would go for all eternity to worship Him. So everything the boys had said was true.

Peace had come to his life, Haribo said, and he had no more pain, nor had he seen any suffering among the people who worshiped Jesus. Haribo also spoke of meeting several important people to whom this being in white introduced him. He gave the names of various Old Testament prophets.

Then the being in white showed him another place—a place of great torment where people go who reject the message of Jesus that

229

these boys had brought to the mountains. Finally the being in white explained that it was necessary for Haribo to go back to the Kwaio people for a short time to tell the elders of his village that the message was true. They needed to listen to what the young men from the coast were saying about this Person called Jesus. This Jesus was their only way to experience eternal life.

Finally the old chief commissioned runners to find the workers from the coast and bring them back to preach to the people.

This time Jack and Japta were found and brought back. Astounded at what had happened to the old chief, they presented the message of salvation again, this time to the entire village. Every person, including Chief Haribo's immediate family of 21 members, received Christ as Savior. And soon more than three hundred villagers throughout the area (consisting of ten nearby villages) had surrendered their lives to Christ.

Haribo remained alive all that night and into the next morning. Then he lay back down quietly in his earth bed and went to sleep forever to be with Jesus.

The Healing Stone

In April 1995 I traveled to the island of Malaita and took a helicopter journey into the rugged interior region of East Kwaio. There I talked with a worker who witnessed the events that took place in Haribo's village in May 1990.

Today six full-time EHC missionaries from Fiji continue to work among the Kwaios in Malaita's interior. But the village in which Haribo lived and died has disappeared. After the evangelization of East Kwaio, the new converts burned their huts as an act of repentance in 1993 and moved to Bobota, a larger Christian community near the coast. It is not uncommon, I learned, for new believers to set fire to their huts and all their possessions as a symbol of forsaking the past and separating themselves from the demonic powers they believe once occupied their dwellings.

This helps to explain why Christian workers who enter a Kwaio village are not allowed to pray, especially in a villager's hut. One Kwaio woman told an EHC worker, "We know that your God is stronger than our god. And if you pray in our home, your God may have a victory in that moment, but when you leave, your God will go with you, and our god will stay here and beat us up."

Today as many as eight thousand Kwaios have come to know Jesus Christ, including well over a thousand in the most remote areas of the island where our helicopter landed. I saw firsthand the way unconverted villagers seem to come out of nowhere, fascinated to hear the Gospel.

I was also amazed that our helicopter trip from the capital city of Honiara on Guadalcanal Island into the interior of Kwaio took little more than an hour. And from the place our helicopter landed on the coast of Malaita, where coastal Kwaios first heard the Gospel a century ago, it is only a seven-minute helicopter flight into the remote areas where many had never heard about Jesus even once. Unchecked satanic bondage must have held this area in darkness for generations.

One subsequent dramatic event in 1992, two years after Haribo died, proved to be another supernatural breakthrough for the interior Kwaio people. Like the miracle at Haribo's village, this was the result of a sustained call to fasting and prayer. And it affirms a premise made by missions strategist Ed Silvoso: "It always takes a power encounter of some sort to establish the Church for the first time, because the Church has to displace the existing satanic structure."[1]

This power encounter concerned a prayer confrontation with a Kwaio stronghold called "the healing stone." The stone was a large boulder in a village called Cinaragu, located deep in East Kwaio in an area especially revered by the Kwaios. The stone, easily the size of the two-man tents we stayed in during our visit to Kwaio territory, represented a key site for pagan worship in the area. It was there that the people of the hills had offered sacrifices to their gods, perhaps for generations.

Christian workers who had been in East Kwaio for only a matter of months soon learned that the healing stone and its immediate surroundings were off-limits to outsiders. Even walking on the ground close to the giant stone could endanger their lives. The healing stone, they recognized, was a stronghold of Satan representing obvious control over the region. It was a "power point" (a symbol or place that seems to be a focal point for demonic activity) more significant than a mere taboo held by the locals.

So another week of fasting and prayer was scheduled, this one specifically targeting the huge stone. For seven days several Christian workers stood on a mountainside opposite the healing stone— their "prayer mountain," as the evangelists called it—praying against this pagan object of worship.

On a cloudy day, as the warriors concluded their seven days of prayer and fasting, a Kwaio priest made his way to the stone to offer a sacrifice. At that moment a bolt of lightning darted from the cloudy sky and struck the stone, splitting it in two. Half of the huge stone rolled down the steep mountain. The priest turned and ran, dropping his sacrifice in the confusion.

Several village priests of the region testified later that when they heard lightning had hit the rock, they were overcome with fear. And a few days later, one of the chiefs of the area near the stone invited the evangelists to come and preach about their Jesus.

Not only did all those present invite Christ into their hearts, but the priests asked the evangelists if the villagers could move with their families to Bobota, the new village peopled by Kwaio converts. The evangelists agreed, and these new converts from several villages promptly burned their huts, too, as an act of repentance, and moved to Bobota.

The breaking of the huge healing stone by a divine lightning bolt was one more outward sign that a powerful stronghold of Satan had been broken over the interior region of East Kwaio.

Mountains of Majesty

During our visit to the new Christian village of Bobota, I was given the privilege of cutting a special red ribbon brought up from the coast that adorned the entrance of the area's first-ever primary school. Seven non-Christian chiefs, who had pleaded for their children to attend the school and learn to read, came from neighboring villages to watch our ribbon-cutting ceremony.

Later I learned that of the first 25 students enrolled in the school, fourteen were children from unconverted villages. And not long afterward, the chiefs from those villages came to the pastor in Bobota and announced that they, too, wanted to become followers of Jesus. One of the chiefs, who had moved with his family to the village just before we arrived, was an old head chief for the Kafu tribe—a smaller tribe from within East Kwaio.

The Kafu people, I learned, are much like the Pygmies of Africa. They do little if any planting and harvesting, instead living off the land. But the Kafu people, unlike the Pygmies, subsist primarily by stealing whatever they can. They also have been known to kill, if necessary, to survive.

Now the old chief, Sumete, stood before me smiling brightly, though most of his teeth had been eaten away by decay. Through an interpreter, he told me his story.

He had been the priestly chief of the entire Kafu people, a small tribe of at most three thousand people. As Kafu high priest as well as tribal chief, Sumete had stolen three hundred pigs in his lifetime and sacrificed an additional five hundred pigs to their "devils" on behalf of other Kafu people.

About two months before, Sumete had become deathly ill and, seeking a cure, had offered thirty pigs (an amazing number for a Kafu) to an evil spirit. But his condition only worsened. Then the devil told him he must go kill somebody. For the first time, a strange new voice within Sumete told him this would be wrong. (This happened soon after the healing stone was destroyed by lightning just a short distance from where Sumete lived.)

Never had he received such an impression. And when the Kafu chief heard what was happening in the Christian village, he decided to visit. There he surrendered his life to Christ and, a few days later, changed his name to Peter, after that of the apostle.

When I met Peter in April 1995, he and his family had just burned their hut and all their possessions, even though they had no place to live until a new hut was built in Bobota. And this would take several weeks, because huge stalks from a special kind of palm tree near the coast had to be transported by foot up the jagged mountains to make the thatched roofs for huts in Kwaio villages, and each trip to bring a single armload of the unique palm fronds required eight to ten hours. So, until their new hut was finished, Sumete and his family were sleeping under the trees, trying to avoid the often-torrential rains.

My heart was touched, especially knowing that joining Peter and his family are hundreds of Kwaios and Kafu alike, scattered throughout the remote regions of Malaita, who have met Jesus as Savior. They are the fruit of a small army of courageous young believers who made house calls throughout the rugged interior of East Kwaio. Their sacrifices have helped transform those once-feared mountains of mystery into glorious, Christ-honoring mountains of majesty.

16

Shining in the Son

It would take eleven days traveling by canoe up the mighty Zaire River (also known as the Congo) before the two Every Home for Christ pioneer missionaries from Kinshasa would reach their destination deep in the equatorial rain forest. From the Zaire River they would journey several days more against the strong current up the smaller Momboyo River. From the Momboyo they would journey still deeper into the forest on small tributaries, until they reached the heart of the rain forest rarely seen by outsiders. It was a dangerous journey few ever made.

The farther these missionaries plunged into the forest, the more difficult their task became. The larger motorized canoes available for hire along the enormous Zaire River could not be used on the smaller tributaries.

Deep in the forest the missionaries enlisted Pygmy guides to take them even farther into the jungle. Sometimes along the tiny tributaries they all had to get out of their canoes and push them through the thick vegetation. Once back in their small vessels, they quickly pulled blood-sucking leeches off one another's bodies.

The guides knew where their fellow nomadic peoples lived. They were hidden in the trees.

On their journey the workers would visit a tribe with six thousand Pygmies. Their young chief, Lendongo, like the old priest Haribo in the Solomons, would be one of the first of the tribe to profess Jesus as Savior. Then multitudes would follow, and two rain forests on opposite sides of the world would shine brightly in the light of God's Son.

People of the Trees

It is, quite simply, the world's most horrible way to die. The virus is called Ebola Zaire because it was first traced in 1967 to an outbreak along the Ebola River in northern Zaire, an area containing some of the deadliest diseases known to man. The 1967 outbreak occurred at the Yambuku Mission Hospital run by Belgian nuns and killed almost all of the nurses, followed by the nuns, in a matter of days. Soon the disease erupted (seemingly simultaneously) in 55 villages surrounding the hospital.

I would have known little of the disease or its origin had it not been for the intensity with which the woman at the visa service office pleaded with us not to go to Zaire.

Wes Wilson, an associate at Every Home for Christ, and I had planned for some time to travel deep into the rain forest of Central Africa. We wanted to see firsthand the amazing results being reported about remote Pygmy tribes coming to Jesus. The numbers of new converts in such a short time, as well as churches planted among these indigenous peoples, were so remarkable as to seem beyond imagination.

If the reports were true—and we needed to confirm them ourselves—a powerful model was emerging that we believed could help touch scores, if not hundreds, of similar unreached peoples globally. And the results would have a significant bearing on Every Home for Christ's "Operation *Oikos*," a plan I will explain in the next chapter to reach these unreached peoples, right where they live, in the next five years.

But first we had to get to Zaire, and the visa service woman that Saturday considered it her obligation to warn us of the dangers.

"The State Department has issued a travel advisory for the region because of the instability of the government," she said. "It's probably the most dangerous place on earth you could visit right now. And I'm sure you're aware they have the worst diseases in the world."

Neither the woman nor Wes nor I knew the Ebola virus was just resurfacing in the heart of Zaire, not too far south of where we were heading in the coming week. And just north of our destination of the Momboyo River was the Ebola River, where the disease had first appeared a little more than two decades earlier. We were headed right for the middle of it all.

For one of the few times in my extensive travels, I inwardly questioned going on a trip. Little did I realize that the enemy did not want us to see the fruit of what can happen in so remote a region if believers will simply go there with the Gospel.

Heading for a Hot Zone

The same weekend Wes and I talked with the woman in the visa office, a popular motion picture titled *Outbreak* was released, based on the ravages of the Ebola Zaire virus. The film begins with a scene depicting the heart of Zaire's rain forest, precisely where we were heading.

A few days later Richard Preston, author of the *New York Times* bestseller *The Hot Zone,* appeared on "The 700 Club" with Pat Robertson to discuss not only the seriousness of diseases like the Ebola virus, but the fact that similar, if not more deadly diseases, might be lurking in other regions of the world like Zaire's rain forests. (The AIDS virus is thought to have originated in the same region of northern Zaire.) The term *hot zone* used by Preston is a medical description given to any area of the world in which a deadly virus such as Ebola is currently active and transmittable.

A friend who knew of our plans to go to Zaire that week and who had watched "The 700 Club" called with a strange feeling she had had during prayer. She wanted to warn me not to go.

Having read Richard Preston's description of the Ebola virus, I could understand why. When the virus attacks a human body, every organ and tissue (except skeletal muscle and bone) is affected. Preston calls the virus the perfect parasite, because it transforms virtually every part of the body into something like a digested slime of virus particles that cannot wait to find their way into other hosts— meaning other human bodies. Once this happens, as the author explains, the virus simply "turns the body to mush, and the under layers of skin die and liquefy."

Next, spontaneous rips appear in the skin, and blood begins to pour from the small rips. Red spots on the skin appear, grow and spread, and then combine to become huge, ugly bruises. The skin becomes so loose it almost falls off the body. Everything begins to bleed. The mouth begins to bleed, as well as the gums and nose. Blood oozes from even the ears and eyes. In fact, the person attacked by the Ebola virus will have eyeballs so filled with blood that they literally weep blood. Soon every opening in the body, no matter how small, bleeds. And all this happens in only a few days.

Finally the victim, whose brain has become clogged with dead blood cells, experiences *grand mal* epileptic convulsions. And as the whole body twitches and shakes, blood spreads everywhere, allowing the virus to spread easily to others who are unprotected.[1]

Ebola is indeed a horrible disease, and anyone heading into the region where it all began should think twice before going. But what occupied my thoughts most, in March 1995, was how much the Ebola virus reminded me of the ultimate ravages of sin that so totally destroys its host—the human soul. Zaire, I knew, with its huge rain forests—along with every other region of the world controlled by Satan—is a spiritual hot zone, sending lost humanity to a fate far worse than any deadly earthly virus.

Jesus is the only cure, I was convinced, and I had to see with my own eyes how the Cure was coming to the rain forests of central Africa.

The Power of a Prayer Shield

Despite what I knew was the harassment of the enemy, Wes and I soon found ourselves in Kinshasa, Zaire, loading our small tents and other supplies—including one hundred pounds of salt for the Pygmies—into a small Mission Aviation Fellowship plane. It would take us deep into the equatorial rain forest.

Central Africa, including the nation of Zaire, is host to many of the world's great rain forests. After South America, Africa holds more intact tropical forests than any continent on earth. And the largest share of these forests is in Zaire, followed by the Republic of Congo, which borders Zaire to the west.

Thankfully we had found a courageous MAF pilot willing to take us to a rugged landing strip at an encampment called Boteka, located along the Momboyo River. It would serve as the launching pad for our trip still deeper into the forest. Had we made the journey that the EHC workers had made two years earlier, it would have taken eleven days from Kinshasa by canoe up the mighty Zaire (Congo) River before we even reached the Momboyo. Then it would have taken several more days of canoe travel to bring us to Boteka. From there we would have faced an even longer journey to our final destination, the village of Bosuka, where hundreds of Pygmies were turning to Jesus. But, as it was, the MAF flight took us only three hours.

Beneath us, dense jungle seemed to stretch endlessly like a plush shag carpet of a hundred shades of green. The canopy of lush foliage was broken periodically by small lakes and what seemed to be countless snaking rivers. *How impossible it would be,* I thought, *to land a single-engine plane like this in such a dense jungle if there were an emergency.* As if to heighten my concern, we were flying straight into huge, billowing clouds with raindrops ripping against the windshield and lightning dancing just beyond our wingtips. Yet the plane flew steady as an arrow.

Having flown more than 25 times around the world in every kind of weather condition, I was amazed how the Lord guided our MAF pilot straight through the weather with hardly a bump. Then, as we neared the Momboyo River, I looked down at the handmade booklet of several hundred names that I had been clutching in my hand for the last three hours. Did these names have something to do with the smooth flight?

Prepared by my secretary, Debbie Lord, it was a booklet of about twenty large, 8 1/2-by-11-inch pages of single-spaced names of people praying for us every minute Wes and I were on this journey. It was part of the new Operation Prayer Shield launched by Every Home for Christ.[2] Each name appeared under the specific time that person would be praying. Not a moment of our entire journey, day and night, lacked at least a few people praying; and during the three hours we had been in the air, even though it was the middle of the night back home, more than forty intercessors had been praying continuously.

Because we had an extra seat in the small MAF plane, we had taken along with us a Belgian nun from Zaire who had close friends she had not seen in several years at the encampment at Boteka. She had been concerned about taking the rigorous, almost two-week journey by canoe and was excited about being able to travel with us by plane. So she had contacted the sisters of Boteka by ham radio to ask if we could use their large, forty-foot canoe, with not one but two outboard motors. Because we were providing free travel to their fellow nun, the sisters of Boteka were pleased to let us use their large canoe, once we arrived in Boteka, for continuing our journey even deeper into the forest.

Already we were seeing how beautifully God was putting things together for our journey.

The Cry of Death

The plane landed safely on a patch of grass in Boteka, which I soon learned had been a Belgian Catholic mission since the early 1950s. (Zaire was known then as the Belgian Congo.) I also discovered that the Every Home Crusade ministry had already seen significant results in the region around Boteka. In fact, many of the Pygmies and Bantu people (taller Africans) who stood cheering along the small grass landing strip when we arrived were converts of EHC's systematic every-home evangelism ministry in the Boteka area.

Teams of EHC workers from throughout the region also had come, some traveling by motorless canoes for days, traversing some of the many smaller rivers of the region. Our African leadership had had no contact with these evangelists for months, but we soon learned how plentiful the harvest of souls had been since the work began in this part of the forest not much more than 36 months earlier.

That night Wes and I and three other workers, including our French-African EHC director, Diafwila-dia-Mbwangi, slept in a shelter provided by the sisters of Boteka. We got our first taste that night of what it was like to be deep in the jungle.

We drifted off to sleep listening to the two-tone sound of African drums sending out messages deep into the forest. These drums,

240

which sounded much as they had for generations, were not to leave our hearing the entire time we were in the forest. Village after village, even while we traveled the winding Momboyo River, seemed to be sending constant messages, perhaps letting other villagers know that strangers were entering their territory. It reminded me of the old Tarzan movies I had seen as a child.

I was awakened suddenly by a cry unlike any I have ever heard. At first I thought I was dreaming. Then, sitting up on my cot, I thought I was hearing the sounds of some strange African animal. As the sound came closer, I realized it was that of a wailing human. Then another shrieking voice joined in. I could not tell if the voices were laughing or moaning. Soon the sound of many voices wailing together surrounded the outside of our small dwelling.

Diafwila-dia-Mbwangi (whom we call "Dia"), lying on his cot across the room, began to pray fervently and softly. I could hear him commanding the satanic oppression of the night to depart. I wondered if we were in danger. Did Dia know something we did not? Then, well past midnight, the sounds subsided.

Early the following morning, Dia asked if we had heard the wailing in the darkness. A young Pygmy mother, as it turned out, had died in the night, and the wailing was the cry of death. It had come from family members and friends joining in the chorus of mourning as each received word of the woman's passing. The mourning process included a unique Pygmy dance. (Pygmies dance not only for celebrations, I learned, but even in death.) When they finally reached our dwelling, they were in the process of letting the entire village know that one among them had died.

I was learning quickly that we had stepped into a culture far different from anything I had ever known.

At daybreak, just before six A.M., we climbed into our borrowed forty-foot canoe to begin what would be a fourteen-hour journey against the current along the snake-like Momboyo River. We would not arrive at our destination, an encampment called Imbonga, until eight o'clock that night. In the same time it would take to travel by canoe from Boteka to Imbonga, probably little more than 75 miles, a Boeing 747 could take us from San Francisco to Hong Kong.

241

The Every Tree Crusade

The Momboyo was one of hundreds, if not thousands, of rivers that flow throughout the several rain forests of Central Africa. As I looked at a map, I noticed, not too far north, the name of another river I recognized—the Ebola. Being reminded of that name made me a little uneasy.

As we motored down the Momboyo River, it seemed to me again that the forest was a vast carpet of greenery, thirty to sixty feet high, reaching to the water's edge as if to drink incessantly. On our entire fourteen-hour journey, we never saw another motorized canoe. Frequently, however, we saw Bantu (the taller Africans) in their small, one- or two-man canoes, darting in and out of tributaries that seemed to flow from everywhere into the river.

Finally we arrived at Imbonga, an encampment even more remote than Boteka that would launch us still farther into the jungle. Again we discovered a small group of humanitarian Belgian nuns and several African priests caring for the needs of the people along the river. We faced an additional 32-kilometer (twenty-mile) trek by foot, or possibly bicycle, even deeper into the forest the following day.

The Catholics of Imbonga had the only vehicle within hundreds of kilometers—an old, beat-up Land Rover—but according to a report we had received by "canoe courier" earlier in the week, we would not be able to use the vehicle because numerous log bridges along the narrow jungle road had decayed and were no longer passable. So we were happy to discover, upon arrival, that two EHC workers who had heard of our coming several weeks earlier had mobilized a small army of Bantu and Pygmies to repair the bridges.

Then we learned that the narrow road—not much more than a twelve-foot-wide jungle clearing stretching for 32 kilometers—included 22 separate log bridges, crossing over an equal number of small rivers and tiny streams. Each bridge consisted of little more than ten or twenty thick logs. Often our team of five had to get out of the aging Land Rover because the logs appeared too weak. But only once did any of the logs give way, and thankfully, with a hand-operated winch and a long chain that our Bantu guide attached to a huge tree, we were able to pull the Land Rover from the ravine and make it to our final destination.

Along the 32-kilometer journey from Imbonga to the Pygmy settlement of Bosuka, we saw numerous Bantu villages—not uncommon in the area. Pygmy villages, on the other hand, were highly unusual, since Pygmies tend to be nomadic, seldom settling down to live in conventional huts or dwellings.

It reminded me of when the Every Home Crusade began in the forest three years earlier. None of the initial progress reports from our workers had indicated how many homes were being reached, even though this statistic appears on every report coming to our central office from the field. Only as we know the precise number of homes being visited in a region can we measure the approximate number of people being reached daily with the Gospel. (The world average is 5.2 persons living in each home.) But our Brother Dia had been reporting only the numbers of conversions (and subsequent baptisms) among the Pygmies. So we asked him for updated reports that included the number of actual homes being reached.

Dia responded in writing that the Pygmies live in trees, not homes.

Remembering those old Tarzan movies that depicted natives living in tree houses, I wrote back that even a tree hut is a home, and asked Dia to report the number of tree houses reached.

Dia wrote again suggesting we still did not understand. The Pygmies do not live in homes, houses or even huts in the trees. They just live and sleep in the trees, sometimes on the thick leaves, sometimes under them and sometimes in temporary thatched shelters assembled hastily when a tribe moves to a new area for hunting. Occasionally they even tie themselves into a tree, he wrote, so they will not *fall* asleep (quite literally!) from a high tree and injure themselves.

This report from Dia ended with his unusual African humor: "Brother Dick, we have now launched EHC's very first Every Tree Crusade." Then he modified our long-standing goal, which speaks of reaching "the last home on earth with the Gospel," by printing in large letters on his report: "WE WILL NOT STOP UNTIL WE REACH THE LAST TREE ON EARTH WITH THE GOSPEL!"

Now, as the well-worn Land Rover finally rolled into the village of Bosuka, I realized instantly we were in Pygmy territory. The broadened path now became a road filled with Pygmy believers waving palm branches joyously and greeting us with Pygmy dances. They were singing a lively song, which I soon learned was declaring repeatedly, "Jesus is Lord and He's coming back soon!"

The settlement called Bosuka means "the end" in their Pygmy dialect, for not much lies beyond Bosuka but dense forest. Indeed, the very village of Bosuka did not even exist until relatively recently. But here I was, standing among these usually nomadic "people of the trees" and seeing with my own eyes that they had formed a village with a church at its center. It was a Christian phenomenon, I was told, and had resulted in thousands of Pygmies in the area giving their lives to Christ.

Half an Arm's Length

The work had gone slowly at first. The two EHC workers who had come to this part of the forest fourteen months earlier—not for a visit but to live—were a married couple, both Bantu.

But as far back as anyone can remember, the smaller Pygmies have feared the larger Bantu. They learned to trade with them for precious commodities not available in the deep forest, commodities like salt and metal (the latter to make tools and weapons), but for generations the Bantu slaughtered the Pygmies and drove them even deeper into the forest.

Pygmies are the world's shortest people. Because they are unable to process the hormones needed for normal growth, adults reach an average height of only four feet six inches.[3] Pygmies feel they are second-class human beings—like monkeys, perhaps, or a category of human just above the animals. Their very name derives from the Greek word *pygme,* which means "half an arm's length."

The Pygmy sense of inferiority made it difficult at first for the Bantu workers to make even an initial presentation of the Gospel. So they had to be unusually creative. They would go to a clearing, for example, where they knew Pygmies could see them, and leave a quantity of salt on an old tree stump or mound in the clearing. Then they would retreat into the trees, waiting for the Pygmies to come and take the salt. Initially the Pygmies did not come until nightfall, when they left monkey meat or fish in place of the salt.

The following day the Bantu workers would place salt again near the tree stump or in the center of the clearing. This time, however, they would not retreat into the shadows of the forest but stand near the edge so the Pygmies could see they were still there. Soon the Pygmies would come, ever so slowly, because they wanted the salt so desperately. Then they would snatch up the precious substance, leave monkey meat or fish in its place and rush off into the forest.

The Christians would come a third day, but this time they would wait only a few paces from the salt. Now it would take even more time for the Pygmies to cultivate the courage to come. But because salt is priceless to a Pygmy, a brave adult (usually a young warrior) would soon step into the clearing and move toward the salt. As he did, the Bantu Christians would walk very slowly toward the salt, trying to send a signal that they meant no harm.

Eventually at least one of the Pygmies, sometimes more, would muster enough courage to approach the believers waiting nearby with the salt. In this moment—through interpreters, if necessary—the Christian workers would begin to tell them they had come in a spirit of love with Good News for their people. The Pygmy listeners almost never looked into the eyes of the speaker, reflecting their conviction that they were less than human.

These first close encounters usually lasted only a few minutes, but they were crucial for building trust that might later lead to longer meetings. Still, in these first moments of contact, the Christians sought to share the Gospel message as quickly as possible. They never knew if they would get another opportunity.

Sometimes it took two or three encounters before there was an indication the message was being understood. When it was, it was clear something was happening in the heart of the recipient. The pattern was almost always the same. The Pygmy would agree to say the sinner's prayer, still not looking into the eyes of the believer. Then he or she would begin to weep, sometimes uncontrollably. Then, just as suddenly, as one worker described the process to me, "The Pygmy will lift his head boldly, look you straight in the eye and laugh with joy. We know then that something has really happened. The Pygmy has met Jesus."

A Cornelius Conversion

When our team arrived at Bosuka, we discovered that a groundswell of conversions had taken place over an amazingly short time. Our last report some six months earlier had indicated that as many as twelve hundred Pygmies in the Bosuka area had received Christ. But because of a lack of radio transmitters in this village, or any other communications from this deep in the forest, we did not know this number had grown significantly. There were now four thousand converts from a tribe of little more than six thousand. Two-thirds of the tribe had come to Jesus!

One of these special converts—and one of the very first ones— was Lendongo Botshemba, the thirty-year-old chief of the tribe, who greeted us graciously on our arrival. His conversion, EHC's Brother Dia told me, had been like that of Cornelius in Acts 10.

The young chief had grown up worshiping the snakes and trees of the dense rain forest along the Momboyo River, just as his parents Bokimba and Bolanza had before him. Most, if not all, of his tribe did not know they lived on a continent called Africa or in a nation called Zaire. And neither Lendongo nor his parents had any idea that David Livingstone and other missionary pioneers had come to Africa more than 150 years earlier to bring the good news of God's Son to their land.

But the miracle of the Gospel was now transforming these parts of the rain forest. Lendongo's entire family had been converted, affecting some forty persons in all. And churches were being planted to help nurture and sustain these new believers. Lendongo was responsible for the formation of at least eighteen additional Christian villages in the region, each one established around a church.

In a neighboring part of the equatorial rain forest, where we had heard that 32 churches had been planted by EHC workers 36 months earlier, we now learned that an astounding three hundred additional fellowships of new believers had been born.

The "Every Tree Crusade" launched in the rain forest had been responsible for more than fifteen thousand Pygmy conversions—*in just 36 months!*

Unfortunately we soon learned that in some parts of Africa's rain forests, the supposed "conversions" of Pygmies seem short-lived, or else they do not fully understand repentance. Some Pygmies have been taught erroneously that mere church attendance makes a person a believer.

To counteract this, Brother Dia, a trained African missiologist with two doctoral degrees from prestigious Canadian universities, has developed a bold discipling plan to help equip full-time Pygmy leaders to disciple these thousands of new believers. Initially the course consists of three months of intensive training, with a month given to a School of Prayer, another month to a School of Discipleship, and a third month to a School of Evangelism.

At the heart of the plan is what Brother Dia calls "H–15." The *H* comes from the French word for man (*homme*), and the 15 represents the number of persons who make up a well-trained discipleship group. The group is divided into three categories of five persons each—the first group representing prayer, the second, evangelism, and the third, resources or support.

Each person in a particular category has an assignment that relates to the overall focus of the group. The resource team, for example, is responsible to oversee whatever is necessary to enable the group of fifteen to be self-sustaining. In areas like the rain forest, they gather the food to feed their entire H–15 group. The five responsible for evangelism go out in continuous evangelism. And the prayer team members spend most of their time in intensive,

247

focused prayer or in mobilizing others to pray. Naturally, all team members cooperate with the others in all three focuses.

The result has been amazing multiplication. One H–15 group in Zaire grew from fifteen members to a church of more than two thousand in just 24 months. And Dia reports that 450 Pygmies are already involved in initial training to form H–15 groups. The goal: one thousand trained Pygmy leaders in a two-year period.

I knew as I heard this plan and saw the fruit of Bosuka that there is great hope for closure (or fulfillment) of the Great Commission in our generation.[4] And as my journey to the people of the trees ended, and our large canoe headed back down the Momboyo River, I could not get a verse from Isaiah out of my mind: "The earth will be full of the knowledge of the LORD as the waters cover the sea" (Isaiah 11:9).

It is happening, and closure is closer than we think!

PART 4

Harvest Finishers

The Closure Factor in Reaching Our World for Jesus

We are inspired, richly and understandably, by the remarkable testimonies of signs and wonders in the harvest—including the mass conversions among the Kwaios led by Chief Haribo, and those of the Pygmies served by their young warrior leader, Lendongo. Yet the really great miracle in world evangelization is only now emerging. It is the unfolding answer to Christ's prayer nearly twenty centuries ago that His disciples "be brought to complete unity to let the world know that you sent me. . . ." (John 17:23).

Today just such a spirit of unity and cooperation of strategy and vision is focusing on the final frontiers of world evangelization— the never-before-reached and least-evangelized peoples. And, most exciting, ordinary warriors like you, your family, your prayer group and your Christian friends are poised to engage in extraordinary warfare accompanied by hands-on partnerships to see the task finally completed—in our lifetime.

All these are Christ's "harvest finishers" who hold in their praying, sacrificial and generous hands the fate of the world. And, as we will see in the final section of this book, they are moving in on closure of the Great Commission.

17

The *Oikos* Agenda

For almost three-quarters of a century, one of the most beloved devotional classics in Christendom has been *Streams in the Desert* by Mrs. Charles Cowman. But many who treasure this unique compilation of inspirational insights may not know how the book came to be. It was born out of many long nights spent by a devoted missionary wife watching her husband succumb to heart disease—which many believe was brought on by his passion to see literally every person on earth given the Gospel.

It all began when young Charles left a promising career with the Western Union Telegraph Company, and he and Lettie decided to become missionaries to Japan. The Cowmans set sail by faith on February 1, 1901. It was a long and arduous voyage across the Pacific on the steamer *China Maru*. As soon as they arrived in Japan, Charles and Lettie were confronted with the stark challenge of evangelizing a "heathen" nation—a challenge Lettie described in a biographical account of her husband's missionary calling:

> During this first month, Charles saw at once the utter impossibility of evangelizing the Orient by western agencies alone. It would have to be done by devoted Japanese.[1]
>
> p. 51

Charles Cowman's conviction that nationals would have to do the job of evangelization was supported by the view of J. Hudson Taylor, the Yorkshire missionary who in 1865 established the China Inland Mission. Cowman often quoted him:

I look upon foreign missionaries as the scaffolding around a rising building; the sooner it can be dispensed with the better; or rather, the sooner
it can be transferred to other places, to service the same temporary use.

p. 81

In those early days in Japan, young Charles became convinced
that the fulfillment of the Great Commission meant going right to
where people lived. Lettie Cowman described an experience they
had not long after their arrival in Japan:

> One day at sunset, Charles and I climbed a high mountain near a large
> city in Japan. Wearied with the climb, we sat quietly looking out over the
> broad valley. In every direction were villages by scores, hundreds, yet
> untouched, unreached. We sat thus till darkness fell. There seemed to be
> One who said, "Do you see those villages? I have been there today and
> seen the broken-hearted people, the weary pilgrims bowing before cold
> blocks of stone seeking for peace." . . . A still small voice whispered, "Will
> you not go to the villages?"

p. 124

A few weeks later Charles and Lettie joined a small group of
newly arrived missionaries for an evening of language study. No
one was permitted to speak a word of English. At one point a young
missionary who had just arrived turned to Charles and asked, in
broken Japanese, "Brother Cowman, have the villagers of Japan
been given an opportunity to hear the Gospel? If not, why not?"

These words were, according to Lettie Cowman, like an arrow
to the heart of her husband, and they transformed the language
class into a prayer meeting. At ten P.M., when the prayer meeting
ended, Charles returned to his room weeping and burdened in a
way Lettie had never seen. At midnight he was still at his desk weeping. Lettie encouraged him to get some sleep.

"I cannot," he said through his tears. "The burden is too great."

Dawn found Charles still in prayer. But he greeted his wife with
a cheery *good morning* and told her he had met the Lord in the night.
God had unfolded to him a plan whereby every person in Japan
might hear the Gospel in only five years.

252

The population of Japan at the time was 58 million. The people lived in an estimated 10.3 million dwellings. Charles estimated the cost of printing Scripture portions at about $100,000, a huge sum in those days. Nevertheless, he planned a systematic campaign, convinced that two missionaries and ten Japanese nationals could visit the homes of an entire province in just six months.

In a challenge to his fellow missionaries in 1912, Cowman explained the historic lack of missionary progress in Japan:

> We have just skirted the borders. 80 percent of the people have never heard one word of the Gospel after a 60-year effort. There is no need to wait for councils, conferences, and committees. To get at the work and do it, that's the thing. This is God's set time. We must act as if we are the only ones to act and wait no longer. Why not in these days of colossal business schemes undertake the King's business as something that requires haste, and summon every loyal disciple?
>
> p. 126

After the "Every Creature Crusade" began (forerunner to the Every Home Crusade), Charles wrote passionately to his friends at home:

> The great village campaign has been launched, and it is the subject of much comment throughout missionary circles. It was quickly noised abroad that the Oriental Missionary Society, a faith mission with no guaranteed funds or influential home committees, a mission that would not go into debt even if worse came to worst, had undertaken to take and to place the Gospel in 10,300,000 homes in Japan.
>
> p. 126

The whole campaign, astoundingly, was begun with only five dollars in the treasury of the mission society Cowman had founded, but with faith that God had ordained it.

The first distribution of Scriptures began in 1913 in Tokyo, where three million homes were visited. Then workers were sent out into the provinces. After four months the first province, where more than one million people lived, had been reached with a printed message of the Good News, and fully nine hundred Japanese had tossed away their idols and given their lives to Christ.

On January 19, 1918, on the first page of the *Oriental Missionary Standard* appeared the word *Hallelujah!* printed in inch-high letters. The Japanese village campaign was finished. The article declared:

> By the time this reaches our homeland readers, the great work of taking the Gospel to every home in Japan will have been completed. Shout the victory with us, and give Jesus all the praise! Sixty million Japanese have had the Gospel put into their individual homes. There waits but the touch of fervent prayer to set this land aflame with a mighty revival. Let us mingle with our shouts and prayers the faith-inspired cry, "On to Korea!"

p. 136

Charles Cowman would live only six more years, most of them in pain, but his passion to see people reached right where they lived, at their *oikos* (the Greek word for *house*), never left him.

After his death Lettie Cowman sought to continue the vision of the Oriental Missionary Society, only to see the ministry focus more on training nationals for Christian service than on systematic, house-to-house evangelism. An amicable parting of the ways came a few years later, and Mrs. Cowman began a new ministry called World Gospel Crusade which, more than a half-century later, merged with The Bible League.[2]

But God was not finished with Charles Cowman's *oikos* vision, and in 1946 planted it in the heart of a young Canadian radio preacher named Jack McAlister. It was clearly God's agenda, and He was not about to let it die.

The *Oikos* Premise

My purpose in writing this book is not only to chronicle the fact that taking the Gospel to every person on earth (at their *oikos*) is possible, but that its greatest triumphs lie ahead. What the Cowmans began early in this century, and what Jack McAlister developed in the early 1950s (the story I told in chapter 3), is giving rise to a final thrust of global evangelism. This thrust, when linked with many evangelism strategies and covered with intensive, focused prayer, could lead to the evangelization of the world in our generation.

In this regard, a basic premise comes to mind: *The Great Commission of Jesus Christ cannot be fulfilled measurably unless the Church goes with the Good News directly to where people live.* Period. Every other strategy for reaching vast masses of people, no matter how incredible the results might appear, must end with going to where people live, if every person is to have reasonable access to the Good News. Technically no other way is measurable.

We often hear the global battle for the souls of men, women and children likened to a military strategy in which air attacks, naval assaults and ground troops are all employed to defeat the enemy. Some view the air assault in world evangelization as the use of television and radio beaming the Gospel to those who have never heard. We might view the naval campaign as taking the Good News to the thousands of remote islands in all the seas and oceans of the world. We might compare the ground forces with evangelists, missionaries and church planters as they conduct mass evangelism crusades and plant churches. Like their military counterparts, they are capturing a hill here or a fortress there.

But one aspect of this battle analogy falls far short in its application. The objective of a military campaign is to defeat and subjugate the enemy, not to take out every single enemy troop, whereas the objective of a spiritual campaign is to disciple a nation—an objective far more sweeping in its scope. We are to make contact with *every* person. Human beings are not our enemy, but Satan, who controls human beings. And the power to release them is the Gospel.

Thus, although the air power and all other aspects of the spiritual conflict for souls are vital, for the campaign to have ultimate success, we must deploy foot soldiers who go physically to every person who has not yet been touched by any other method. And

255

because there is no other way to be certain every person has had reasonable access to the Good News unless we go at least once to where people live, direct *oikos* contact is essential.

In the early years of the twentieth century, a gifted American Bible teacher, S. D. Gordon, expressed his view on what it would take to evangelize the world in a single generation. He wrote the following in 1908, less than a decade after an ambitious attempt by missions-minded Christian leaders to mobilize the Church to evangelize the world by the year 1900. The group fell far short of their goal, partly because no one sought to organize a campaign similar to the one Gordon described:

> The great concern now is to make Jesus fully known to all mankind. That is the plan. It is a simple plan. Men who have been changed are to be world-changers. Nobody else can be. The warm enthusiasm of grateful love must burn in the heart and drive all of one's life. There must be simple, but thorough, organization.
>
> The campaign should be mapped out as thoroughly as a presidential campaign is organized in America. The purpose of a presidential campaign is really stupendous in its object and sweep. It is to influence quickly, up to the point of decisive action, the individual opinions of millions of people, spread over millions of square miles, and that, too, in the face of a vigorous opposing campaign to influence them the other way. The whole country is mapped out and organized on broad lines and into the smallest details.
>
> Strong, intelligent men give themselves wholly to the task, and spend tens of millions of dollars within a few months. And then, four years later, they proceed as enthusiastically as before to go over the whole ground again. We need as thorough organizing, as aggressive enthusiasm, and as intelligent planning for this great task our Master has put into our hands.[3]

The *Oikos* Promise

As Christ's Body reaches out to evangelize our world—*oikos* by *oikos,* as S. D. Gordon suggested—we soon recognize that a home-to-home strategy will be essential if we are ultimately to witness the scene around the heavenly throne described by the apostle John:

> I looked and there before me was a great multitude that no one could count, from every nation, tribe, people and language, standing before the throne and in front of the Lamb.
>
> Revelation 7:9

Note the song by which the four living creatures and the 24 elders (categories of angelic beings, as we saw in chapter 14) exalt Jesus Christ, the Lamb:

> "You were slain, and with your blood you purchased men for God from every tribe and language and people and nation."
>
> Revelation 5:9

Consider the scope of the promise embodied in that song. It includes four distinct categories of the redeemed.

From Every Tribe

First, this melodic prophecy speaks of humankind as being purchased "from every tribe." *Tribe* comes from the Greek word *phule,* which is translated "kindred" in the King James Version. Most often *phule* is used to describe kinds of people or tribes, like "the tribe of Reuben" or "the tribe of Judah." A tribe is not a full nation, but a smaller group within a nation. It can refer to the cultural characteristics—whether social behavior or the arts or beliefs or institutions—of certain groups within a nation.

Most ethnic groups within a nation have clearly defined patterns of behavior or beliefs that differ greatly from the beliefs of the nation as a whole. No matter how we define the word *tribe,* we know that the promise that men have been purchased "from every tribe" includes every such group.

257

From Every Language

Second, the song sung by the heavenly beings speaks of the redeemed as representing "every . . . language." The Greek word used for language is *glossa,* which can mean any language or dialect.

There may be as many as ten thousand languages and dialects throughout the world. (India alone has an estimated sixteen hundred languages and dialects.) We are also told that three thousand of the world's languages and dialects have no alphabet or script.

But according to Scripture, the vast multitude of the redeemed at this final climactic worship scene in heaven will represent "every" language group on the face of the earth. This implies that the Gospel *will* be made available in some form to all the people speaking those languages and dialects, so as to produce converts from among them.

From Every People

Third, the melodic promise of Revelation 5:9 speaks of "every . . . people" being represented before the throne. The Greek word for *people* is *laos,* which appears 143 times in the New Testament, and refers to races of human beings. The emphasis here is on every category or race of people.

The fact that "the song of the redeemed" touches several similar categories is no accident or coincidence. God wants to make it clear that the scope of fulfillment of the Great Commission is sweeping. Every race will be represented.

From Every Nation

There is yet a final category. We learn that the redeemed come from "every . . . nation" (or people group). The Greek word for nation is *ethnos* (which we examined when we discussed Matthew 24:14 in chapter 1). Appearing 164 times in the New Testament, *ethnos* most commonly is translated *Gentiles,* and generally refers to people groups other than those of Jewish ancestry.

Here it is clear that not a single people group or clan will be missed at the throne. This suggests that research attempts to identify and locate least-evangelized peoples, and the resulting strategies to evangelize these groups, will ultimately be successful!

But first let's assess the challenge. And for a place to begin, let's go back to an ancient biblical procedure inaugurated in Joshua's day.

The *Oikos* Procedure

Joshua Project 2000, headed by Luis Bush, is a primary focus of the A.D. 2000 & Beyond Movement for the years leading into the twenty-first century. This sweeping plan focuses on what it will take to assure not only that all previously unreached or least-evangelized peoples have access to the Gospel, but that reproducing bodies of believers (churches) are planted within every group. To arrive at that goal, a procedure is needed to assess, clarify and ultimately win these peoples for Jesus.

An effective pattern for such a procedure is found in the "Moses model" for possessing new territory promised by God. The procedure unfolds as God instructed Moses to "send some men to explore the land of Canaan, which I am giving to the Israelites" (Numbers 13:1a). Then God told Moses precisely where to find these explorers (or spies): "From each ancestral tribe send one of its leaders" (verse 1b). The explorers were to be top leaders from each tribe in Israel.

Let's draw on this analogy as we look toward the research needed to penetrate the least-evangelized peoples today with the Gospel. Wouldn't it please God for all "tribes" (or streams) in Christ's Body to become involved *at a leadership level?*

When these explorers or spies were finally selected, Moses gave them specific instructions: "Get you up this way. . . ," he commanded them (verse 17, KJV). The patriarch was suggesting that God had a specific plan and process for information-gathering that would lead to ultimate victory.

The biblical plan continues with these exhortations from Moses:

"See what the land is like and whether the people who live there are strong or weak, few or many. What kind of land do they live in? Is it good or bad? What kind of towns do they live in? Are they walled or fortified? How is the soil? Is it fertile or poor? Are there trees on it or not? Do your best to bring back some of the fruit of the land. (It was the season for the first ripe grapes.)"

verses 18–20

As we draw an analogy from this lesson, we discover eight possible applications for a procedure today to touch every *oikos* of these least evangelized peoples, systematically and literally, with the Gospel.

First, *we must observe the land.* Moses told the spies (we might even consider them researchers) to "see what the land is like." Applied today, this would suggest obtaining a general overview of the challenge before us. It might even include determining the geographical implications of pursuing spiritual victory within a desired area of focus.

We learned the significance of this first step at Every Home for Christ when we were developing a plan to reach every *oikos* of the numerous Pygmy tribes scattered throughout Africa's rain forests. Observation soon told us it would be impossible logistically to reach these people in a conventional sense of visiting each *oikos*—hence, our Every Tree Crusade. Similarly, among some remote tribes in the South Pacific, EHC's on-site "explorers" discovered people still living in caves, so we planned an "Every Cave Crusade."

Second, *we must observe the people.* Moses commanded his spies to "see . . . whether the people who live there are strong or weak." In military terms this suggests an assessment of a people's physical capacity to withstand an attack. In spiritual terms it suggests something different: What are the people like? What are their cultural characteristics? And how might our knowledge of these factors help us reach them with the Gospel?

Third, *we must observe the numbers.* Moses told his band of explorers to see if the inhabitants were "few or many." The numbers challenge is critical in matters of world evangelism if the goal is to reach everybody. Precisely where do the people live and exactly how many are there? This information is essential if we are literally to reach all of a people group or nation with the Gospel.

Fourth, *we must observe the conditions.* Moses' instructions continue, "What kind of land do they live in? Is it good or bad?" No doubt Moses wanted to know something of the capacity of the land to produce crops. So, applying the analogy to reaching the least-evangelized, we might ask questions like these: What is the moral and spiritual climate of the people—the condition of the soil of their hearts? Do their values and way of life tend to make them more or less open to the Gospel? And how might this affect the manner in which the message of salvation is written or recorded for systematic, home-by-home communication?

Fifth, *we must observe the opposition.* Moses told his spies to see "whether the cities [the people] inhabit are like camps or strongholds" (NKJV). In the NIV: "What kinds of towns do they live in? Are they walled or fortified?" The enemy strongholds in a land keep its inhabitants, spiritually speaking, from receiving or responding to the Gospel. These strongholds need to be categorized for specific prayer if we are to make progress in evangelizing a people or nation.

Sixth, *we must observe the needs.* Moses directed his spies to test the soil to see if it was "fertile or poor." The New King James reads: "See . . . whether the land is rich or poor." Is the region we are moving into an area of prosperity or poverty? Will the inhabitants need substantial humanitarian assistance to accompany our systematic evangelism and church-planting initiatives?

Seventh, *we must observe the resources.* Moses instructed his band of explorers to "see . . . whether there are forests there or not" (NKJV). He was asking his spies to determine the capacity for building habitable structures with local resources rather than bringing them in.

Again, let's apply this concept to reaching the least-evangelized. After the Church penetrates such a group, can these indigenous peoples (once a modest percentage is converted) support and sustain continued evangelistic outreach on their own with little or no outside help? This is, after all, God's ultimate desire.

Finally, *we must observe the opportunity.* Even at the outset of research, the actual work of evangelism must begin. Moses told the spies "to bring back some of the fruit of the land." The old prophet wanted to see fruit from the very first stages of the campaign.

Sadly, too much emphasis on research regarding unreached or least-evangelized peoples can actually hinder the task of evangelizing them. Some researchers seem so fascinated with numbers and statistics that they almost forget our primary goal: to reach these people for Jesus. Surely we want to present souls to our Lord when we stand before His throne, not file folders of well-intentioned but unproductive research. Moses was telling his spies not only to bring back the facts, but to *bring back the fruit.*

The *Oikos* Prospectus

Today a simple plan is emerging to incorporate the above biblical pattern into an overall strategy that will not only clarify the status of evangelism among all the remaining least-evangelized peoples in the world, but reach them physically right where they live. This plan focuses on two distinct categories: first, on nations that as a whole have had little or no substantial evangelistic activity due to political, sociological and religious hindrances; and, second, people groups themselves (often within nations included in the first category) that have had little if any penetration with the Gospel.

Every Home for Christ is working with the Body of Christ globally to help place on-site "explorer" teams (like those Moses appointed to search out the land) among these two groups. Prayer and intercession teams will either precede the evangelism teams (to identify, pray against and bring down strongholds, as happened in the Solomon Islands) or, in some cases, work hand in hand with them. Then the teams of evangelists will systematically visit every *oikos*, whether hut, home, tree or cave within that people or nation, giving each a personal presentation of the Gospel.

This plan, Operation *Oikos*, is already underway in at least six hundred of the estimated 1,739 least-evangelized people groups of the world, even while efforts continue in scores of other nations that technically do not have least-evangelized people groups but still need to be reached systematically with the Good News.

The ultimate goal of Operation *Oikos* is to reach a minimum of one billion of these unreached people over a five-year period, while planting reproducing fellowships (of at least two hundred believers per unreached people group) for all 1,739 groups.

Because most of the least-evangelized peoples can be found within the geographical boundaries of what mission leaders refer to increasingly as "the 10/40 Window,"[4] and because many hundreds of millions of people live outside those boundaries who have yet to receive a clear presentation of the Gospel, Operation *Oikos* includes plans to reach every family of every nation in which no known *systematic* plan of total evangelism has ever been completed.

To reach every family of a nation, of course—a nation like Egypt, with an estimated 12,664,740 homes, or one like Mali in North Africa, with some 1,902,118 families—is to reach every unreached people group within that nation. Reach an entire nation literally, and all its people groups are reached. It is really that simple!

Can It Be Done?

But can the whole world literally be reached, home by home, in our generation? Some Christian leaders, unfortunately, are casting a negative vote with their pessimistic comments and lack of tangible support for those committed to the task.

I thought about this sad reality recently while reading God's Word. Then I noticed an interesting list of key leaders from Israel's ancient history. Do you recall these names?

There was Geuel, son of Maki, and Nahbi, son of Vophsi. Then there was a respected leader named Sethur, and another named Ammiel. This who's who list of top leaders in Israel also included Gaddi, Palti, Igal and Shaphat, as well as Shammua and Gaddiel. Each was hand-picked for one of the Old Testament's most memorable military strategies, and was prominent enough to have his name forever recorded in the archives of holy Scripture.

I would not be surprised, however, if these names do not ring a bell, even though each one listed represented the cream of the crop in Israel's military leadership at the time. It must have been quite an honor for each of those selected, since there were at least six hundred thousand men in Israel, and only twelve made the final list!

If you count the names I listed above, however, you will note only ten. I deliberately excluded two, Joshua and Caleb, to make a point. Here is what the Bible says about this list: "These are the names of the men whom Moses sent to spy out the land" (Numbers 13:16, NKJV).

Sadly, the majority of the twelve spies, about ninety percent, were convinced ultimate success was impossible, even though God had already told them He had given them the land. These men were what we refer to today as naysayers.

They *did* report that the land flowed with milk and honey, of course, and even presented Moses with samples of the fruit (see Numbers 13:26–27). But they added this negative evaluation: "The people who dwell in the land are strong; the cities are fortified and very large; moreover we saw the descendants of Anak there" (verse 28, NKJV).

Caleb, speaking not only for himself but for Joshua, quieted the people, declaring, "Let us go up at once and take possession, for we are well able to overcome it" (verse 30, NKJV).

Unfortunately, the majority drowned him out: "We are not able to go up against the people, for they are stronger than we" (verse 31, NKJV).

So the majority cast their vote, and history shows that God honored it. He kept the entire generation from entering the land of promise—all except the two who were convinced it could be done. Forty years later, only Joshua and Caleb of the original twelve and of the generation that had accepted the negative report, went in to claim the promise. An entire generation missed the possibility of closure regarding God's promise to possess the land, simply because they agreed it could not be done.

The task of completing the Great Commission in our generation is within reach of a praying, courageous Church. But, like Joshua and Caleb, we must cast our votes—first with our prayers, then with our resources, finally with ourselves. We must be convinced it is God's agenda to touch literally every *oikos* with the good news of Jesus, and that it is possible, if we will just set out boldly and systematically to accomplish the task.

Doers of Today

Don White and Ralph Barris did just that when facing the challenge of evangelizing the Alaskan Eskimos. Don and Ralph were ex-Marines who had seen action in the Korean War and who launched one of the very first Every Home Crusades, an Alaska-wide initiative in the mid-1950s. This crusade provided ample proof that it is possible to reach every dwelling in a remote and difficult region, literally and systematically, with the Gospel. And their persistence and courage in taking the Gospel to scores of villages along the mighty Yukon River, and to even more villages scattered throughout Alaska's interior, has provided more than four decades of encouragement that no unreached people group is beyond the reach of determined Joshuas and Calebs.

Don White, in the spirit of a Joshua, first spent four years exploring the land of Alaska, often by light plane, meticulously mapping out the countless villages that had to be reached. Later a respected missionary leader looked at Don's voluminous pages of research and commented that never in his entire missionary career had he seen so complete a survey! But Don knew research was essential if no one was to be missed.

He was especially concerned that most mission groups coming to Alaska converged on just a few of the larger communities, while almost none went to the more remote villages. One small town he visited, with just two thousand inhabitants, had been visited by *nine* different evangelical missions, whereas several villages only two hours away by small plane had never had any Gospel witness.

265

So in 1956 Don linked up with his fellow Caleb, Ralph Barris, and the two began a systematic effort to touch every family in every known village, town and city of Alaska.

First they set their faces toward the mighty Yukon River, along which hundreds of villages and hamlets awaited the Good News. It seemed more like an ocean than a river. Indeed, in the Yukon Flats it is a river of rivers, between fifty and one hundred miles wide. But Don and Ralph, confident of the unceasing prayers covering them in the EHC prayer chain back home, set out with a modest, fourteen-foot-long craft they aptly named *Good News.*

Natives gave skeptical, even humorous glances at the little boat—bright, shiny, short, fat and almost round in comparison to their own seaworthy, 25- to 30-foot crafts. Little did they know that the *Good News,* with its tiny five-horsepower motor (which could go downstream but not upstream), would encounter and survive six- to seventeen-foot waves during its first journey, conquer the muddy river and discharge its sacred mission faithfully.

During the weeks that followed, Don and Ralph learned first-hand the hazards of the Yukon. For one thing, they learned the importance of keeping their one-gallon gas tank full, since they could not afford to run out of gas in rough water. They also learned that falling overboard in this river could be fatal, because fifty percent of the Yukon is silt, and the person who falls overboard has only a few seconds to tear off all of his clothes before the silt filters into his clothing and drags him to the bottom, life preserver and all. Once, when an old-time stern-wheeler passed, they found themselves in a huge wake and were certain they would capsize—but an angel, Don believes, kept the *Good News* upright.

Don and Ralph lived off of C-rations and an occasional salmon, and at night they camped along the banks of the river. Carefully they read the maps that were available, along with Don's own aerial surveys. They learned to read the water with its treacherous sandbars that might extend for three-fourths of a mile. (Once they had to push the heavily loaded boat against the current for more than half a mile to get off a sandbar.)

At night the men were exhausted and often terribly thirsty. Finding fresh drinking water was a continual problem, because the muddy Yukon water was not fit to drink and, even after extensive boiling, tasted like dirt. But the occasional mountain stream flowing into the Yukon would provide them with fresh water for several days at a time.

A Vote for the Possible

It was worth it all as they visited village after village where the Gospel had never been. In each one Don and Ralph attempted to visit every dwelling and present the Good News to every family. Often they conducted nightly evangelistic meetings. Rare was the occasion that no one accepted Christ.

After a fruitful visit to one village, the duo headed downriver looking for the next village, said to be only a few miles away. Instead they got lost in the vast Yukon Flats—where the river resembles an ocean—and saw no sign of civilization for two days and nights as they motored along the remote expanse of water. To make matters worse, the tiny motor finally quit. Ralph realized he had been using gasoline without adding oil to it, and the lone piston had frozen tightly in its shaft. He worked over the motor feverishly, pouring oil into the shaft as Don guided the boat downstream, paddling furiously with the oars to avoid getting caught in one of the hundreds of dead sloughs. Finally, after much prayer and many pulls on the starter cord, the little five-horsepower motor turned over with a cough and sputtered back to life.

After two days and nights of drifting aimlessly on the water, they had no idea where they were. Suddenly they heard movement behind them. They turned to see a white man and an Indian running toward them down the bank of the river, apparently surprised to see so tiny a boat in their remote area.

The white man turned out to be a missionary named Don Nelson. He told the duo they had missed their targeted village by more than seventy miles—such had been the strength of the Yukon's current over the last two days. Don's heart was heavy with disappointment. He realized their little motor could never power them back upstream to evangelize the missing village, and they had set out determined not to miss a single one.

Then he was stunned to hear from Don Nelson that this mission outpost had its own three-seat airplane.

"It's too bad I can't fly it," the missionary apologized, "or I could fly you both back to that village."

Ralph reached into his pocket and pulled out his wallet.

"That's all right," he said with a smile, producing his own pilot's license. "I have a license if you'll just let me fly the plane."

They decided to fly to the village the following day. But first they would minister here.

Spiritually hungry Indians from throughout the area filled a Quonset hut that night, taking every available spot to hear Don preach for more than three hours. Each time he tried to end his message, they refused to go home. Finally when he did end the meeting, and Don and Ralph retired to Don Nelson's log cabin, the Indians came to the cabin one by one pleading for more. They soon filled the little dwelling, even standing alongside the walls. Fellowship, singing and preaching continued until well past midnight.

The following day the three-man team flew back to the village Don and Ralph had missed. The trip took less than an hour. There they visited each home, sharing the Good News with family after family. And in the evening the missionaries conducted an evangelistic service in which seven people surrendered their lives to Jesus.

God had provided Don and Ralph with an airplane so that seven souls might find Christ. Those seven would become the nucleus for a small New Testament fellowship that began that very night in a remote Alaskan village.

As for Don White and Ralph Barris, they had become early *oikos* strategists and proved it could be done. Like Joshua and Caleb, they had cast their votes for the possible.

We, too, must cast our vote for the closure of the Great Commission in our generation. But is there a key that will bring it about? I believe there is, as we will see in the final chapter. But first let's look at a way we can bring it about sooner.

18

Cords of Closure

He was a man with a vision for "closure"—that elusive term missiologists and evangelism strategists use to define the ultimate fulfillment of the Great Commission. Even though his most productive years of ministry came at the end of the last century, Dr. A. T. Pierson's passionate pursuit of closure, a term he probably never actually used, is almost legendary. His heart beat for the completion of world evangelization in his lifetime and he spread this vision to all who would listen.

It was Dr. Pierson, a pastor and gifted writer with a missionary's heart, who trumpeted the cause of finishing the task of world evangelization by the year 1900. As far back as 1870, when the vision gripped his heart, Pierson was convinced it was possible.

The preaching of the great American evangelist Dwight L. Moody in England had been stirring up the Church in the British Isles. Young people especially were being touched. In early 1885 seven outstanding students from Cambridge University, soon to be known as the "Cambridge Seven," set sail for missionary service in China under the famous China Inland Mission, founded by J. Hudson Taylor.

In 1885, with a full fifteen years remaining until the turn of the century, the vision to fulfill the Great Commission was spreading. Closure actually seemed possible. At a conference in Northfield, Massachusetts, attended by a thousand key leaders and lay Christians, A. T. Pierson, accompanied by D. L. Moody, presented the vision.

Pierson preached with passion about finishing the task of global evangelization by the year 1900. His words were filled with hope. Boldly he declared,

> If ten million out of 400 million nominal Christians would undertake
> such systematic labors that each one of that number should in the course
> of the next 15 years reach 100 other souls with the gospel message, the
> whole present population of the globe would have heard the Good Tid-
> ings by the year 1900![1]

It is reported that D. L. Moody leaped to his feet, interrupting Pierson and shouting to the crowd, "How many of you believe this can be done?" The crowd cheered in agreement as if to cast their unanimous vote to move ahead toward the goal. The same night Moody appointed a committee of six and agreed to participate him-self in seeking God's direction to finish the task of global evange-lism "now!"

In three days the small group had prepared a document entitled "An Appeal to Disciples Everywhere." It was presented to the entire delegation still in session and approved by another thunderous cheer. Included in the document was a call for a global conference of key leaders in which plans could be set forth for finishing the task.

A year later, in 1886, Dr. Pierson published a book, *Crisis in Mis-sions,* that spelled out the incredible opportunities that lay before a stirred-up Church. "An Appeal to Disciples Everywhere" appeared in its appendix.

The Church seemed poised to finish the Great Commission Christ had given His disciples nearly nineteen centuries earlier.

Then in 1888 another world missions conference took place, this one in London. It had been in the planning stages even before the Northfield Conference. Some hoped it would set into motion strategies (as suggested by "An Appeal to Disciples Everywhere") that could be implemented to fulfill the Great Commission. Instead it emerged as an inspirational conference only, stirring up the par-ticipants' emotions but resulting in no significant world evange-lism strategy.

As the millennium approached, hopes dimmed for reaching the goal. By 1895 A. T. Pierson finally declared, "We're compelled to give up the hope."[2]

270

The Quest for Closure

At least two factors were at work hindering the achievement of what had been a plausible goal. The question today is whether the Church will succumb once again to the same hindrances.

It is said that when Dr. A. T. Pierson and his colleagues felt "compelled to give up the hope" to evangelize the world by the year 1900, he attributed the failure to two primary areas of neglect. First, the corporate Church did not cooperate fully in the task. They talked about it and preached about it but never sat down and planned practically how they could do it together. And second, the Church did not mobilize enough prayer.

These two obstacles are far less formidable today as we move into a new millennium. In fact, there are more hopeful signs today regarding global prayer movements than at any previous time in history. At the end of the last century, what was happening regarding the mobilization of prayer could not even come close to what is taking place at present. Further, an ever-increasing spirit of cooperation among missions groups, organizations, denominations and strategies is breaking down sectarianism and ministry isolationism that have slowed the Church so often in her past quests for closure.

Prayer Mobilization

First, regarding prayer mobilization, Anglican researcher David Barrett suggests there may be as many as 170 million Christians worldwide committed to praying every day for spiritual awakening and world evangelization. Of this number, he says, as many as twenty million believers actually see intercession as their primary calling and ministry within Christ's Body.[3]

There may be as many as ten million groups meeting regularly, adds Barrett, with the primary focus of praying for world revival. Equally astounding, the researcher says there may be as many as thirteen hundred separate prayer mobilization networks seeking

271

to motivate and mobilize the Church to pray for global spiritual awakening and the evangelization of the lost.[4]

Prayer is the key to closure of the Great Commission, and we will look in the next chapter at a brand-new category of intercessor.

Working Together

Something else extraordinary is happening, which we will look at in this chapter: Ministries, denominations and strategies are uniting to work together toward the common goal of fulfilling the Great Commission in our generation. According to David Bryant in his book *The Hope at Hand* (Baker, 1995), a global network of evangelical missions has emerged over the last 25 years, including such strategic alliances as the Lausanne Committee for World Evangelization, the A.D. 2000 & Beyond Movement, the International Charismatic Congress on World Evangelization and World Evangelical Fellowship.[5]

Bryant further points out a spontaneous networking of plans worldwide focused on the year 2000. As many as seventy international strategies are focused on total world evangelization by the early part of the twenty-first century. In addition, Bryant says, there are currently 56 "Great Commission global networks" uniting ministries concentrated on all the two hundred–plus nations in the world and seeking the fulfillment of the Great Commission.[6]

The Rallying Cry

Whether or not the Great Commission is completed literally by the year 2000, it is healthy to see the extraordinary way so many global evangelism strategies are coming together to cooperate toward the goal. Others who applaud the goal are convinced the year 2000 will become the launching pad for finishing the task, rather than the culmination of it, and will thus mark the beginning of the end.

One organization God is using in a unique way toward this objective (a strategic alliance I have mentioned already) is the A.D. 2000 & Beyond Movement. Born largely out of the heart of Beijing-born Thomas Wang and led by missions strategist Luis Bush, the A.D. 2000 & Beyond Movement was formed in the early 1990s to help facilitate a cooperative effort toward global evangelization in this generation.

Because an estimated two thousand evangelism plans are focusing specifically on the year 2000 (a number that is increasing almost monthly), it was suggested that these organizations be brought together strategically so they could focus their individual energies more effectively on the ultimate objective of "a church for every people and the Gospel for every person by the year 2000" (a phrase that has become the rallying cry for the A.D. 2000 & Beyond Movement).

It was only logical that Every Home for Christ become involved in the movement, since EHC represents a vision and strategy for working with all Christ's Body to present a clear Gospel witness, home by home, throughout the world. I agreed to help direct one of the organization's networks, or "tracks," the God's Word and Literature Track (GWALT). This network seeks to unite Bible agencies and literature ministries in an overall strategy to give every person on earth reasonable access to the message of salvation—something that can be done measurably only by going to where people live.

As I prepared for the first consultation of GWALT in Colorado Springs in 1993, intended to establish a clear purpose and measurable objectives toward the twenty-first century, I became convinced that the task of world evangelization cannot be completed by any one group. On the contrary, it will require something of a miracle of cooperation not yet seen in Christendom—a miracle many believe is well within grasp as the Church enters the twenty-first century.

I thought of the many times I had been in prayer settings (including each morning with our staff in the office) when prayer was offered for ours and other ministries, that God would knit us all together. Often I joined in that prayer, intending to ask God to give us a "spirit of networking." But each time I tried to say the word *networking*, it came out *knitworking*.

At first it seemed like a slip of the tongue. Then I began to realize it was something the Holy Spirit was orchestrating—a new picture of cooperation. We needed to weave our strategies and ministries much more closely together, I realized, just as something *knit* together is woven more tightly than something that is simply *strung* together.

Mustering Our Joint Forces

Two passages of Scripture come to mind. First, the Old Testament account of Israel's rebellious tribe, Benjamin, in which a concubine was raped and her dead body cut into twelve parts and sent throughout all Israel. The eleven other tribes attacked the Benjamite city of Gibeah because of the crime (see Judges 20:1–11). Three times in this brief passage (verses 1, 8, 11) we are told that Israel joined together "as one man." Note especially the description from verse 11: "All the men of Israel were gathered against the city, knit together as one man" (KJV).

The Hebrew word for "knit together," *chaber*, means "to be in association with; to be united; to be a close companion in a task or cause." *Chaber* comes from a Hebrew root meaning "to join together; to partner together." Moffatt translated verse 11 this way: "They mustered their joint forces."

Each of the eleven tribes, to an extent, had its own goals and objectives. Each had its own warriors and, no doubt, its own ideas as to how the situation ought to be handled. Any of the tribes could have mobilized its individual resources in an attempt to punish the tribe of Benjamin. But instead "they mustered their joint forces" toward a common purpose. And although the final victory did not come until the third wave of attack, and then only after a season of weeping before the Lord with fasting (see Judges 20:18–26), any one of the eleven tribes attempting the task alone might well have been annihilated. Being "knit together as one" was the key.

The same is true, I am convinced, if closure of the Great Commission is to be achieved in our generation.

A Fabric of Harmony

The other Scripture that comes to mind when I think about how we need to weave our strategies and ministries more closely together is Paul's "knitworking" portrayal of the Body of Christ. He described the uniting of various functions of the Church, specifically involving the use of the various apostolic gifts. These gifts, he wrote, are to help bring God's people to His overall objective—to be

> built up until we all reach unity in the faith and in the knowledge of the Son of God and become mature, attaining to the whole measure of the fullness of Christ.
>
> Ephesians 4:12–13

Paul went on to describe Christ's role in this process:

> From him the whole body, joined and held together by every supporting ligament, grows and builds itself up in love, as each part does its work.
>
> verse 16

The King James Version refers to the whole body as being "fitly joined together." The Amplified Bible uses the equally accurate expression *firmly knit together.* Each of these versions is translating the Greek word *sumbibazo,* a combination of the Greek *sum,* a prime root meaning "union with" or "together," and *bibazo,* meaning "to force" or "to drive." *Sumbibazo* is thus speaking of something that is driven together or even forced together for a purpose.

When we first started getting together in that GWALT consultation in 1993 to consider ways to cooperate toward closure, God had already begun a process of *sumbibazo* throughout Christ's Body, especially regarding ministries with a focus on world evangelization. He was driving us together for a purpose. Indeed, in some ways it even seemed we were being forced together.

For one thing, most missions (including the participants in our consultation) were facing declining resources, even as opportunities for expansion were increasing dramatically. For another thing, not only the old Soviet Union but all of Eastern Europe was open to evangelistic activity for the first time in seven decades. Also, it was becoming increasingly obvious that there were still significant enemy strongholds blocking the path toward closure—countries like the Arab-Muslim nations that still blocked public or open evangelization.

All these factors can easily hinder any one strategy or group from achieving its objectives. But by mustering their joint forces, these groups might overcome all such challenges. Could it be the Lord is compelling His Church to come together? Is the Lord of the harvest weaving His "cords of closure" on a loom of adversity and opportunity because He knows this is the only way His people will work together to complete the task?

Networking is essential, of course, but in a spirit of greater closeness, which we might think of more as knitworking. Knitworking is what you and I do to weave our lives and ministries with others in such a way that we create a beautiful fabric of harmony. And when it comes to world evangelization, this fabric will help cover all the earth with the good news of Christ's love.

An Example of Knitworking

Already there are encouraging signs suggesting it is possible for many ministries to pool their resources for a more effective end result.

In South Africa, for example, a united effort called Operation Every Home, headed by Hendrik Hanekom, an Afrikaner, has emerged with the goal of taking a clear presentation of Christ in printed form to every family in that nation of some forty million people. When this task is concluded—and it has already involved taking the Gospel message to almost two million households—a total of 7.5 million personal visits will have taken place to homes in South Africa.

The outreach is a joint effort involving Every Home for Christ, World Missionary Press, Campus Crusade for Christ and the South African Bible Society, in direct cooperation with at least 25 other ministries and denominations. It involves hundreds of church fellowships, which ultimately will touch the entire nation of South Africa systematically with the Good News. Best of all, praying believers will do the task, praying over each house as they go.

Translations of Gospel booklets into eleven main languages of South Africa have been completed by a team of 21 translators from various regions where the languages are spoken.

Every Home for Christ is mobilizing and training the churches for the actual home-by-home evangelism outreach.

World Missionary Press, a highly respected literature ministry led by Jay and Vicky Benson, is providing all the Gospel booklets needed for every black family (six million homes in all—about 75 percent of the nation). The remainder of the literature for approximately 1.5 million "first-world" homes will be provided by South African Christians. In order to print this special order, WMP purchased a state-of-the-art, four-color press worth $250,000 principally to accommodate the project. (The press will be put to significant use in future WMP outreaches.)

Every Home for Christ priced the quantity of Gospel booklets WMP is providing for the project in South Africa. Within South Africa, the cost would be almost two million dollars. Thus, the first victory of this spirit of cooperation was the provision of literature.

Another victory occurred when the South African Bible Society became an official participant in the project. The SABS usually charges a royalty on the printing of Scriptures for which they hold the copyright. The royalties alone on the Scripture translations used in this project came to about fifty thousand dollars. But when the SABS joined the project as an official sponsor, it waived the royalties and instead charged only an administrative fee of fifteen dollars.

One of the key lay leaders involved in the project, who owns a large automobile-importing company, heard about the great cost of shipping the literature to the various points of distribution. He contacted a major automobile company with which he does business, and it agreed to allow the use of its containers to transport the literature at no cost. The saving on shipping: another fifty thousand dollars.

The Key to Closure

Albania is another example of a unique cooperative effort and model that can be applied elsewhere.

Several organizations—Christian Evangelism in Frontier Areas (CEIFA), Every Home for Christ, Operation Mobilization (OM), Youth With A Mission (YWAM) and several others—are working together, in conjunction with local churches, to reach every dwelling in Albania with printed Gospel messages over several years. More recently the Christian Broadcasting Network (CBN) became involved as a part of their year 2000 WorldReach strategy, which also brings the use of television into the effort.

Two ministries, EHC and CEIFA, coordinated the initial effort and provided funding, while others such as OM and YWAM provided teams at different times to help the small number of Albanian believers visit every home systematically in the ten major cities and towns in Albania with populations ranging from 25,000 to 300,000. Since then, full-time evangelism teams have branched out toward the estimated three thousand smaller towns and villages of Albania with a home-to-home Gospel witness.

As the plan was just getting underway, a team of thirty intercessors from Colorado Springs, led by Pastor Ted Haggard of New Life Church, traveled to Albania during the October 1993 "Pray through the Window" campaign. (It is estimated that more than twenty million believers participated in this month-long prayer campaign focused on the region referred to as the 10/40 Window,[7] including about 249 teams of intercessors that actually visited the 10/40 Win-

278

dow countries during that month.) Strategic prayer was offered by Ted Haggard's team at various key sites, including at least one major "high place"—a specific geographical demonic stronghold—in the mountains above Albania's capital of Tirana.

On returning to his congregation in Colorado Springs, Haggard not only mobilized his church for further prayer for Albania, but he enlisted their financial support to put feet to their prayers. New Life Church alone helped provide a Gospel message for every family in at least two thousand villages of Albania.

At this writing, the task of reaching every home in Albania is almost complete. Recent estimates indicate that as many as thirty villages are being reached in a single week. Many of those remaining are accessible only to evangelism teams traveling on donkeys or, in a few cases, by helicopter. More than 25 villages have been found so far that do not appear on any government maps, indicating that Christian workers are going to places even census-takers have not visited.

One thing is certain: Cooperation is key to closure. It is also essential to speeding up the process.

A literal fulfillment of the Great Commission is not as complex as it may seem. And as we all work together, it can happen far more quickly than you might imagine. Look at one specific example, which came to my attention while I was doing research for this book. It shows how quickly a task can be accomplished, and how significantly results can be enhanced, when believers cooperate with one another.

Billy Graham's crusade to his largest crowd physically in one location—in Seoul, South Korea, in 1973—happened as the result of a spirit of cooperation throughout Seoul and its neighboring communities. At least one and a half million people are estimated to have filled the great Yoido Plaza in Seoul to hear Dr. Graham preach.

Little is known, however, about the work that took place in the days leading up to the huge rally. Following many weeks of preparation, including much intensive prayer and the mobilization of hundreds of churches, two consecutive Saturdays were set aside for more than one hundred thousand believers to take the Good News (including invitations to the Crusade) to one million households in the greater Seoul area. It was estimated that between four and five people lived in each home visited. So an estimated five million people came in contact with the Gospel in just two days as the result of this cooperative effort.

And this, in turn, opened the way to Dr. Graham's powerful presentation of the Good News to one and a half million people in Yoido Plaza.

A Catholic Canoe and Campus Crusade

In 1995, when I traveled deep into the equatorial rain forest of Zaire to see the miracle harvest among the Pygmies (a story I recounted in chapter 17), our team witnessed firsthand the beauty of knitworking. The journey, as I said, would have required an eleven-day canoe trip up the Zaire River, followed by several more days of canoeing up the Momboyo River, had it not been for the availability of a gifted Mission Aviation Fellowship pilot stationed in Zaire. He flew us deep into the forest in just three hours.

Then there was our need for a huge canoe to take us still deeper into the jungle. I explained in chapter 17 that Catholic nuns at the encampment in Boteka were gracious to provide us that canoe. They were grateful we had allowed one of their sisters to fly with us from Kinshasa, saving her the arduous, eleven-day canoe trip, and the loan of their forty-foot canoe with not one but two outboard motors was their way of saying thank you.

In all this it was obvious Jesus had begun to do some knitting.

When we arrived at Boteka, we were joined by several Christian leaders of the forest who had heard we were coming. Most had traveled several days by canoe to meet us. One of them was the Campus Crusade worker for the area, who was responsible for showing the *Jesus* film that has had such a remarkable evangelistic impact worldwide (see the Epilogue on p. 311). But he had never been able to show the film in the region where we were heading—

the Pygmy settlement of Bosuka, in the heart of Zaire's rain forest. He had brought with him a gasoline generator, the film and a huge portable screen, since the EHC director for the area had asked him to show the film at an outdoor rally in Boteka.

So it was an easy matter to ask the brother from Campus Crusade to join us in our "Catholic canoe" for the journey farther into the forest to where EHC workers had labored for more than a year and seen several thousand converts. Seeing the *Jesus* film would be a marvel, we knew, to those Pygmies, who would invite many more of their people to come from even deeper in the forest.

And that is exactly what happened. The huge portable screen was set up in possibly as remote a place as the *Jesus* film has ever been shown. The story of God's Son, which many had heard by word of mouth from EHC evangelists, could now be pictured physically. Pygmies ran into the forest to tell their friends about this living "picture miracle." Native drums sent a message throughout that part of the forest inviting others to come. All through the night, Pygmies continued to gather, even long after the movie had ended.

It happened because Every Home for Christ workers, flying with a Belgian nun in a Mission Aviation Fellowship plane, were provided a canoe from a Catholic mission, facilitating the transport of a Campus Crusade for Christ worker deep into the rain forest of Central Africa, all so that lost Pygmies could "see" *Jesus*.

That's Jesus knitting the cords of closure. And Jesus really loves to knit!

19

The Fate of the World

Writing in his classic book *Destined for the Throne,* Dr. Paul E. Billheimer reminds us that "the fate of the world is in the hands of nameless saints."[1] Billheimer was speaking of the unseen servants and soldiers in the battle for men's souls who give, go and pray but rarely get the credit. Billheimer's quote always reminds me of F. C. Case, a quiet woodcutter who lived his entire life in the same North Carolina cabin where he was born.

F. C. Case was not a man of great means. In fact, even when he was well past seventy, he still read by the light of a kerosene lantern. Only a few years before his death at age 86 did Frank finally bring electricity into his cabin—and that was mainly because it took so many batteries to power his radio (which he kept tuned to Christian programming)!

The old man's diet often consisted of little more than a ten-dollar bag of pinto beans, which he said might last him almost a month. His sole income in his later years came from cutting and chopping wood in the Carolina hills (although he never owned anything as modern as a chain saw) and selling it in nearby towns. Yet this man was responsible for providing printed Gospel messages for more than eight million people in scores of countries around the world.

F. C. Case entered life, as he put it, "a full-blooded Baptist," and he joined his church officially at age sixteen. Shortly after becoming a Christian, Frank began giving to missions. He tithed faithfully to his church and often doubled and tripled that amount to missions.

During the Depression Frank earned as little as fifty cents a day working on bridge construction, even less when he made bricks or sold wood. Because fifteen people were eating from his table, he had to stretch a bag of pinto beans for up to two months, though he was never quite sure how he did it! But he never wavered from his commitment to give to missions. By the end of the Depression, he was giving ten dollars a month to missions—a remarkable sum when you consider that it was equivalent to the price of two months of food.

Early in the 1950s, at a church missions convention, the Lord spoke to F. C. Case about giving a thousand dollars to buy literature for India. Until then he had never heard about the impact of literature in evangelism. Now he felt God leading him to give a huge sum for this purpose. A few weeks later Frank heard Jack McAlister over the radio talking about conducting Every Home Crusades throughout the world, using Gospel literature. Frank sent an initial gift of two dollars. He considered it a small down payment toward his overall goal.

Through the years Frank's gifts grew remarkably. It often seemed he was giving everything he had except the few dollars he needed to eat. In many months Frank sent as much as six hundred dollars, earned from cutting wood in the North Carolina hills. And always he covered his gifts with prayer.

When Frank Case heard about how inexpensive and effective systematic literature evangelism is, he was inspired to do much more. He calculated how many people he could reach with a dollar (at that time, one hundred families could be reached!), and he set a personal goal of reaching ten million people with the Gospel in his lifetime.

When F. C. Case died in 1976, he was two million short of reaching his goal. But he knew that eight million people had been given access to the Gospel because of his faithfulness.

Not Many Noble

The self-giving life of F. C. Case reminds me of the apostle Paul's words:

> Brothers, think of what you were when you were called. Not many of you were wise by human standards; not many were influential; not many were of noble birth.
>
> 1 Corinthians 1:26

These words of Paul's, coupled with Paul Billheimer's wise insight, remind us that it really *is* a host of "nameless saints" like F. C. Case who will make possible the ultimate fulfillment of the Great Commission.

When Paul spoke to the believers at Rome about what was necessary for spreading the Gospel everywhere, he made a sweeping declaration: "Everyone who calls on the name of the Lord will be saved" (Romans 10:13). Then the apostle asked a series of questions:

> How . . . can they call on the one they have not believed in? And how can they believe in the one of whom they have not heard? And how can they hear without someone preaching to them?
>
> verse 14

Finally Paul asked the pivotal question:

> And how can they preach unless they are sent?
>
> verse 15

The apostle added quickly, quoting the prophet Isaiah,

> "How beautiful are the feet of those who bring good news!"
>
> verse 15 (see Isaiah 52:7)

Paul was speaking of those behind-the-scenes senders without whom the fulfillment of the Great Commission would remain a dream. They are the givers and pray-ers, the nameless saints who, in Jesus, control the destiny of human beings and nations.

And at the heart of their calling is the ministry of prayer.

Change the World

From the moment Jack McAlister knelt prayerfully with Ken McVety in 1953, studying a map of Tokyo and contemplating what it would take to give the Gospel to every family in that city as well as the whole nation of Japan, it was clear that prayer was essential. The 29-year-old visionary flew home from that ministry trip convinced God had shown him the key to accomplishing this every-home vision, not just in Japan but in the whole world: continuous prayer.

Within days of his return, Jack began mobilizing believers to contribute not just dollars for desperately needed literature, but one or more quarter-hours every day to pray for world evangelization. There are, Jack pointed out, 96 fifteen-minute periods in every day. The average person sleeps about 32 of these (or eight hours), and many work an additional 32. Then Jack would ask, "What are you doing with your remaining 32 fifteen-minute time periods?"

McAlister devoted a substantial amount of time on his radio program to prayer mobilization, and did so for more than three decades of regular broadcasting. He devoted two full months a year, January and June, exclusively to mobilizing prayer (instead of money) for missions.

In one remarkable step of faith in the late 1970s, Jack produced a five-hour television program, telethon-style, titled "Change the World." Its exclusive purpose: to mobilize people to give fifteen minutes every day in prayer for a lost world. By that time more than two hundred million quarter-hours of prayer had been mobilized for missions. But through the telecast, which was aired for a year in almost every television market in America, Canada and Australia, *double* that amount was mobilized![2]

Prayer was the reason, Jack was convinced, that literature distributed through the global Every Home Crusades often generated response percentages as much as ten times higher than other distribution programs, some of which used literature printed far more colorfully and creatively. Later I saw with my own eyes, and heard from many of our global EHC leaders, the confirmation of his observation that *prayer made the difference.*

Take the significant upheaval that took place in Nepal during the early 1980s. As many as two hundred Christians were jailed for between three and seven years for their evangelistic activities, while EHC workers continued providing the Gospel to as many as thirty thousand families every month—systematically, house to house. Not a single worker was detained for more than a few hours, let alone convicted or sentenced to prison. And during those years of village outreach, more than fifty thousand written response cards requesting Bible study lessons were received at various post office boxes (which were often changed for security reasons) in Katmandu.

After democratic reforms came to Nepal in the early 1990s, I traveled to that Himalayan nation to see the work firsthand. I asked our EHC director there if he had an explanation as to why so many workers had escaped detection, and what he felt accounted for the amazing results, including the planting of more than 1,500 village house churches (which today have multiplied to more than four thousand). He was convinced, he told me, that these blessings had resulted from prayer.

Just after his own conversion to Christ in the 1970s, during severe days of persecution, he had heard that perhaps forty or fifty years earlier, believers in India (including Nepalese Christians living in India) had stood in long lines shoulder to shoulder along the India-Nepal border, facing Nepal and praying for the salvation of Nepal's people.

Our Nepalese director was convinced that when the every-home campaign was launched in Nepal in 1983 during difficult times, God was honoring all those prayers, including the tens of millions of quarter-hours of prayer EHC had mobilized outside Nepal.

One way God did this, our director told me, was by keeping the workers safe. Another way was by giving them unique ideas on how to go about their house-to-house campaign.

Since the government approved of using literature as a means to teach proper hygiene in Nepalese villages, for example, the Holy

Spirit whispered to the director's heart the idea of developing a small booklet explaining the importance of health and hygiene.

The booklet gave many suggestions contributing to good health. It included illustrations about how to kill germs and even how to build an outdoor latrine. Then it warned of enemies of the spirit and soul—invisible poisons that cannot be seen or washed away. It spoke openly of the greatest enemy of our lives, Satan, who seeks to destroy our souls and lead us to an eternity of pain and suffering in a place called hell. The only cure for Satan's scheme, the booklet explained, is knowing and trusting the Creator of the universe, the one true God, who sent His only Son, Jesus Christ, to make possible the ultimate cleansing of the soul.

The booklet concluded with a simple presentation of the Gospel in language the average Hindu could comprehend, so that every reader could learn how to repent of sin, trust in Christ and become His true follower.

What a creative way to present the Gospel legally in that nation! Our Nepalese director knew the idea had come from God and that the booklet easily gained the approval of the censors because so much prayer had covered the project.

But now the workers had to deal with Nepal's law forbidding the open distribution of Christian literature. The law did not permit "free" distribution of religious propaganda, so EHC workers began going house to house selling these booklets on hygiene (physical and spiritual) at a price so ridiculously low—a little more than a U.S. penny—that anyone could afford to buy one. For those who lacked even that tiny sum, the Christian workers would say, "Please take a copy anyway; others have given enough extra, so it's already paid for"—which was true, because when many Christians in Nepal heard about the campaign, they gave extra gifts to help.

According to the EHC director, not one worker could remember a single person refusing a booklet. Before long thousands of requests for further information on how to overcome "the great Satan" came in to Every Home Nepal's various post office boxes in Katmandu.

Today, more than ten years later, the law permits use of a much wider range of Christian literature and follow-up materials, and the number of response cards that have been received at the EHC office in Katmandu has now exceeded two hundred thousand. The director there does not know the nameless saints who have prayed so passionately for Nepal, but he does know their prayers are responsible for the remarkable harvest.

Warring Saints

Much of this passionate praying is the kind some prayer strategists call "warfare prayer." Warfare prayer is a more focused level of prayer, often of an intense nature, directed against demonic powers hindering God's plans and purposes in a region. This kind of prayer has been around far longer than we might realize. Some call it "strategic-level prayer" because it deals with the unseen powers of darkness (see Ephesians 6:10–12) at a strategic level, thus opening the way for the evangelization of dark regions of the earth.[3]

Ed Silvoso labels such prayer "the main vehicle to take the gospel to every creature," suggesting that the "heavenly realms" of Ephesians 2:6 are "the battleground where the Church must face and defeat the forces of evil." Silvoso describes what he calls a key principle for prayer evangelism: "The believer is a deputy of the Court of Calvary assigned to enforce the judgment awarded to Jesus: the salvation of the lost. The believer is to use this delegated authority mainly in prayer."[4]

Of one thing I am certain. Increased levels of intensive, focused prayer produce unusual results.

Recently I heard about an Every Home Fiji evangelism team that determined warfare prayer was essential if they were to reach every home in the resort city of Nadi, Fiji. While planning their assault, the team learned that a particular boarding house had been rented and turned into a brothel by a group of prostitutes.

The workers recognized this as a stronghold of Satan requiring a special prayer strategy before any evangelistic attempts could possibly be successful. So the team set aside a full week for fasting and warfare prayer before even approaching the house. They confronted the powers of darkness in prayer and commanded them boldly to depart in Jesus' name.

When the day came for "storming the fortress," they did so not in a warlike way, but quietly and gently. As a result, four of the young women in the brothel, including the head of the group, gave their lives to Jesus. The stronghold had been broken.

Three days later all the young women, along with their leader, showed up for a youth fellowship rally and declared their commitment to Christ publicly.

More unusual victories followed as the Nadi team of prayer warriors learned more about the power of warfare prayer. Sometimes signs and wonders followed as these believers confronted the powers of darkness over their island nation, and more souls were saved.

On one occasion, their prayers had a particularly unusual impact.

A Fijian army intelligence officer, whose cousin served on the EHC Nadi team but who was not himself a Christian, grew increasingly frustrated with his inability to track down suspected arms smugglers. There was ample evidence that arms were being smuggled into Fiji—as they thought, in preparation for a coup attempt against the government. But all the efforts of this officer to catch the culprits or locate the weapons had been fruitless. He was ready to give up.

One night a man appeared to the officer in a dream.

"Go to your cousin Mosese," said the man, "and he will tell you what you need to know."

That was all the army officer could remember from his dream. But about 5:30 A.M. he dressed and set out for his cousin's workplace, the Every Home Fiji Nadi base several miles away.

Unknown to him, the team was fasting and had spent the night in prayer.

The officer told his cousin of his brief dream and the dilemma that had caused it. Then he looked at Mosese and asked, "Can you really tell me what I need to know?"

"There is one thing I know for sure that you need to know," Mosese replied. "If you know it, nothing else matters."

Then Mosese told his cousin about Christ, and how receiving Him into his life was the answer to every question. In that very instant, although Mosese had not even answered the question he had been asked, his cousin believed.

The officer stayed at the Every Home Fiji base for several days to read discipleship materials and soak up all he could from other believers. As he shared with them his concerns about illegal arms shipments, he became convinced demonic activity was involved. Soon he, too, was involved in warfare prayer with the rest of the Nadi team.

The officer phoned his superior and told him in detail everything that had happened. Soon his superior arrived at the Every Home Nadi base and gave his life to Christ, too. Now he became involved in the praying.

That very day Every Home Fiji mobilized a prayer chain and called on prayer warriors to pray from six to ten P.M. every Saturday night about the matter of the suspected arms shipments. Within days of the first prayer meetings, the flow of information increased dramatically. God gave intercessors key insights that prompted authorities to look in areas they had never suspected. About two weeks later, a large container of arms was discovered on board a ship in an Australian port hundreds of miles away, destined for Fiji. A few days later, weapons that had been hidden for months in Fiji were also found and confiscated.

Warfare prayer clearly had done its work. Had a nation been spared bloodshed as a result?

A Word for the Wind

In 1992 I was able to witness firsthand something of the power of warfare prayer during a trip to Fiji for a great harvest celebration. I was there as EHC's international president to welcome a special delegation of representatives from the Kwaio tribe in the Solomon Islands. They had come to talk about the incred-

291

ible spiritual breakthrough among their people in the interior of Malaita. We were also commissioning six full-time Fijian missionaries to work among that previously unreached people group in the Solomons. To our knowledge they would be the first full-time missionaries ever to live and work among the mountain Kwaios.

We were meeting in a makeshift auditorium consisting of huge sheets of corrugated steel resting on top of bamboo pillars. Almost three thousand Fijians had gathered for the commissioning—most of them converts from the ten-year, island-to-island, door-to-door evangelism campaign throughout their 106 inhabited islands.

One afternoon, shortly before a key session was to begin, I was chatting with several EHC leaders from the islands. People were gathered around the outside edges of the makeshift auditorium, enjoying fellowship. Suddenly a terrible wind began blowing. All heads turned toward the eastern boundary of the EHC property. Several began shouting something in their language as several small but powerful tornado-like whirlwinds swirled in different directions. One of them crossed the boundary and headed straight toward our meeting place.

The whirlwind ripped off part of the roof and tossed several huge sheets of metal onto the ground. One of the sheets gashed into the side of a woman's leg. Though we were standing at a considerable distance, we could see blood begin to pour from the cut.

The whirlwind hovered for a moment above the area, then began to move almost tantalizingly toward another piece of metal roofing, lifting it slowly from the bamboo scaffolding. I was too dumbfounded to speak.

The EHC leaders from the islands with whom I had been chatting moments earlier knew instinctively this was no ordinary whirlwind. In fact, I learned later that the words the Fijians had been shouting when the tornado-like whirlwinds first appeared represented the name of a demonic spirit that often disrupted meetings in this precise manner. They actually had a word—a specific name—for the wind when it created such a condition.

292

Our director from Vanuatu, Raynold Bori, turned toward the sound of the metal roofing flapping in the wind. He pointed authoritatively at the swirling, tornado-like gust of wind.

"Leave right now," he commanded fervently, "in the name of Jesus."

Almost simultaneously our director from Papua New Guinea, William Pukari, rushed to his side and joined him. Then another joined them. Each of them, raising both hands in the direction of the swirling wind, joined with Raynold in commanding the wind to leave.

It all happened so quickly that I stood mute. Finally I was able to voice my own affirmation.

"Yes, Lord," I said. "I agree with my brothers."

What happened next was amazing. The tornado-like gust, though continuing to spin, dropped the huge sheet of metal into its original place and began to retrace its path back to the eastern boundary of the property. I knew the exact border because a day earlier our Fijian director, Suli Kurulo, had explained to me how God had given them this large piece of land through the generosity of a sugar plantation owner, and Suli had pointed out to me all the boundaries of the property.

Now I stood transfixed as this swirling wind, which moments before had seemed to display a personality, rushed back to the very boundary from which it had come. When it got there, the leaders beside me let up in their praying.

Immediately the wind crossed the boundary again and started heading back in our direction, as if to say, *I'm returning!* Once again the level of prayer intensified, with hands lifted toward the funnel.

What happened next is impossible to forget. One of the brothers commanded the spirit boldly to leave the property.

"This property belongs to Jesus!" he shouted.

As he continued to pray, I watched the swirling wind, still looking like a miniature tornado, follow the eastern boundary of the EHC property line. It headed directly south and never crossed the boundary. When it reached the southern boundary of the EHC property, it made an amazing ninety-degree turn and moved west, once

293

again not crossing over the boundary. Three thousand pairs of eyes watched its every movement. When the swirling wind reached the southwest corner of the property, it turned sharply toward the north.

The outstretched hands of the praying leaders never dropped. Their prayers were as intense as they had been at the outset.

The tornado-like wind was now about thirty yards west of the tin-roof auditorium and moving northward along the western boundary of EHC's property. It continued in that northerly direction, never crossing back over the property line. It had now almost circled the property. When it finally reached the exact boundary of the northwest corner, it hovered for a moment and seemed to turn briefly in the direction of the auditorium, as if to say, *You've beat me this time, but I'll be back.* Then it swirled into the canefields to the northwest and disappeared.

That day in Fiji I saw Billheimer's nameless saints in action. They were the ones who did the praying, while I just stood by saying, "Yes, Lord, I agree."

The Harvest Warrior

The fate of the world lies not only in the hands of nameless saints who pray, but in the hands of those like F. C. Case who give even as they pray. I call these saints *harvest warriors,* because they war for the harvest through both praying and giving.[5]

Charles and Lettie Cowman, about whom we talked in chapter 18, were two such harvest warriors. In Charles' last message in 1900 before leaving the United States for Japan, he spoke of what had driven him and Lettie to make that decision:

> Some years ago I read a book entitled *Dawn on the Hills of Tang.* It said, "The investment of life is the most momentous of all human decisions." The investment of influence gave me a larger vision, that it is not a light thing to live out a whole human life and to live it in such a way as to bring large returns. The paramount question that towers above every other, at

whatever point we may have reached, is: "How can I now invest the rest of my life so it will bring the largest return?"[6]

Lettie Cowman never forgot those words, even long after Charles died in 1924 and she was left with the task of carrying on the vision for the "Every Creature Crusade" that had been conducted in Japan.

She liked to recall an experience on a wintry December afternoon in 1932 during the height of the Great Depression. Funds had become so scarce that the Koreans serving with the Oriental Missionary Society were informed at their yearly convention that the 24 new graduates of the Bible Training Institute who had expected to open new missions would be unable to do so. It seemed the enemy of their souls was sitting directly beside the empty treasury, Lettie wrote later, and telling her, *Now the work will fail!*

But the students at the convention began to pray fervently. They sang and shouted with voices of triumph. They seemed to sense the answer was on its way.

Then, according to Lettie, out of their deep poverty many Korean Christians of the surrounding area came and placed their gifts into the offering plate. It soon became too small to hold all the sacrifices. Although the weather outside was freezing cold, men took off their overcoats and placed them in the offering. They gave leather shoes, watches, briefcases, eyeglasses and blankets. Women took silver pins from their hair and put them in the offering. No one was coaxing them on but the Holy Spirit. One small Korean woman, whose mission station was located high in the mountains 340 miles away, walked down the aisle and placed her return railway ticket into the offering plate. She said she would walk home.

According to Mrs. Cowman, this giving meeting began at two in the afternoon and continued until ten that night, when a missionary whose heart was full of emotion went to the platform and commanded them to give no more. "I can bear it no longer," he said.

After that meeting, all the workers returned to their stations. The sacrifices were converted into cash, and the amount received was nearly $3,500 (a sum that today would be twenty times that amount). The 24 new graduates had exactly enough to make it to their pioneer assignments far inland, as planned. God had supplied every need.[7]

The Money Box

I believe the fate of the world today depends on this kind of sacrificial spirit. It is reported that Christians worldwide have a total annual personal income of approximately eight trillion dollars. The same Christians, it is estimated, give only 1.5 percent annually—less than a sixth of a tithe—to all aspects of church ministry, both locally and nationally. And only a meager 0.1 percent goes to foreign missions—about a tenth of a penny out of every dollar.[8] The resources to evangelize the world are available if only believers will release them!

Jesus spoke frequently of the need for a right perspective on how we manage our resources. He cautioned His disciples:

> "Do not lay up for yourselves treasures on earth, where moth and rust destroy and where thieves break in and steal; but lay up for yourselves treasures in heaven, where neither moth nor rust destroys and where thieves do not break in and steal. For where your treasure is, there your heart will be also."
>
> Matthew 6:19–21, NKJV

One nameless saint in Europe just a few years ago took this passage to heart when he thought of a special treasure he had kept for years that might help build Christ's Kingdom, if only he would release it.

This German saint, whom we will call Franz, knew about the tremendous need for Gospel messages to reach the lost in Germany and beyond, and he had long believed in the vision of Every Home for Christ globally. So he visited Jörg Enners, EHC director in Germany. At this time, East and West Germany had just reunited, and the opportunities for spreading the Gospel seemed endless. But

Jörg lacked even enough money to pay the monthly bills for the ministry.

Franz listened intently to the need and promised to pray.

A few days later he came back to Jörg and handed him a small metal box. It was filled with rare gold and silver coins representing his entire life savings.

"Why have you brought me these?" Jörg asked, stunned.

"I struggled with myself," Franz admitted. "But the Lord told me three times to give my collection away. So I want to give these coins to your ministry."

Jörg, amazed at the man's unselfishness, was able to sell the coins to a collector for three thousand dollars, which he promptly used to settle urgent needs for the EHC work in Germany.

But that is not the end of the story. A few weeks later Franz called Jörg to tell him he had just received a telephone call informing him that he had won second place in a special contest. The prize was worth more than four thousand dollars. Franz could not believe it—it was a thousand dollars more than the gift of coins he had given.

The story still does not end there. Shortly afterward, the man who had bought the coins from Jörg showed up at the EHC German office. Something was troubling him.

"I know someone gave you these coins so you could sell them on behalf of the ministry," he said. "But I believe God wants me to give them back to you, so you can give them back to the person who gave them to you." He added, "And you can keep the money I gave you for the coins."

When Jörg gave Franz back the coins, Franz could hardly believe it. The value of the contents of the money box, when added to the prize money he had collected, meant that God had blessed Franz' faithfulness by more than doubling his initial gift.

This would seem a fitting end to the story, had God not planned one final surprise. When Jörg told the unusual testimony of the money box in EHC's monthly newsletter for German believers, a reader (yet another nameless saint) was so touched by the account that she sent the ministry her own money box filled with similar rare coins. Now both Franz and Every Home for Christ had been doubly blessed. And because of these sacrifices, many more could hear about Jesus.

A Question in Conclusion

So where do we go from here? Nameless saints, I believe, hold in their hands the key to history's greatest harvest—a thought that leads us, as we conclude, to a vital question:

What do we do about the challenge set before us to finish the task of world evangelization?

Do we join forces with those compassionate Christians like F. C. Case, the Cowmans and the company of courageous Koreans in a freezing cold December who gave so much and kept so little? Or do we retreat from tangible, sacrificial involvement and bask in the comfort of a sometimes uncaring generation too concerned with self-gratification?

One thing is certain: Someday a generation of followers of Christ will arise to finish the Commission Christ gave the Church to tell all the world of His love.

The noted evangelist D. L. Moody said of the ultimate evangelization of the world, "It can be done; it ought to be done; it must be done!"[9]

Do we really believe that? If we do, let's join the ranks of that growing army of nameless saints committed to see Christ's Kingdom come, His will be done and the whole earth filled with His glory (see Revelation 11:15; Habakkuk 2:14). Together we can finish the task!

Epilogue

A Reason to Rejoice!

Writing in his excellent and encouraging book *The Hope at Hand* (Baker, 1995), David Bryant shares so many hopeful signs of an existing and coming awakening that he finds it necessary to add several substantial appendixes to describe them. In one appendix alone, Bryant shares 83 astonishing facts he calls "encouraging highlights of world revival." In another he describes seventy additional "inspiring accounts" resulting from what he calls "distinctive praying."[1]

Bryant cites missiological research indicating that about seventy percent of all progress toward completing the Great Commission has taken place just since 1900. Of that, seventy percent has occurred since World War II. And seventy percent of that has come about since 1992.[2]

Further, it is estimated there are now more than 2,520 Christian radio and television stations around the world providing potential access to the Gospel to 4.6 billion of the world's people in their own tongues.[3]

According to a variety of researchers, as Bryant points out, a mass movement in organized Christianity began to get underway in East Asia only around 1980. In that year there were an estimated sixteen million Christians in all of East Asia. Less than ten years later that number had grown to eighty million.[4]

Other equally inspiring testimonies offer additional hope. In Laos the Church has grown from five thousand to twenty thousand in just five years. Nagaland, India, a region that was once considered ninety percent Christian, is now claiming to be one hundred percent Christian. As many as fifteen thousand Christian baptisms are believed to be occurring per week in Hindu India, and reports indicate that nearly eighty percent of these have responded to Christ through some kind of supernatural encounter.[5]

In Indonesia, the world's most populated Muslim nation (with 195,623,000 people), the percentage of Christians is so high, according to one researcher, that the government will not release accurate figures.[6]

In Mongolia as recently as 1991, there were only about fifteen known believers in the entire population of two million. Today that number is at least one thousand, with many worship places emerging in major population centers.[7]

If God has some amazing developments up His sleeves (as we observed in chapter 13), it seems He has especially opened His sleeves over China, where between 25,000 and 35,000 Chinese are said to be coming to Christ *daily*. So remarkable is the harvest that accurate numbers are hard to obtain. Even the Three Self Patriotic Church Movement (TSPM) in China, which is government-supervised, is experiencing amazing growth. In numbers of congregations alone, it has increased from four thousand to seven thousand in just five years.[8]

And not all Three Self church groups report accurate numbers to the government, for fear of future crackdowns that might hinder their ability to function freely. I spoke with one Three Self church leader who still reports his membership to the government as 150, in spite of the fact it is now well over fifteen hundred. If the authorities knew the real numbers, he fears, they would split up his church.

The old Soviet Union, now the Commonwealth of Independent States (CIS), has also experienced both awakening and harvest. After seventy years of oppression, according to Bryant, the Christian movement there represents an astonishing 36 percent of the population, or more than one hundred million—five times the size the Communist Party ever reached.[9]

Before 1991 Every Home for Christ had not visited a single home with the Gospel in what was then the Soviet Union. But in the 36 months following the official breakup of the nation, with Gorbachev's resignation on Christmas Day 1991, EHC went freely to more than fifteen million homes and received nearly one million responses. Immediately prior to the Billy Graham crusade in Moscow in October 1992, EHC worked with 57 evangelical churches in the city to place a Gospel message and crusade invitation in almost half a million homes in central Moscow.

Africa, too, is seeing an expanding harvest. In 1900 only four percent of the population was estimated to be Christian. Today that figure is said to be well over forty percent and moving rapidly toward the fifty-percent mark, which may come before the year 2000. In the ministry of Every Home for Christ alone, in one twelve-month period in 1994, more than 750,000 Africans sent in responses—and that was only in French-speaking Africa. And in just one African country, Nigeria, in a single mass crusade sponsored jointly by both charismatic and evangelical churches, German evangelist Reinhard Bonnke spoke to crowds in excess of half a million, and more than 250,000 made decisions to follow Christ in the five-night campaign.

Blessings are also pouring forth from God's sleeves over Latin America, where the evangelical movement is said to be growing three times faster than the population.[10] In an article in *The Los Angeles Times*, a Roman Catholic journalist estimated that at the present rate of conversions to evangelical Christianity in Latin America, the entire population of the region will be evangelical by the end of the twenty-first century.[11]

More Miraculous Growth

The zeal of the new believers in the developing regions of the world is not to be overlooked. Statistics indicate, according to David Bryant, that the non-Western missions movement is growing five times faster than that of the West. Bryant cites the fact that currently there are 49,000 missionaries from the two-thirds world—35.5 percent of the total Protestant missionary force worldwide;

and by the year 2000, the number of two-thirds-world missionaries will surpass that of all the Western nations combined.[12]

The DAWN (Discipling A Whole Nation) saturation church-planting movement led by Dr. Jim Montgomery is another example of the incredible acceleration of the global harvest in recent years. DAWN seeks to work with all the Body of Christ to fill a nation with cells of believers (one cell or church per five hundred to one thousand people) by enlisting all evangelism strategies in the process. The systematic house-to-house proclamation ministry of Every Home for Christ, which has resulted in the formation of thousands of Christ Groups (see chapter 6), is a vital part of the DAWN movement.

When DAWN officially began in 1985, four DAWN-type pilot strategies were already in various stages globally. (One, in the Philippines, had existed for about ten years.) By 1995, within a decade of DAWN's launch, full-scale strategies were functioning in thirty nations and had been started in another sixty. The total of these ninety nations represents 85 percent of the world's population. Plans call for DAWN-type strategies of saturation church planting in 145 nations (representing 96 percent of the population of the world) in the next 36 months.

The miraculous results of this saturation church-planting strategy in the Philippines indicates that the harvest is significantly expanding. In the decade before the movement began in the Philippines, churches were multiplying at a rate of about five percent per year. If that rate had continued from 1975, seventeen thousand churches would have been planted by the year 2000. Instead the rate has more than doubled, and already 35,000 new churches have been established. At the present rate, the number of new congregations in the Philippines will surpass fifty thousand by the year 2000—an increase of 33,000 churches over what had been expected.[13]

Students of prayer and God's Word are not surprised at the growing harvest and the miracles accompanying it. For one thing, they have been praying passionately for these developments, and they know and believe God answers prayer. Then, too, they realize Scripture speaks of end-time revival and harvest, with the ultimate result that "the earth will be full of the knowledge of the LORD as the waters cover the sea" (Isaiah 11:9).

The Accelerating Harvest

We are closer to the fulfillment of this promise than many realize. And although many ministries and denominations can attest to this reality, I share examples primarily from the outreach of Every Home for Christ because I am more aware of the results reported from our campaigns.

In less than two decades in French and Anglo-Africa, through Every Home Crusades, more than fifteen million families have been visited and given the Gospel of Jesus Christ. Since according to the World Health Organization about 5.2 people live in each home all over the world, that means that more than 75 million people have been given access to the Good News (within hand's reach) in French and Anglo-Africa in less than twenty years. More than two million of these families have been reached in French Africa alone in a quarter of that time—only five years.

The written responses in French Africa to the printed Gospel messages (in the form of mailed decision cards to African offices), as well as verbal decisions by illiterate peoples as recorded by field evangelists, are especially encouraging. Well over 2.1 million "Decision for Jesus" response cards, as well as registered reports of people praying to receive Jesus, have been processed in five years in this region alone. One-third of this total, remarkably, came during just one twelve-month period, further indicating both the acceleration of the harvest and the amazing receptivity of those receiving the message.

In South Asia, which includes EHC's outreaches in Sri Lanka, Nepal, Bhutan, Bangladesh and the vast nation of India, the results are equally encouraging. Since 1964 more than 459,741,200 Gospel messages have been hand-delivered house to house, each with a decision card. Because two Gospel booklets, one for adults and one for children, are usually delivered to each home, it means that these nearly five hundred million booklets have touched more than 250 million families throughout the region.

In India alone, well over six million written decision cards have been processed in the last three decades. In Nepal more than 200,000 decision cards have been received in less than a decade, most of them just since the democratic reforms in the late 1980s. In addition, more than 4,000 Christ Groups have been formed by Every Home for Christ in Nepal, including many hundreds in isolated villages scattered in the Himalayan mountains.

In Bangladesh, a strictly Islamic nation of 132.3 million people, about thirty million inhabitants representing more than four million families have already been given the Good News personally at their homes, and 217,279 people (an amazing figure for a Muslim land) have responded in writing by sending a decision card to EHC's Bangladesh office. These inquirers have been sent the simple but effective four-part Bible correspondence course.

In East Asia, including Indonesia, Malaysia, Thailand, Korea and Japan, more than 411,210,000 Gospel messages have been hand-delivered to an estimated two hundred million families. And in spite of the strong influence of religions like Islam, Hinduism and Buddhism, more than 1,748,000 decision cards have been followed up with Bible lessons. Most of this has occurred in less than 25 years, further suggesting that God does indeed have something special up His sleeves regarding the ultimate completion of the Great Commission.

Even in Myanmar, where Adoniram Judson preached two centuries ago, 5,472 people have now responded to Gospel messages, including at least one hundred Buddhist monks, more than thirty of whom have been so transformed that they are now themselves giving the Gospel house to house! Again, most of this has happened in less than a decade.

Latin America has also been touched dramatically by these evangelistic house calls. More than 378 million Gospel messages in Spanish, as well as tribal dialects, have been delivered, most of them home by home, throughout all of Latin America. As of this writing, more than 2,441,940 decision cards have been received and processed as a result.

Work is presently underway to take a witness of the Gospel, as well as the love of Christ through humanitarian assistance, to the more than seventeen million children estimated to live in the streets and alleys of Latin American cities. Instead of calling this an Every Home Crusade, organizers are labeling the effort an "Every Street Crusade," since these youngsters literally live in the streets, alleys, parks, dumps, even sewers.

In Europe, in spite of the sometimes lukewarm attitude of the churches toward evangelistic endeavors, more than 225,793,000 printed messages about Christ have been delivered systematically by many hundreds of churches to more than one hundred million families in twenty nations. More than 583,000 Europeans have responded in writing to testify that they have been touched by the Gospel message and want to receive further Bible instruction.

In the CIS and Eastern Europe, more than twenty million families have been visited and given the good news of Jesus Christ just in the decade of the 1990s. Based on the World Health Organization's global estimate of 5.2 people per home, this means as many as one hundred million people in the region have been exposed to the Gospel—within hand's reach, in their homes. And for the vast majority, it was their first encounter with the Gospel.

Already nearly two million people throughout what is now called Eurasia have indicated in writing that they have prayed to receive Christ as Savior or that they want additional materials about Jesus. And because often it is only one person from a family who responds, it is possible that the actual number coming to Christ is considerably higher.

Smaller regions of the world are being affected in a similar way. Although the islands of the Pacific represent considerably smaller populations than those on the continents, the per capita response to house-to-house evangelism is sometimes double or triple that of other regions of the world. In the Pacific, for example, almost ten percent of the Gospel booklets distributed throughout some three hundred islands have resulted in decision cards coming to the EHC offices in the region—or 85,752 decision cards in response to a systematic, home-to-home distribution of 885,000 evangelistic messages. And most of this has happened in just a decade.

A further indication of the acceleration of the harvest in recent years is the unusual percentage of increases of people responding to Christ, as compared to similar outreaches only a few years ago. In 1989, for example, in response to EHC's house-to-house evangelism, just over 342,000 people sent in decision cards to our offices throughout the world. This represented approximately nine hundred decision cards per day. By 1992 that number had increased to 426,031—an encouraging 25 percent increase, but not overwhelming. But by the following year the number jumped to 1,260,288, or some 3,450 decision cards daily for twelve months. By 1994 the number jumped even more, to 1,485,284, or 4,070 per day. This represents an increase of 350 percent in only five years.

Other ministries and denominations report equally astonishing advances in response to the communication of the Gospel. Campus Crusade for Christ has seen a remarkable harvest of responses to the showing of the *Jesus* film, now translated into more than 342 languages. It is estimated that more than 732 million people have seen the film in just over sixteen years.[14]

German evangelist Reinhard Bonnke, best known for his huge evangelistic crusades in Africa with as many as a half-million attending a single meeting, has also caught a vision to reach households with the Gospel. Bonnke's ministry, using primarily the mail, has already touched 24 million homes in the United Kingdom and forty million homes in Germany. According to Bonnke, 3,200 German congregations of many denominations cooperated in the follow-up, as did fifteen thousand groups in the U.K. To date, one hundred thousand decision-card responses have come in from the U.K. and German campaigns alone.[15]

Next Bonnke wants to touch all of the United States and Canada. Then, working in conjunction with ministries like Every Home for Christ, he wants to help fill China and the former Soviet Union with the Gospel (where he will be unable to use the mail). EHC is well underway in laying the foundation for such a campaign in the

CIS, having mobilized thousands of believers in the region who have already reached millions of households. (And as we noted in chapter 9, miracles have already begun for a similar campaign to sweep across China.)

The Christian Broadcasting Network is expanding significantly overseas and reports phenomenal results in response to the communication of the Gospel through television and other media. Pat Robertson, CBN's founder, says it took their ministry almost twenty years to see one million people pray to receive Christ, but in the following five years, the first half of the 1990s, that number increased fifty times.[16]

Billy Graham's use of satellite technology in his twilight years, conducting simultaneous crusades in scores of languages globally, has reached millions of people with the Gospel in a single evening.

No, there is little doubt that the Church is moving rapidly toward that grand event when the seventh angel will blow his trumpet and heavenly voices will declare, "The kingdom of the world has become the kingdom of our Lord and of his Christ" (Revelation 11:15). That is God's epilogue on the history of humankind. And we have reason to rejoice that He is quite possibly writing its final chapter, even in this moment!

Notes

Chapter 1: Back in Fashion

1. Frank Kaleb Jansen, "When Theology, Missiology and Futurology Clash," *International Journal of Frontier Missions,* January–March 1995, Vol. 12:1, pp. 3–6.

2. W. E. Vine, *An Expository Dictionary of New Testament Words* (Old Tappan, N.J.: Revell, 1966), p. 228.

3. Edgardo Silvoso, *That None Should Perish* (Ventura, Calif.: Regal, 1994), p. 60.

4. Jack McAlister, *Alaska: Assignment Accomplished* (Studio City, Calif.: World Literature Crusade, 1960), p. 51.

Chapter 2: Seeds of the Harvest

1. Lettie Cowman, *Missionary Warrior: Charles E. Cowman* (Greenwood, Ind.: OMS International, 1989), p. 34.

2. *USA Today,* September 8, 1995, p. 1.

3. Patrick Johnstone, *Operation World* (Bromley, Kent: STL Books, 1986), p. 467.

4. H. Osberg and J. Hoagland, *Attempt the Impossible* (Studio City, Calif.: World Literature Crusade, 1968), p. 23.

5. Yohann Lee, *Dawn of a New Era* (Studio City, Calif.: World Literature Crusade, 1962), p. 47.

6. Paul Smith quoted in Lee, p. 29.

7. Robert G. Lee, *Everybody* magazine, World Literature Crusade, Vol. 1, No. 2, 1969, p. 16.

Chapter 3: A Prairie Fire Commissioning

1. By May 12, 1995, the ministry Jack and Hazel McAlister co-founded, now known as Every Home for Christ, had been responsible for the distribution of more than 1.8 billion Gospel messages. Since EHC's policy is to distribute two Gospel booklets per home, one for adults and one for children (the latter designed for young readers who may be the only readers in some homes of developing nations), as many as nine hundred million homes or families may have been provided the Gospel within hand's reach, or—using the estimate of the World Health Organization of 5.2 people per home globally—potentially 4.5 billion people living in those homes.

EHC does not believe all 4.5 billion people have necessarily read the message, but that a Gospel message was placed within reasonable access of this number of people in a systematic, measurable way. Nor does EHC suggest that this 4.5 billion represents most of the world, since some countries, like India, have had multiple distribution coverages (almost three times), while at this writing less than five percent of the vast nation of China, using the same house-to-house method, has been covered.

Chapter 6: Graveyard of Siberia

1. Jim Montgomery, DAWN *2010: A Strategy for the End of the Age* (manuscript in preparation for publication by DAWN Ministries, 7899 Lexington Dr., #200B, Colorado Springs, CO 80920), p. 14.

Chapter 7: Captives for Christ

1. For a more complete record of the revival at Olmos Prison, I recommend the booklet *Revival Behind Bars* by Michael Richardson and Juan Zuccarelli (Professional Word Publications, Inc., 5009 W. Royal Palm Rd., Glendale, AZ 85302). This booklet helped me confirm information I received from other sources who have visited or worked at Olmos Prison in recent years.

2. The current director of Every Home for Christ's Good News Behind Bars, Samuel Desimone, continues to conduct regular training sessions for inmates at Olmos Prison. During a riot staged by unsaved inmates at Olmos in 1995, Brother Samuel was chosen by both penal authorities and inmates to serve as their mediator. Pray for brothers like Samuel Desimone and the other leaders mentioned in this chapter who work at Olmos Prison.

Chapter 8: The "Must-Bring" Mandate

1. The full account of Gyalsang has been written from careful, lengthy interviews with the Sherpa convert by representatives of both Gospel Recordings and Every Home for Christ. Several of them have seen the pages of script Gyalsang composed as the result of the visions described in this chapter. Two of the workers were present when Gyalsang was converted and discarded his Tibetan Buddhist objects of worship. And today Every Home for Christ has visited every family in every village of the Syabru district.

2. Information in this chapter about Gospel Recordings is taken from *Count It All Joy* (England: Hodder & Stoughton, 1978) and *Faith by Hearing* (Hong Kong: China Alliance Press, 1960), both books by Phyllis Thompson and used by permission of Gospel Recordings. These books are available through Gospel Recordings, 122 Glendale Blvd., Los Angeles, CA 90026-5889.

3. According to David Tamez, Latin America director for Every Home for Christ, at least 56 native languages and more than 220 dialects are spoken in Mexico alone. Many of the Indians who speak these languages have no access to the Gospel in their native tongues except through recorded messages. With the participation of Gospel Recordings, home-to-home evangelism has already begun among the Tzoltzil, Tzeltzal and Chamulas in the Mexican state of Chiapas, as well as the Mazahua (which GR first recorded in the 1940s) in northern Mexico. Also underway is a systematic effort to reach the Totonacs and Aztecs in Puebla.

4. Cardtalk "talking booklets" are still produced by Gospel Recordings in the United States and South Africa, even though solar-powered and hand-cranked cassette players are being used increasingly among illiterates because more substantial follow-up lessons can be put on audiocassettes.

Chapter 9: Warriors of the Night

1. More recently the thirty prayer pamphlets focusing on China's provinces have been adapted into a *Target China* prayer guide available from Every Home for Christ, P.O. Box 35930, Colorado Springs, CO 80935-3593. In Canada write Every Home for Christ, P.O. Box 3636, Guelph, Ontario, N1H 7S2, Canada.

2. It is unfortunate that for security purposes it is necessary to change our brother's name (as well as some names throughout this book). In time I believe it will be possible to acknowledge this quality servant of the Lord whose heart beats passionately for the lost of China. Pray for Brother Mac. God knows who he is.

Chapter 11: A Child Shall Lead Them

1. Arthur Zich, "Indonesia: Two Worlds, Time Apart," *National Geographic,* January 1989, pp. 112–113.

Chapter 13: The Sleeves of God

1. As told by Pat Robertson on "The 700 Club," October 9, 1995 (program #285-95).

Chapter 14: Agents of the Invisible

1. John Calvin, *Institutes of the Christian Religion,* Book 1 (Grand Rapids: Eerdmans, 1972), p. 145.
2. Billy Graham, *Angels: God's Secret Agents* (Garden City, N.Y.: Doubleday, 1975), pp. 14–15.
3. Silvoso, p. 181.

Chapter 15: Mountains of Mystery

1. Silvoso, p. 128.

Chapter 16: People of the Trees

1. Richard Preston, *The Hot Zone* (New York: Anchor Books, 1995), pp. 105–108.
2. For information on participating in Every Home for Christ's intercessory Operation Prayer Shield, or to inquire about intercessory prayer training books and courses, write Every Home for Christ, P.O. Box 35930, Colorado Springs, CO 80935-3593.
3. Douglas H. Chadwick, "Ndoki—Last Place on Earth," *National Geographic,* July 1995, p. 45.
4. *Closure* is a term used to define the ultimate completion of the Great Commission, whereby everyone on earth has had reasonable access to the Gospel of Jesus Christ. Although no one knows exactly when closure will be accomplished, many Church leaders link it to Christ's words in Matthew 24:14: "And this gospel of the kingdom will be preached in the whole world as a testimony to all nations, and then the end will come" (see chapter 1).

Chapter 17: The *Oikos* Agenda

1. This quotation and the following ones, and the biographical information about the Cowmans, are taken from Lettie Cowman's book *Missionary Warrior: Charles E. Cowman* (see note 1, chapter 2).
2. Today both The Bible League (formerly World Home Bible League) and Oriental Missionary Society (OMS) continue some isolated house-to-house evangelism, although neither ministry declares as its primary mission the taking of a printed message of salvation to every home of every nation on earth, in the way the Cowmans envisioned. OMS does continue to send out some Every Creature Crusade teams and plans to increase that number in the years ahead. The Bible League uses Scripture portions house to house in some areas as part of their church-planting strategy.
3. S. D. Gordon, *What It Will Take to Change the World* (Grand Rapids: Baker, 1979), pp. 41–42.
4. The 10/40 Window is a geographical rectangular box marked by the boundaries of 10 and 40 degrees latitude north of the equator, and stretching from West Africa across the Middle East to East Asia (including China and Japan). First designated the 10/40 Window by missions strategist Luis Bush, the region is home to more than 3.5 billion people. An estimated 97 percent of the people groups defined as least-evangelized live in the 10/40 Window, while only eight percent of the world's missionary force labors there. The 10/40 Window is also headquarters for the world's largest non-Christian religions, such as Islam, Hinduism and Buddhism.

Chapter 18: Cords of Closure

1. Todd Johnson and Ralph Winter, "Will We Fail Again?", a compilation of previously printed works edited by Rick Wood, *Mission Frontiers* bulletin (Pasadena: U.S. Center for World Mis-

sion, July/August 1993), p. 12.

2. Ibid.

3. David Bryant, *The Hope at Hand* (Grand Rapids: Baker, 1995), p. 31.

4. Ibid.

5. Ibid., p. 222.

6. Ibid.

7. For a definition of the 10/40 Window, see note 4, chapter 17.

Chapter 19: The Fate of the World

1. Paul E. Billheimer, *Destined for the Throne* (Fort Washington, Pa.: Christian Literature Crusade, 1975), p. 106.

2. During those days I joined with the ministry of Every Home for Christ to develop the Change the World School of Prayer, which has taught more than a million believers globally to change the world through their prayers. For information on the Change the World School of Prayer home study course or video course for churches, write Every Home for Christ, P.O. Box 35930, Colorado Springs, CO 80935–3593.

3. For further insights regarding strategic-level prayer, see my book *The Jericho Hour* (Lake Mary, Fla.: Creation House, 1994).

4. Silvoso, pp. 18, 177.

5. I have developed a monthly "mentoring" training series on audiocassette for those who wish to become harvest warriors with the ministry of Every Home for Christ. For more information write The Harvest Warrior, Every Home for Christ, P.O. Box 35930, Colorado Springs, CO 80935–3593.

6. Cowman, p. 47.

7. Ibid., pp. 158–159.

8. Bryant, p. 225.

9. D. L. Moody, quoted in *A.D.200 & Beyond Handbook,* Luis Bush, ed. (Colorado Springs: A.D. 2000 & Beyond, 1993), p. 3.

Epilogue: A Reason to Rejoice!

1. Bryant, p. 231.

2. Ibid., p. 221.

3. Ibid., p. 222.

4. Ibid., p. 223.

5. Ibid., p. 224.

6. Ibid.

7. Ibid., p. 225.

8. Ibid.

9. Ibid.

10. Bryant, p. 227.

11. Richard Rodriguez, "Latin Americans Convert from Catholicism to a More Private Protestant Belief," *Los Angeles Times,* August 13, 1989, Opinion Section, p. 1.

12. Bryant, p. 223.

13. Statistics in this chapter regarding the DAWN strategy come from notes I took during a conversation with Dr. Jim Montgomery at DAWN headquarters in Colorado Springs on April 5, 1996.

14. Information from The *Jesus* Film Project, April 10, 1996, Department of Field Information, P.O. Box 72007, San Clemente, CA 92673.

15. From notes I took from a conversation with Reinhard Bonnke at his Frankfurt, Germany, headquarters on March 6, 1996. See also *Christianity Today*, December 11, 1995, p. 63.

16. From "The 700 Club," October 9, 1995 (program #285-95).

Index

For more information on the ministry of Every Home for Christ, write:

Every Home for Christ
P.O. Box 35930
Colorado Springs, CO 80935–3593

In Canada write:

Every Home for Christ
P.O. Box 3636
Guelph, Ontario, N1H 7S2
Canada

In Australia write:

Every Home for Christ
P.O. Box 168
Penshurst, N.S.W. 2222
Australia

In South Africa write:

Every Home for Christ
P.O. Box 7256
Hennopsmeer, 0046
South Africa

For addresses of other offices, write to the Colorado Springs office above.

Dick Eastman is international president of Every Home for Christ (formerly World Literature Crusade), president of the National Prayer Committee, the originator of "The Change the World School of Prayer" and the author of ten books (three of them, *No Easy Road*, *The Hour That Changes the World* and *A Celebration of Praise*, published by Baker; and two more, *Love on Its Knees* and *Seven Keys to a Happy Life*, published by Chosen). Dick has taught and ministered in scores of nations. He received his formal education at Carthage College, Kenosha, Wisconsin; Moody Bible Institute, Chicago, Illinois; North Central Bible College, Minneapolis, Minnesota; and the University of Wisconsin, Madison, Wisconsin. Dick holds a Bachelor of Arts degree (Bible and theology), a Master of Science degree (journalism), and an honorary Doctor of Divinity degree.